I0827988

IMAGES
of America

FARMINGTON

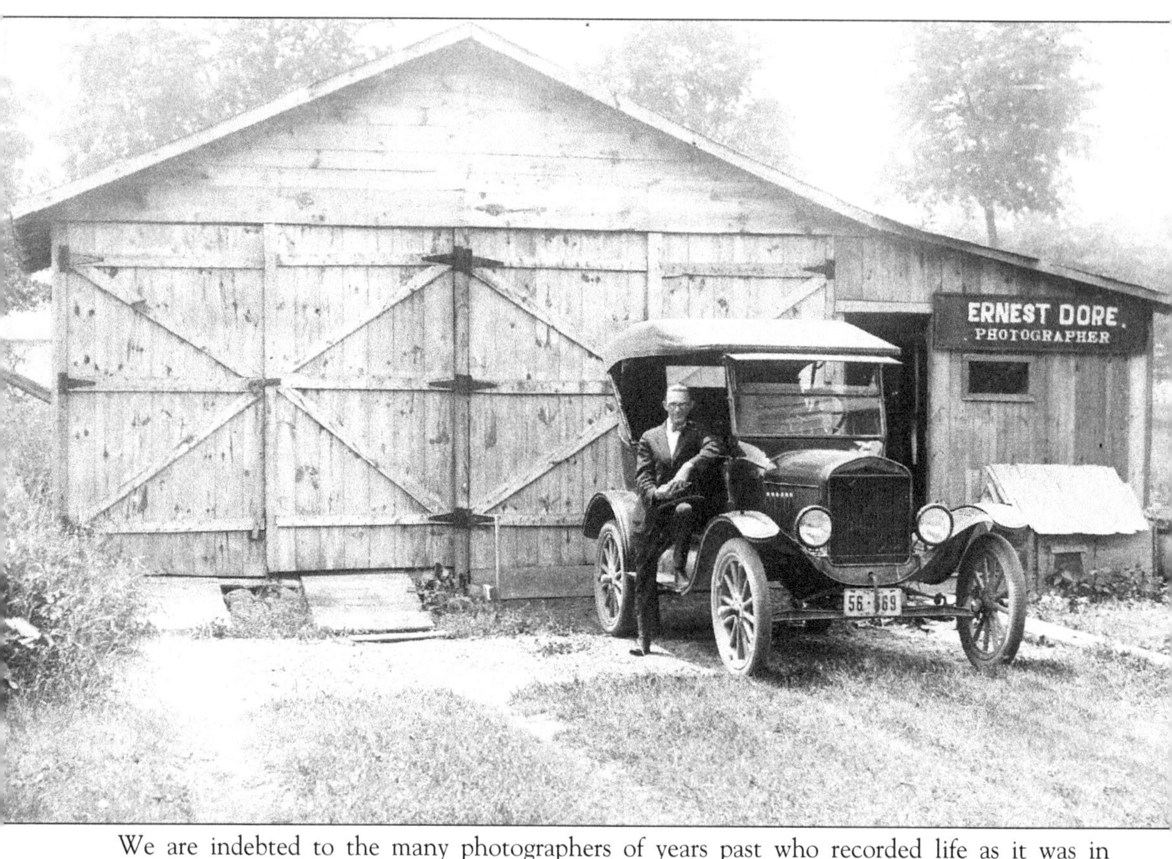

We are indebted to the many photographers of years past who recorded life as it was in Farmington. Their work has made this book possible.

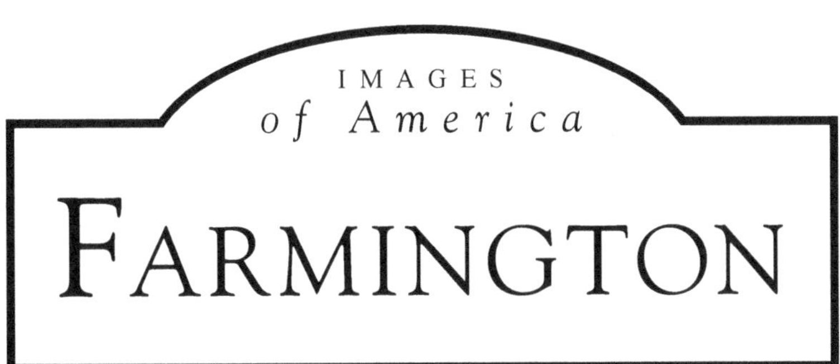

Farmington Historical Society

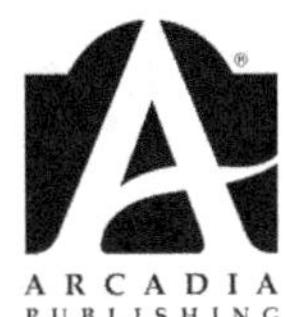

ISBN 978-1-5316-6081-9

Published by Arcadia Publishing
Charleston, South Carolina

For all general information contact Arcadia Publishing at:
Telephone 843-853-2070
Fax 843-853-0044
E-mail sales@arcadiapublishing.com
For customer service and orders:
Toll-Free 1-888-313-2665

Visit us on the Internet at www.arcadiapublishing.com

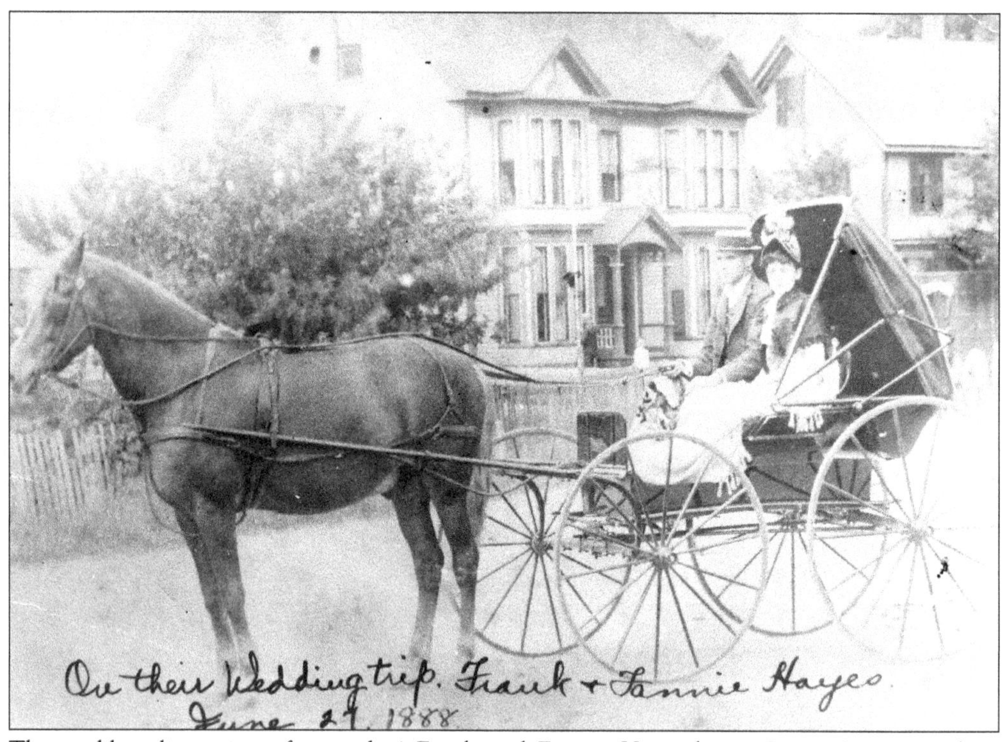

The wedding limousine of yesterday! Frank and Fannie Hayes leave Grove Street on their wedding trip, June 27, 1888.

Contents

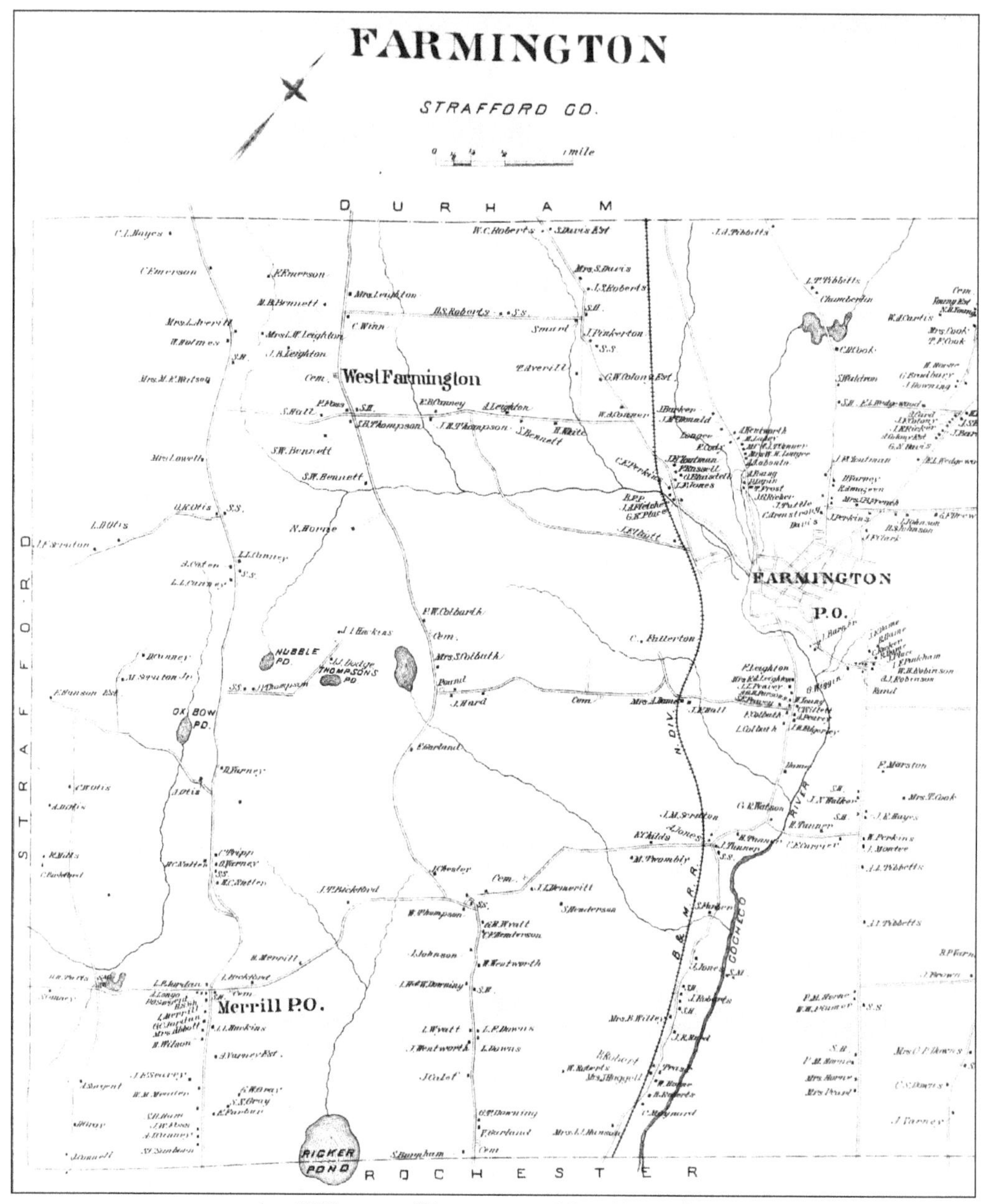

An 1892 map of Farmington, New Hampshire.

Introduction

Small towns abound in New England and the story of their growth and development is an integral part of the history of America. Farmington, located in the southeastern part of New Hampshire, exemplifies this.

The native Indians called the area "Chemung," meaning "canoe place." When settlers arrived in the 1770s, it was known as the Northwest Parish of Rochester. Distance and rough roads made it difficult for these first families to travel to the established church in Rochester, although they were taxed heavily to support it. This age old problem of taxation was the catalyst which caused the citizens to petition for a charter to incorporate a separate township of Farmington, and this was granted on December 1, 1798. The first town meeting was held on March 11, 1799, at the home of Simon Dame. The 141 voters present elected three selectmen: Ichabod Hayes, Lieutenant Ephraim Kimball, and David Roberts. This form of government has been maintained, with the addition of a town administrator, to this day.

Originally an agricultural settlement, the early homes were farms in the Merrill's Corner section, hence the town name. In the 1800s, the establishment of water-powered industries along the Cocheco, Ela, and Mad Rivers caused a population shift, with the present downtown area evolving near these rivers. The subsequent construction, in 1849, of a railroad through the mill area brought further prosperity and cemented the location of the town commercial center. In early days this business area was referred to as "The Dock" or "Puddledock," a name which endures today on the masthead of the local paper, *The Puddledock Press*.

Although Farmington began as an agricultural community, the principal industry to develop was shoe manufacturing. From its beginnings in 1836 when E.H. Badger built the first shoe shop on Spring Street, to its ending in 1991 when the last factory (the Alton Shoe Company) closed its doors, the shoe industry made the town's reputation and employed upwards of 2,000 people. It was as a cobbler that the most renowned native, Vice President Henry Wilson, got his start, journeying to the shoe capitol of Natick, Massachusetts, in 1833 to learn his trade.

Though difficult to envision today, the downtown area once contained several hotels, grocery stores, and even a movie theater and bowling alley. Farmington has had its ups and downs like any other community, with prosperity checked by disasters and economic depressions. Through good and bad times its generations of loyal residents have remained strong and supportive of one another, with deep pride in past accomplishments and optimism for the future.

It is hoped that the photographs presented here of a town and its people, how and where they worked and played, will bring enjoyment to the reader and, also, an understanding of the valuable heritage to be found in a small New Hampshire town.

Book Committee:
Dorothy Bean
Dorinda Howard
Norma Park
December, 1996

Acknowledgments

Publication of a book such as this depends upon many individuals for the contribution of both photographs and information. The Book Committee sincerely appreciates the assistance of the following: Roger Belanger, Pearl Bowden, Robert Cameron, Everett Carlsen, Martin Chagnon, Roscoe Chamberlin, Rosanna Chute, Evelyn Derby, Lois and Prisco DiPrizio, JoAnn and Charles Doke, Ardys Elliott, Jane and Norman Fall, Eileen Ferland, Farmington Fire and Police Departments, Steven Gardner, Uel Gardner, Lena George, Marshall Gibbs, Polly Gilman, Derald Goodwin, Eugene Goodwin, Jewell Gray, Norma Gray, Elsie Hart, Thom Hindle, Helen Houston, Richard Hunneman, Edith Jenness, Paula Kenyon, Esther Krisiak, Gladys Lepene, Jean Merrill, Lorraine Meyer, Eugene Nute, Roger Nutter, Norma Park, Paul Place, Joanne Pulsifer, Nancy Rabb-Cassinari, Louise Rollins, Rufus Rundlett, Barbara Russell, Pamela and George Sansoucy, Robert Schulte, Pauline and Frank Scruton, Nicholas Servetas, Mortimer Sullivan, Beulah and James Thayer, Frances Thayer, Norma and Robert Tilton, Ruby Towle, Charles and Sandra Wibel, and the Trustees and Librarians of the Goodwin Library.

One

Downtown

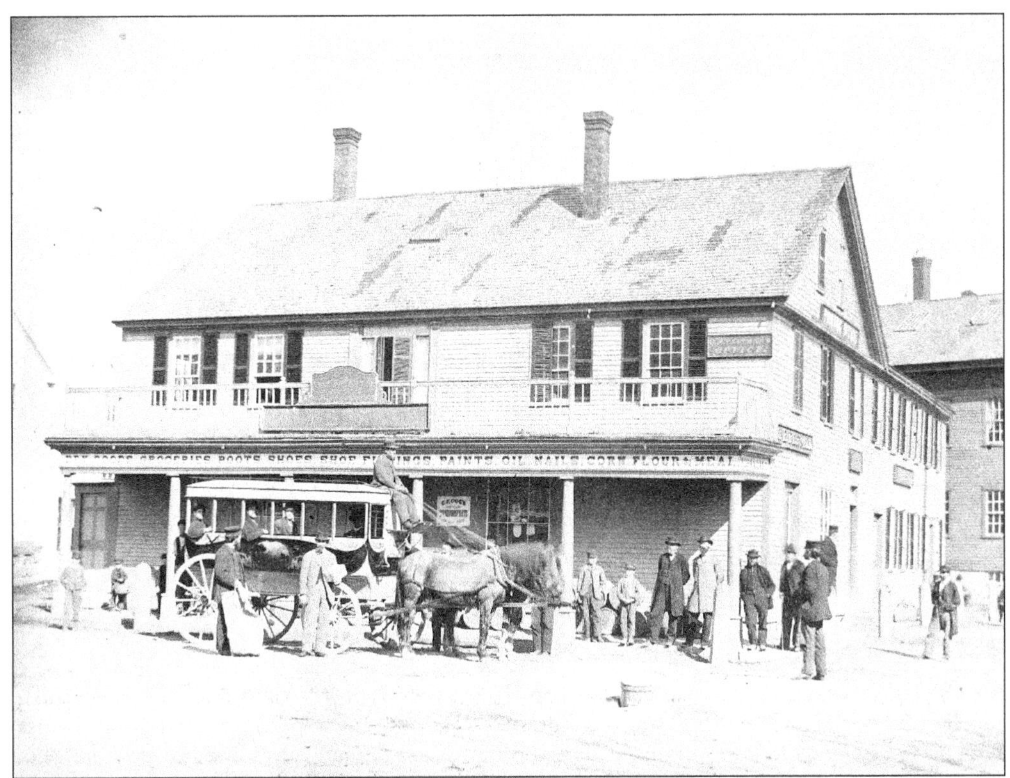

The former Steamboat Hotel, built in 1830 by Gilbert Horney on the corner of Main and Central Streets, appears here with the Perkins Jitney which served as transportation between the center of town and the railroad station. Reported to be the oldest commercial building still in existence, it currently houses a laundromat.

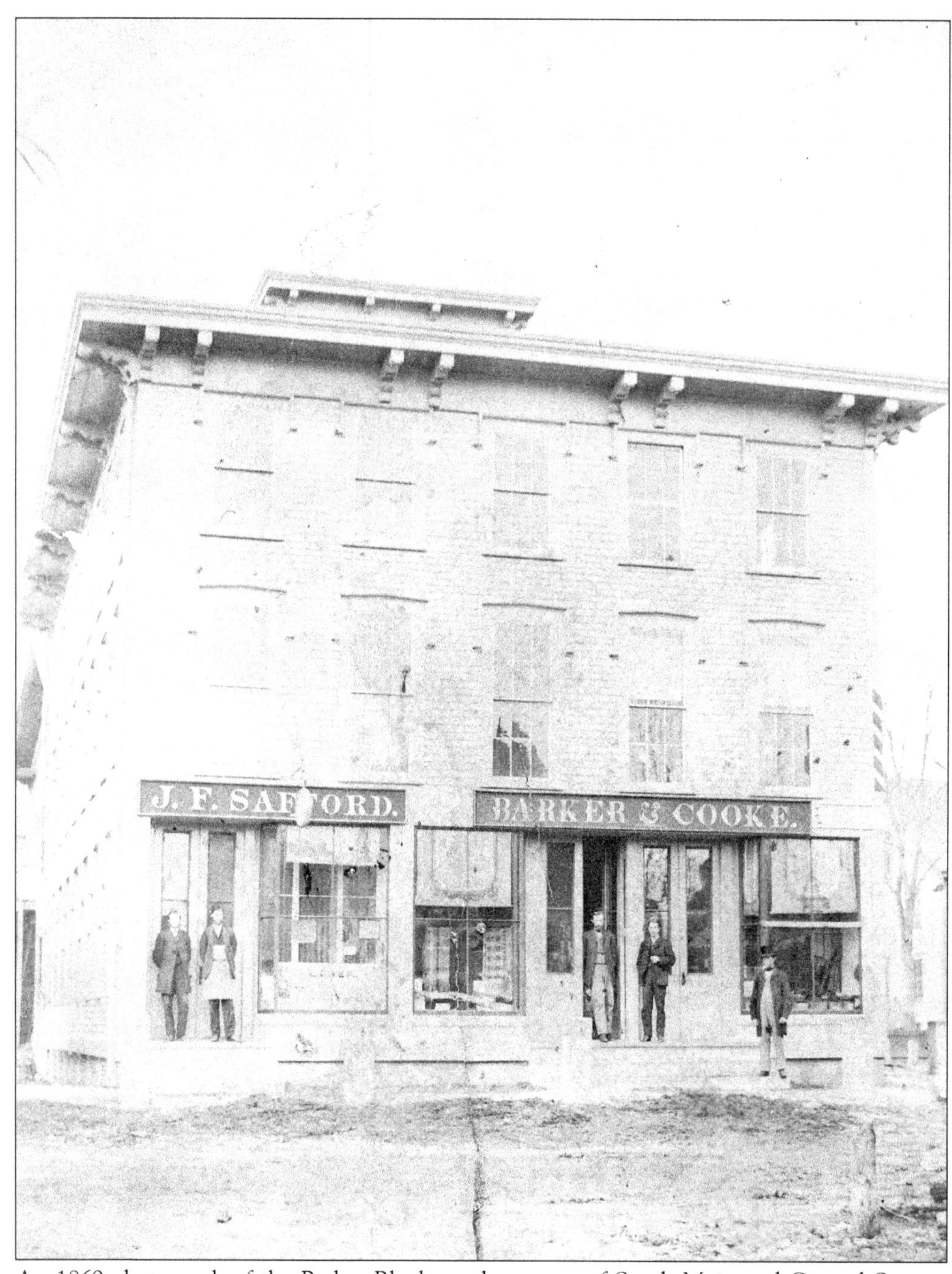

An 1869 photograph of the Barker Block on the corner of South Main and Central Streets. Jeweler and optician James Safford and a friend stand on the steps, along with store owner Thomas Cooke and clerk John Lougee. The top-hatted gentleman is Josiah B. Edgerly, Judge of the Police Court.

The Farmington Savings Bank was organized in 1868 and the Farmington National Bank in 1872, both banks operating in this brick building. A stairway on the left led to the Masonic Hall on the second floor.

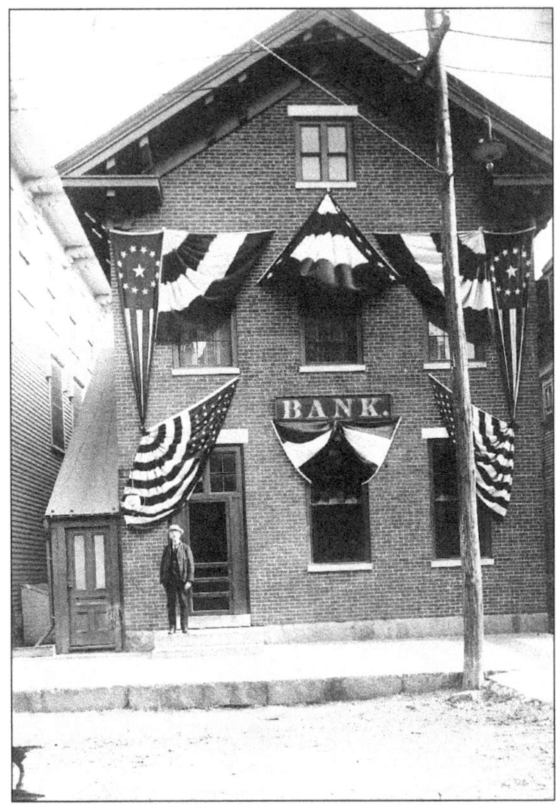

A festively decorated Boston Clothing Company was a later occupant of the Barker Block. Union Hall occupied the top floor. Today the Farmington Bank stands on this site.

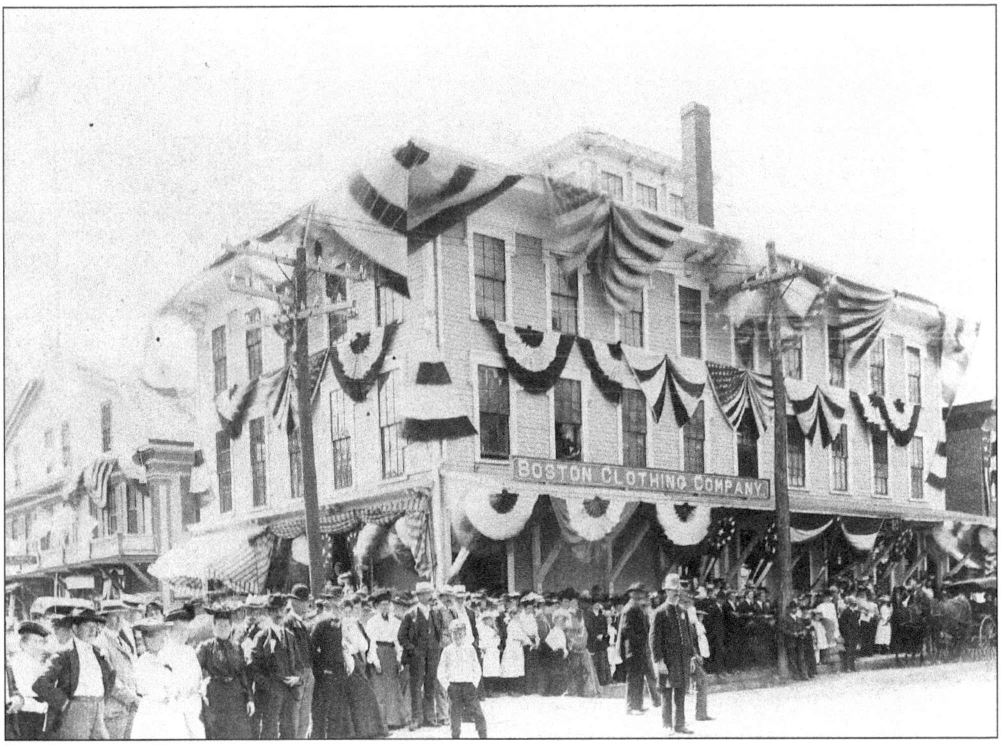

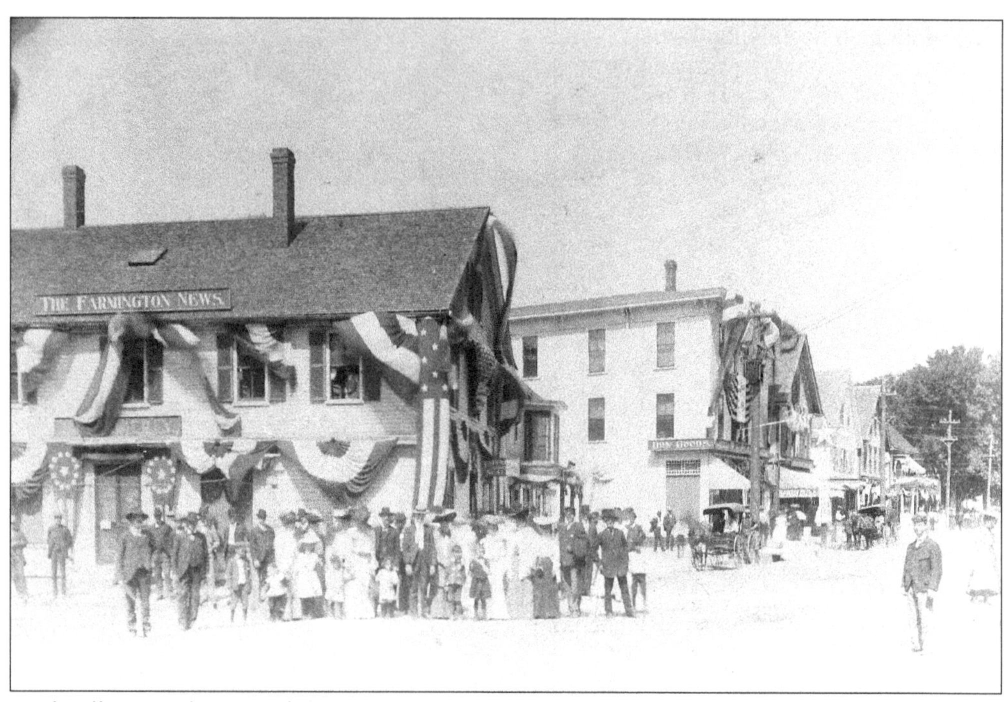

With offices on the second floor of the Steamboat Hotel building, *The Farmington News* was a weekly newspaper originated by James E. Fernald and his son. First issued on March 14, 1879, it was published in this building until 1955.

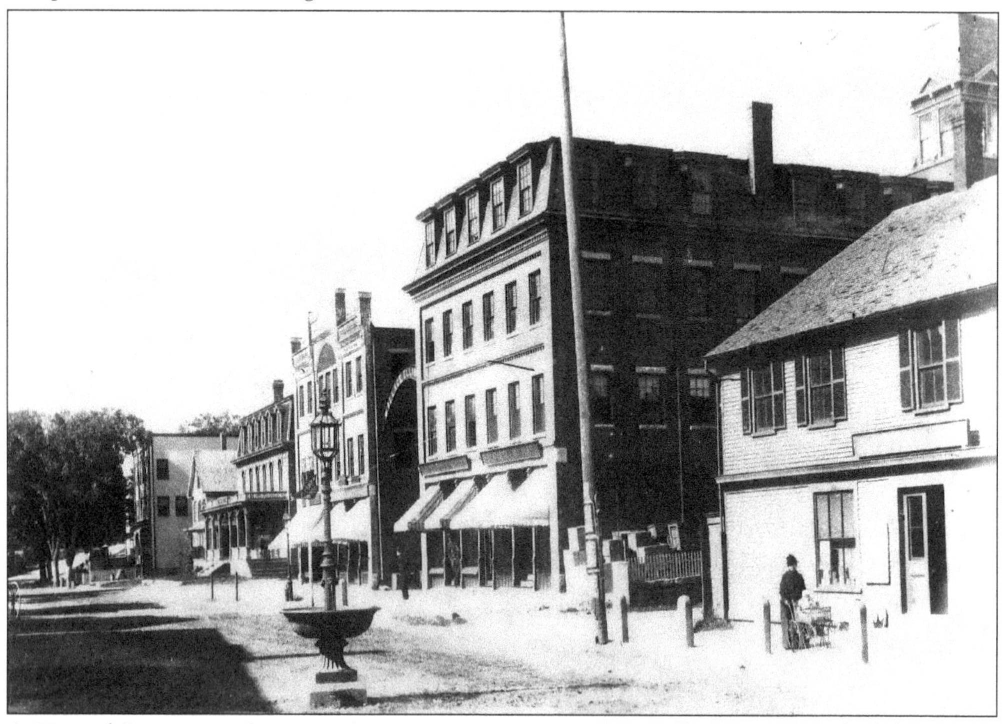

A Central Street view featuring the town watering trough, installed in 1887. It had dippers for people, a high basin for horses and cattle, and a low place for dogs!

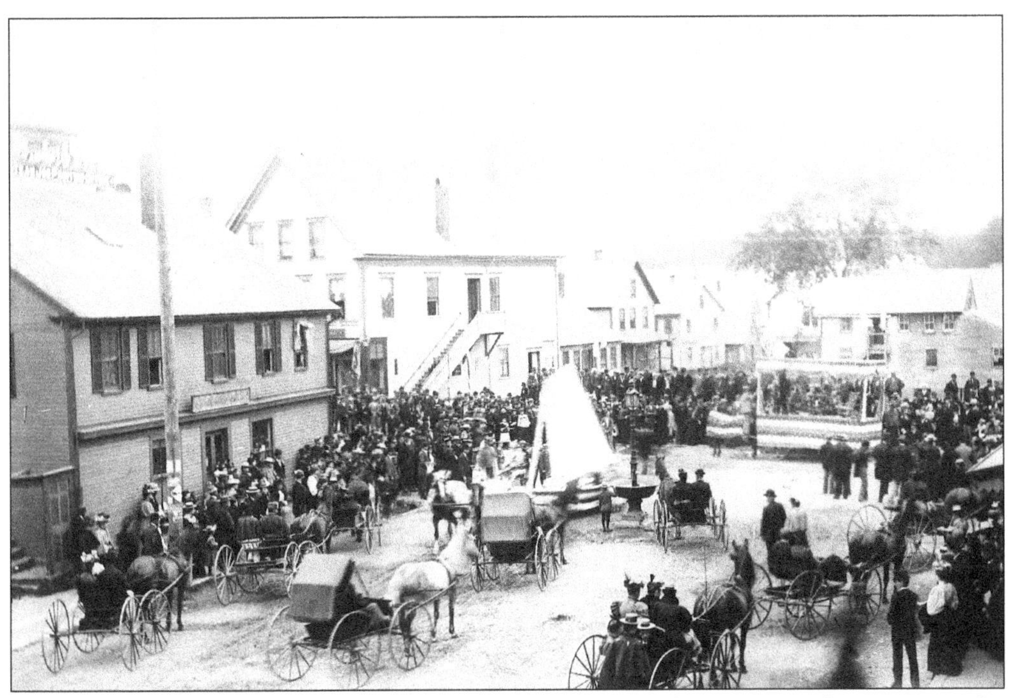

The Square has always been a site for public gatherings. This picture, taken prior to the construction of the Odd Fellows Block, shows the houses on Mechanic Street.

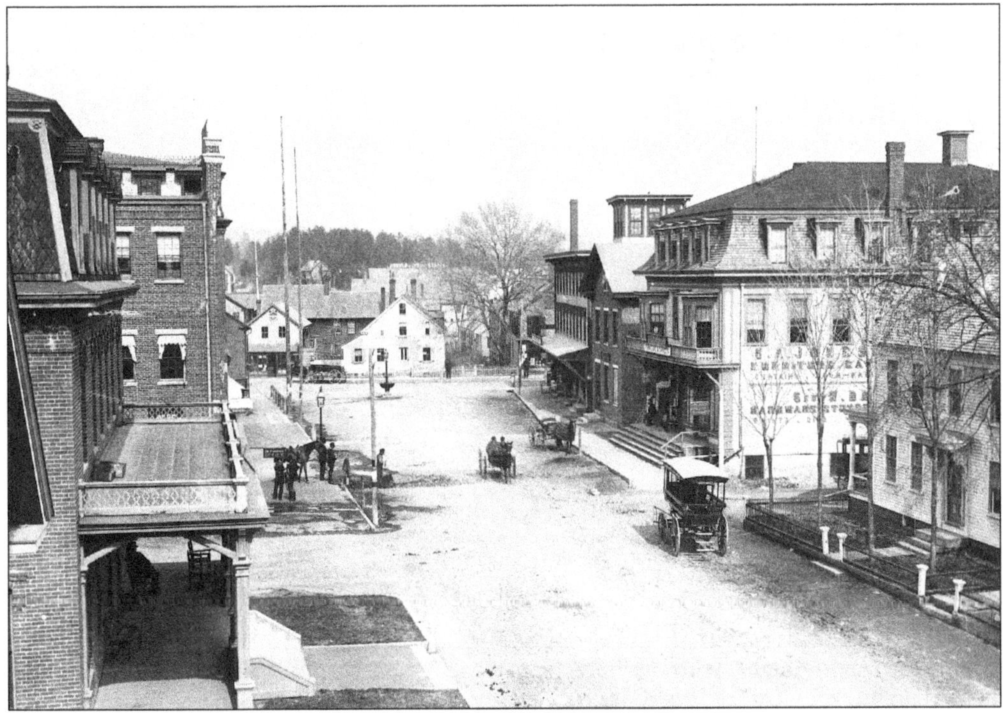

This 1895 photograph by Ralph White records the south side of Central Street when there were still residential dwellings at the Square. The Horn/Schulte House on the right was sacrificed for the bank parking lot in the 1970s.

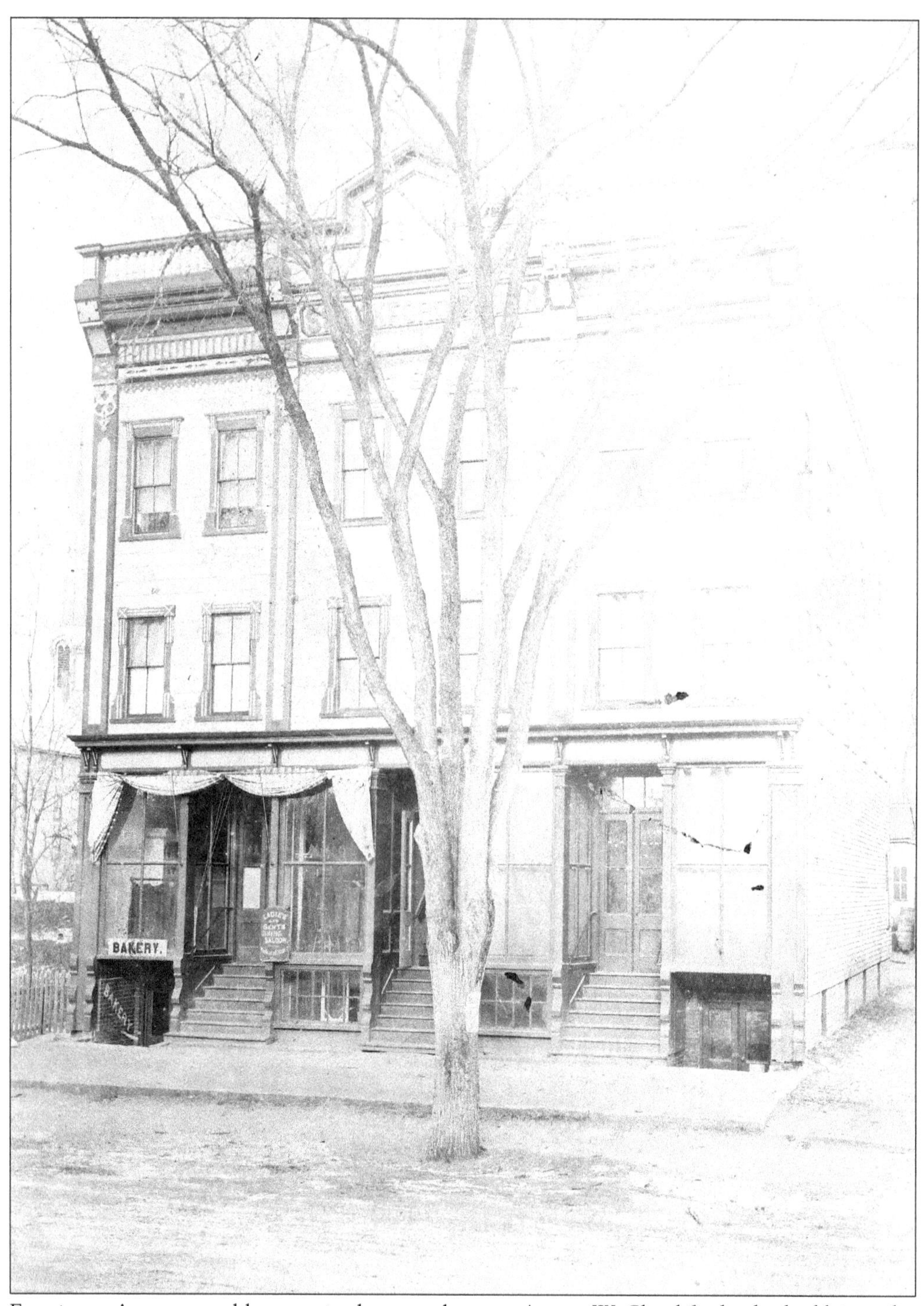

Farmington's most notable portrait photographer was Amasa W. Shackford, who had his studio in this building on Central Street. The U.S. Post Office was located on this site prior to May of 1995.

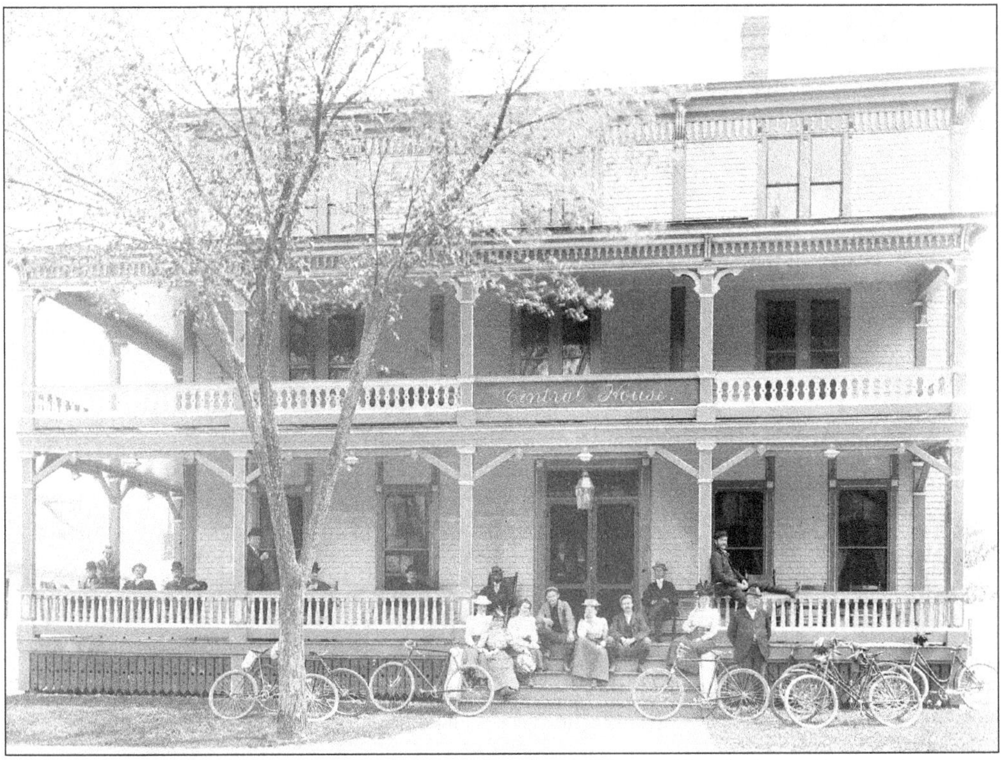

A prominent building on Central Street was the Central House Hotel, shown here with a group of "wheelers" in 1899. It was demolished in 1976.

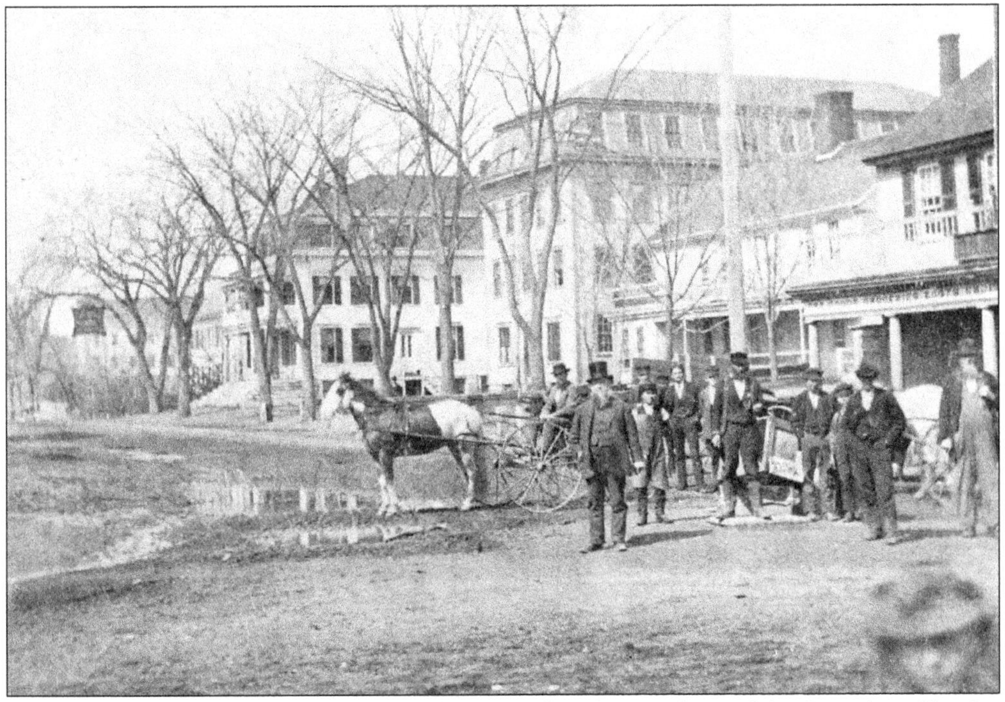

An early view of the north side of Central Street taken from in front of the Steamboat Hotel.

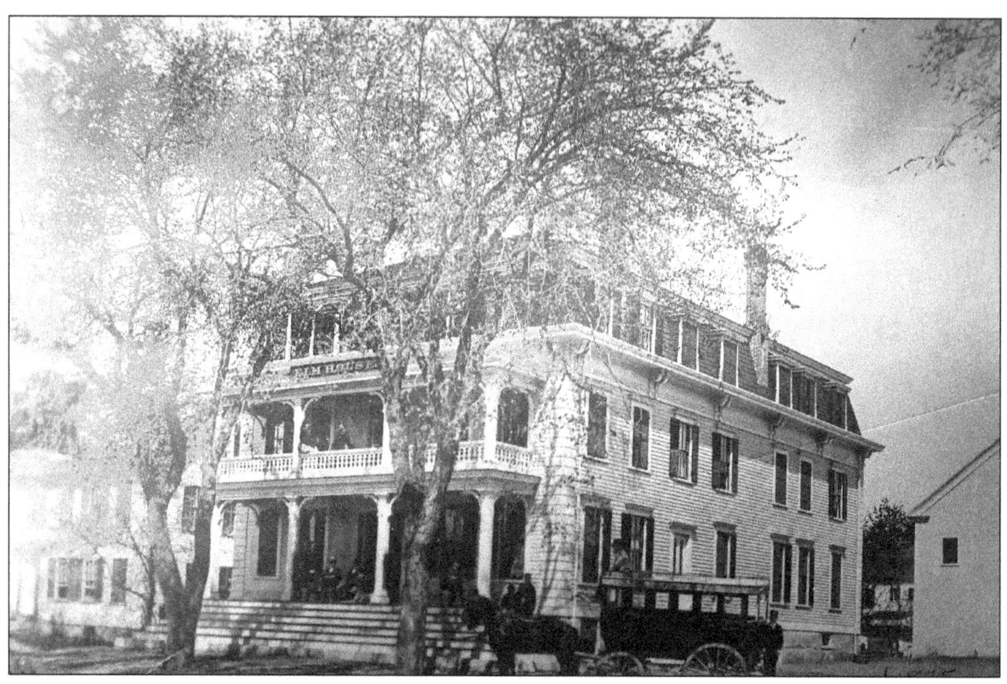

Another handsome hotel on Central Street was Elm House, which fell victim to fire in 1875 but was quickly rebuilt. It later became the Roosevelt House and then the Wilson House.

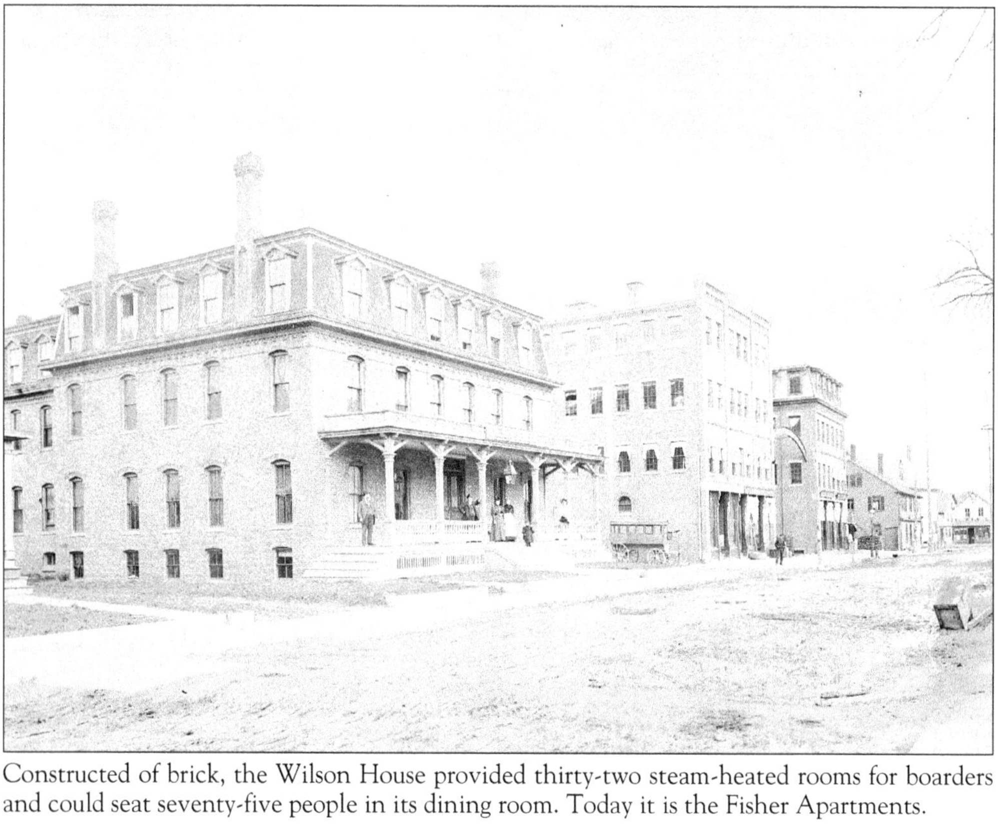

Constructed of brick, the Wilson House provided thirty-two steam-heated rooms for boarders and could seat seventy-five people in its dining room. Today it is the Fisher Apartments.

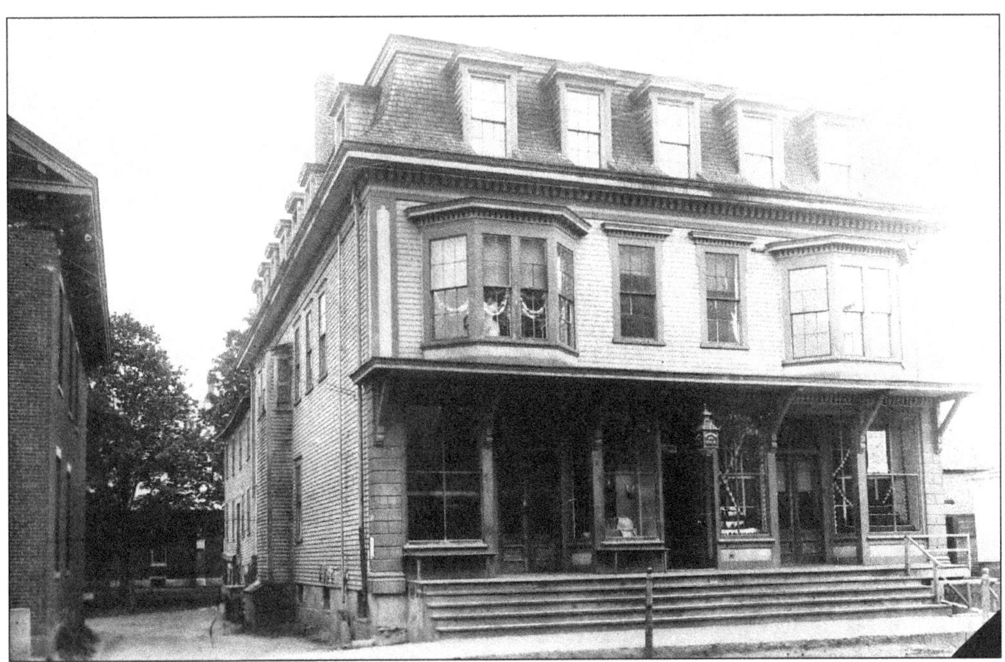

A popular shopping place for the ladies was Lucy Small's Millinery Shop on the second floor, for her ribbons, laces, feathers, and bonnets were much in demand. Stacks of codfish in the basement supplied Marcus Small's first-floor grocery.

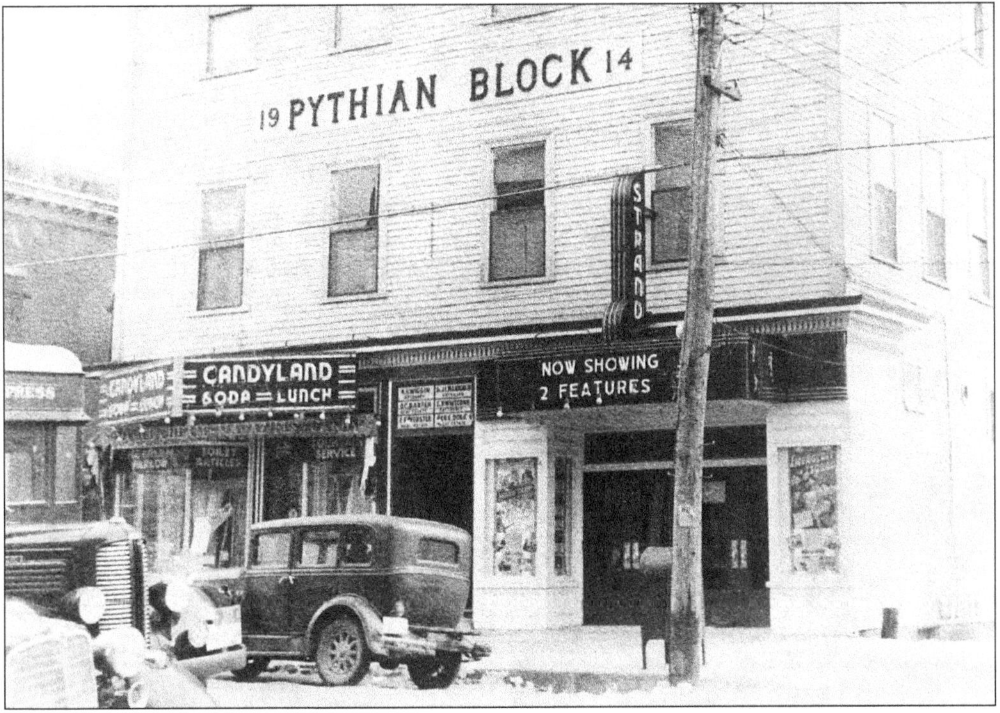

After a fire destroyed the Small Block, the Pythian Block was erected in 1914 as headquarters for the Knights of Pythias. The movie theater and Candyland served as an entertainment focal point until the 1960s.

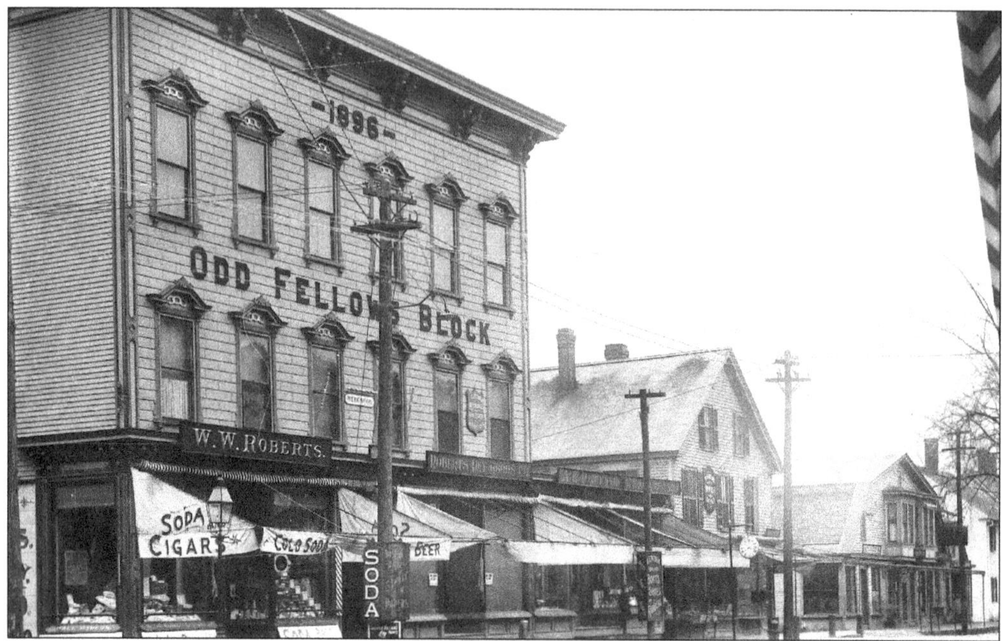

The formal opening of Odd Fellows Hall in October 1896 saw over five hundred people in attendance. For over fifty years the street floor was the location of Roberts Drug Store, which was sold in 1953 to Wilfred "Twink" Osgood, thus becoming Osgood's Pharmacy.

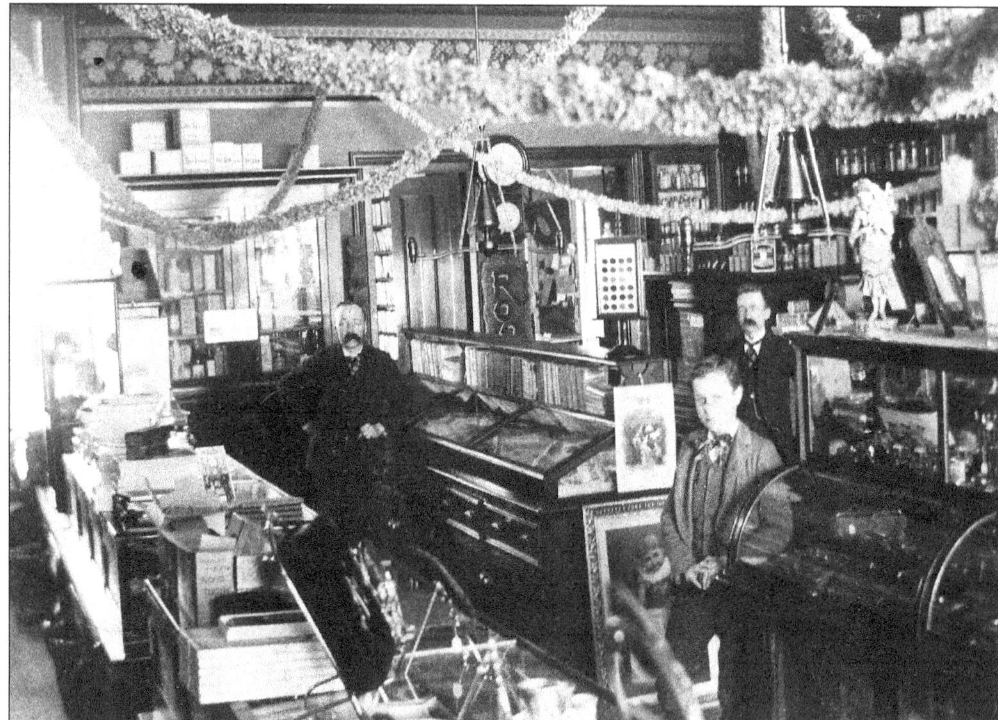
W.W. Roberts (on the left) and Will Peavey (behind the counter), both Farmington natives, formed a partnership in 1889 and opened their drug and stationery store at 21 North Main Street. A young Herbert Browne is in the foreground.

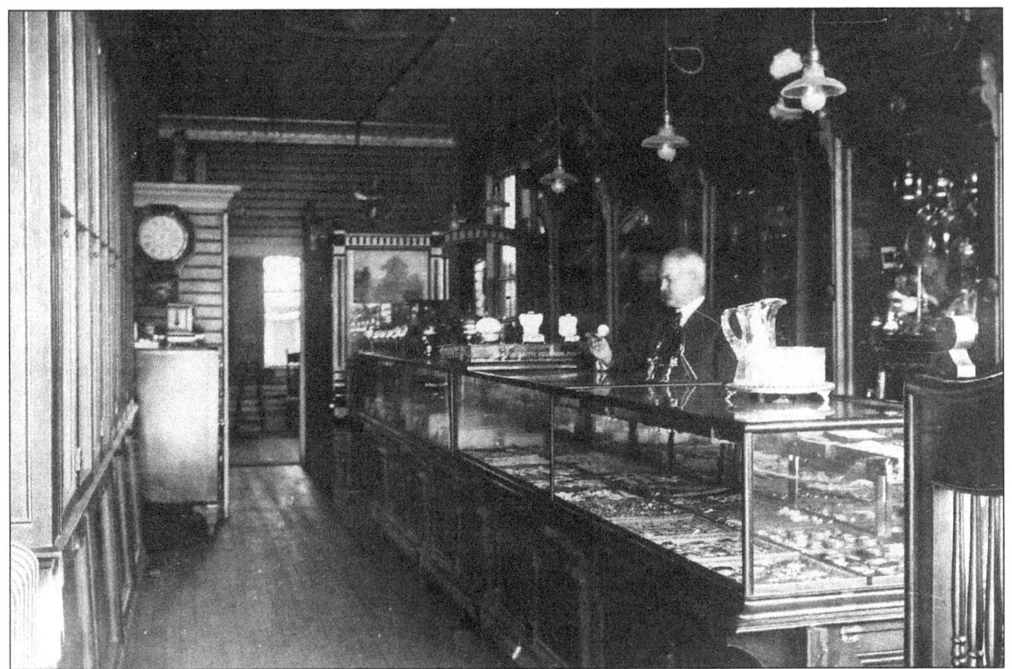

Edwin Legro was proprietor of a jewelry store next to the Odd Fellows Block for a number of years. His store later became the barbershop of Rufus Rundlett.

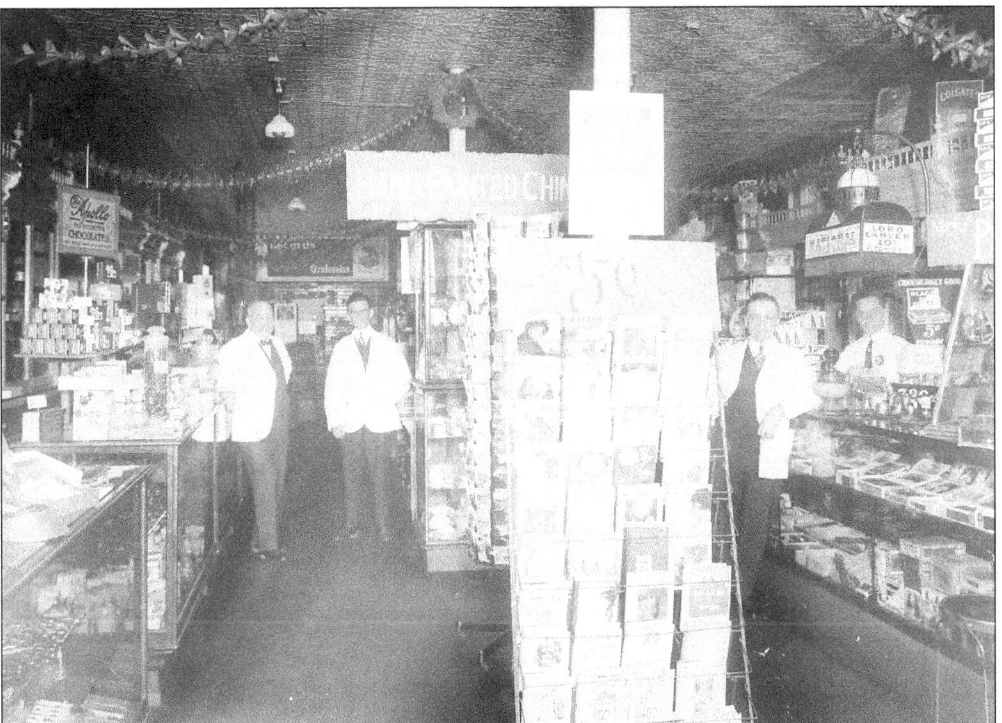

William Roberts purchased complete ownership of the drug store in 1894 when it was moved into the Odd Fellows Block. He is shown here with Clarence Blaisdell, his son George Roberts, and a grown-up Herbert Browne.

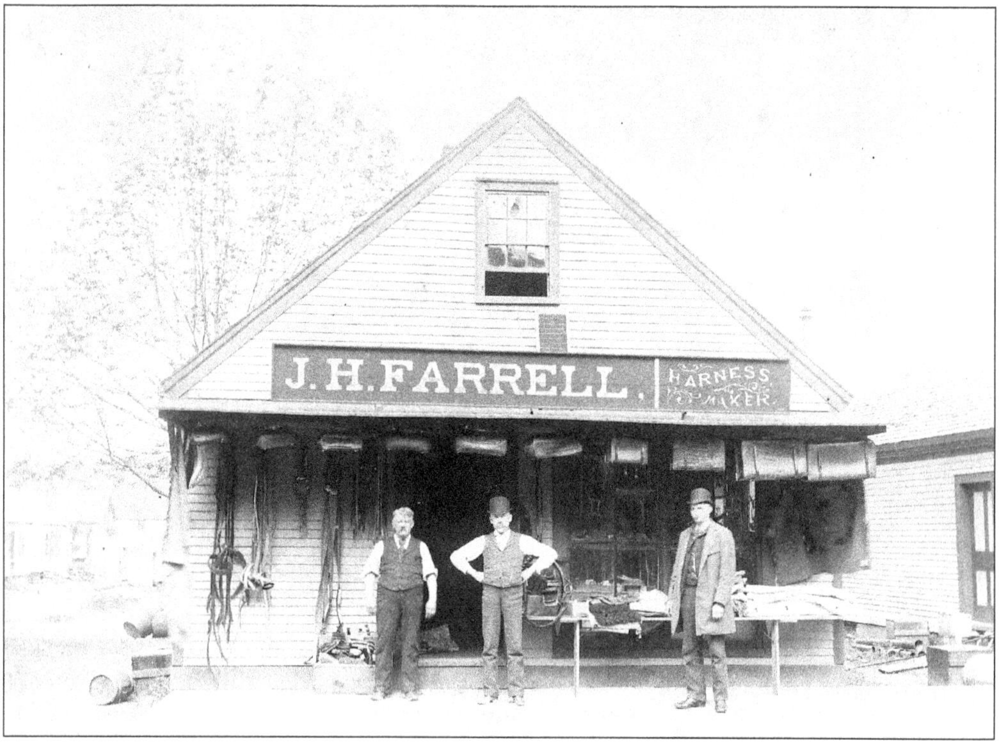

Before the advent of automobiles, harness making was a profitable business as can be seen by this establishment on Main Street.

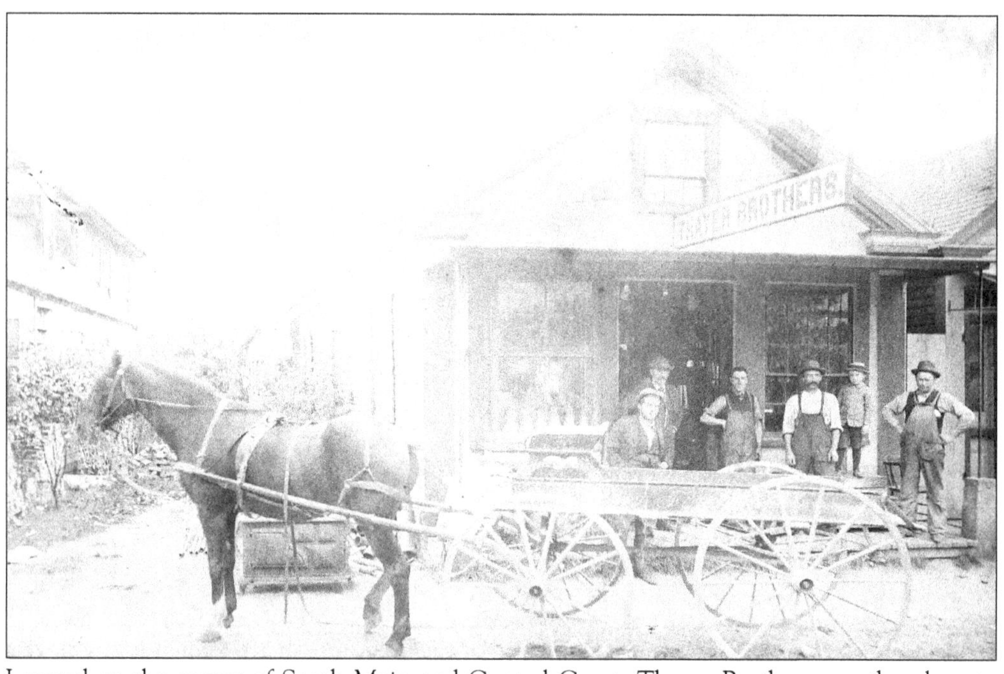

Located on the corner of South Main and Central Court, Thayer Brothers was the place to purchase a stove, pump, or kitchen furnishings.

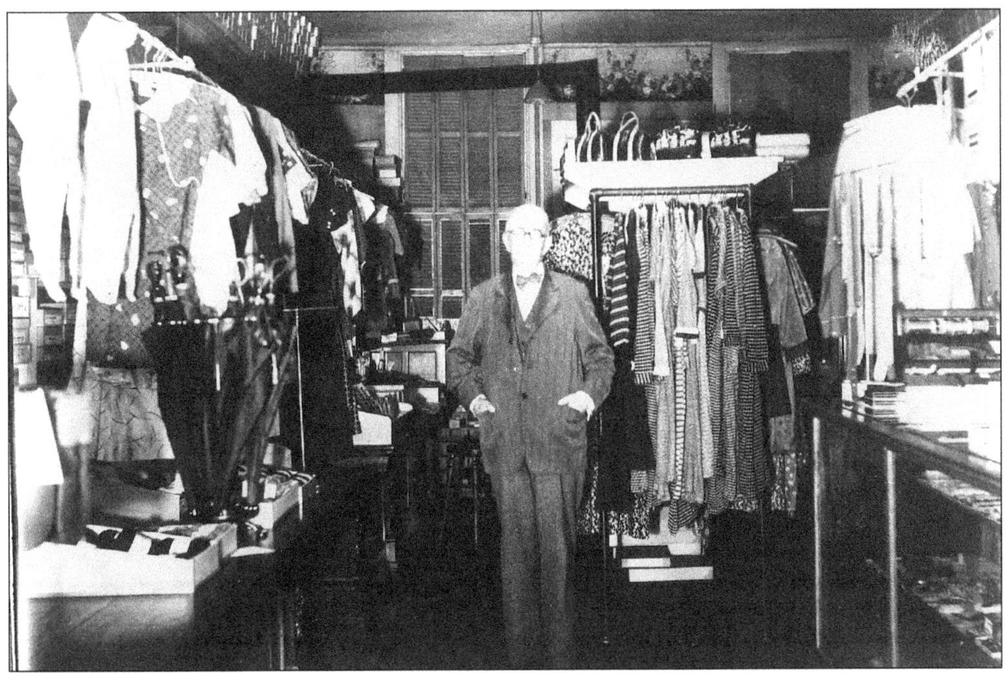

Proprietor of a dry goods store on Main Street until 1936, Ned L. Parker was one of the town's most civic-minded citizens. In addition to several terms in the state general court, he also served as town moderator, library trustee, and school board trustee. He was a frequent contributor to *The Farmington News* of well-researched articles on local history.

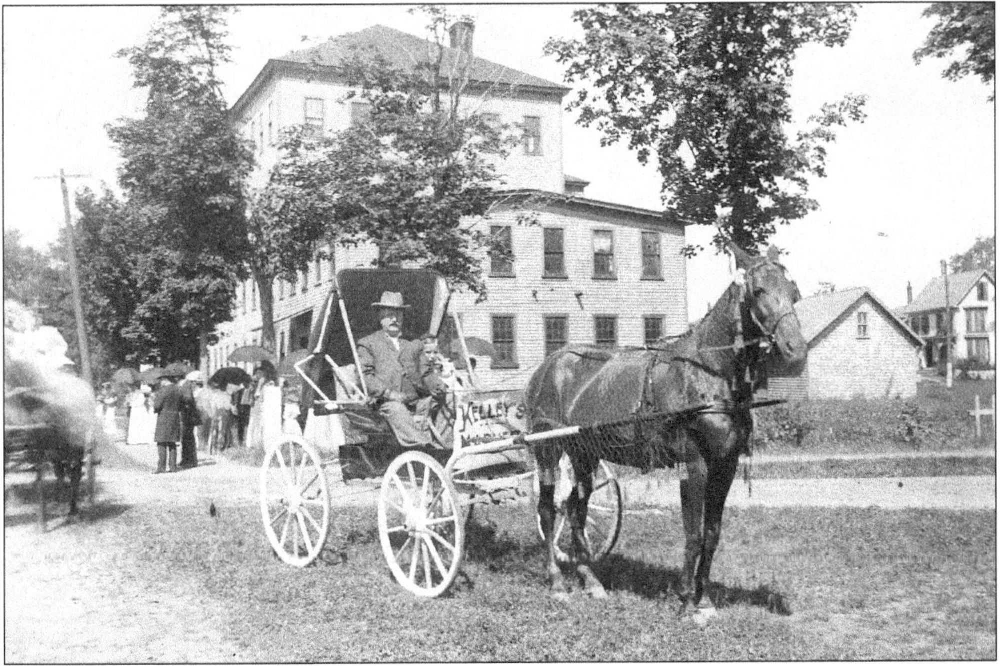

With the Cloutman shoe factory in the background, James Kelley, with son Ernest, advertises his market, which was located first in the Boston Clothing Company building and then in the Steamboat Hotel building. Note the fly net on the horse!

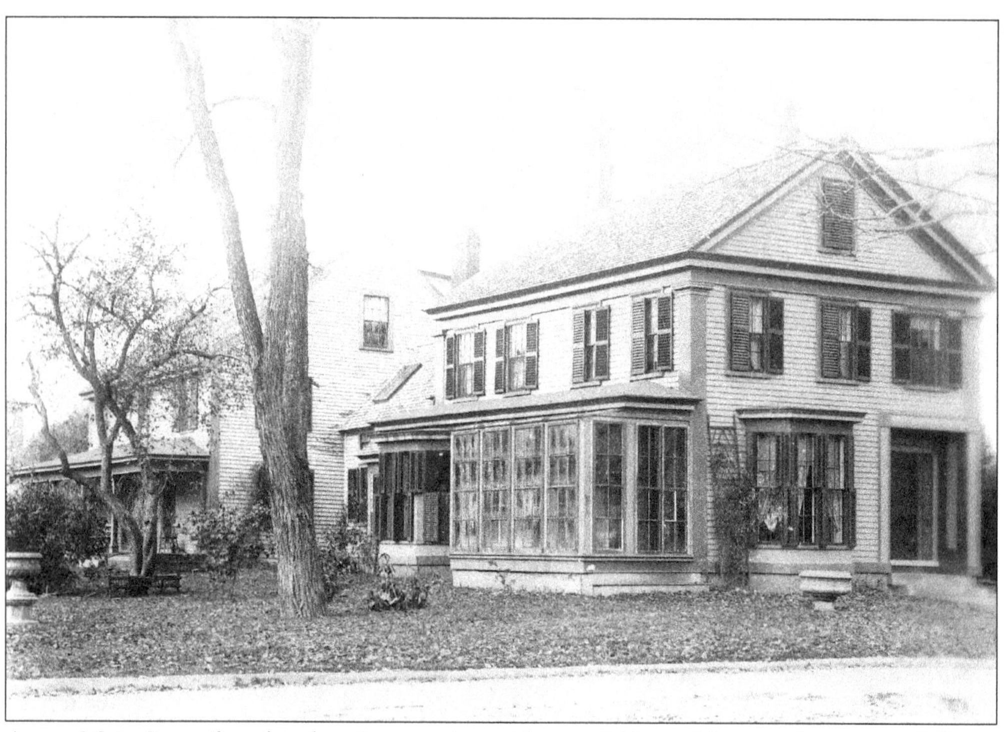

Across Main Street from his shoe factory, the residence of Alonzo Nute on the corner of Grove Street looks much the same today as when it was built in the mid-1800s.

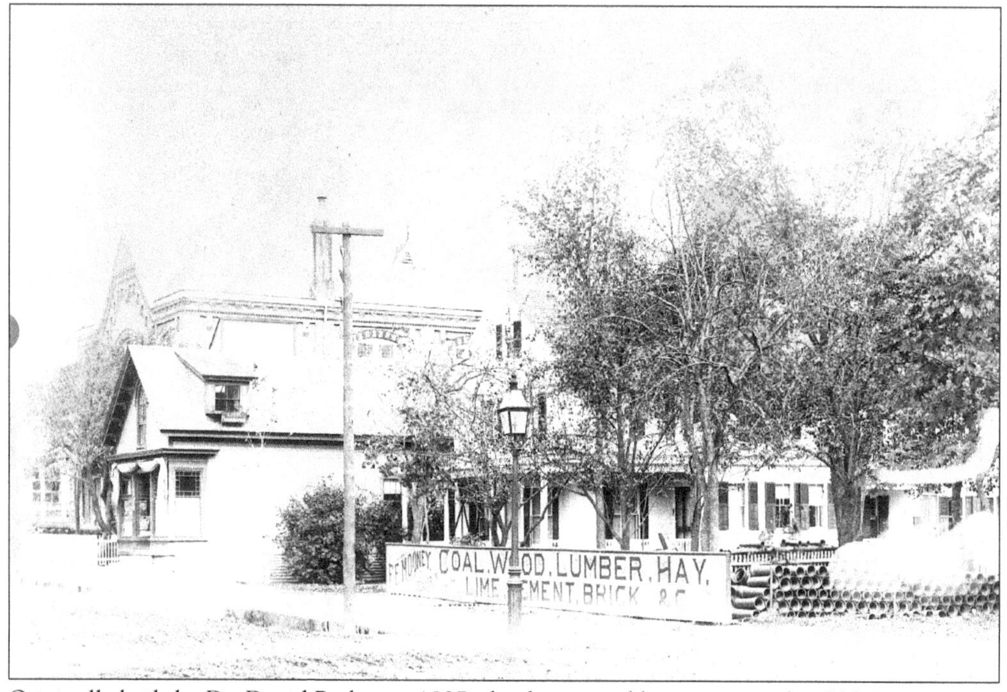

Originally built by Dr. David Parker in 1837, this house and barn next to the Old Court House became Frank Mooney's fuel and hardware business in the 1890s. Today the buildings serve as apartments and a law office.

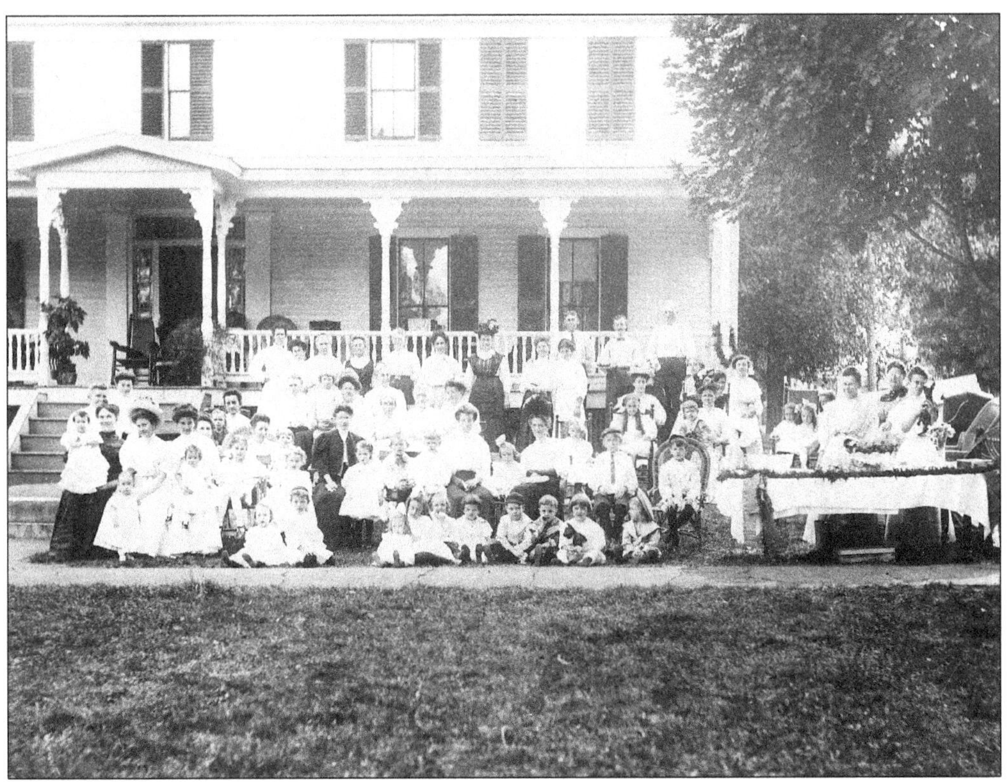

This festive occasion took place in front of the Currier Rooming House. The building later housed the Main Street Restaurant, a most modern establishment as it was lighted by electricity!

TABLE BOARD
AND FURNISHED ROOMS.

CENTRALLY LOCATED.
LARGE AND AIRY ROOMS.

Main Street Restaurant

46 AND 48 NORTH MAIN STREET.

MRS. HESTER E. PINKHAM,
PROPRIETOR.

TRANSIENT CUSTOM SOLICITED.
LIGHTED BY ELECTRICITY.

FARMINGTON,
NEW HAMPSHIRE.

(OVER)

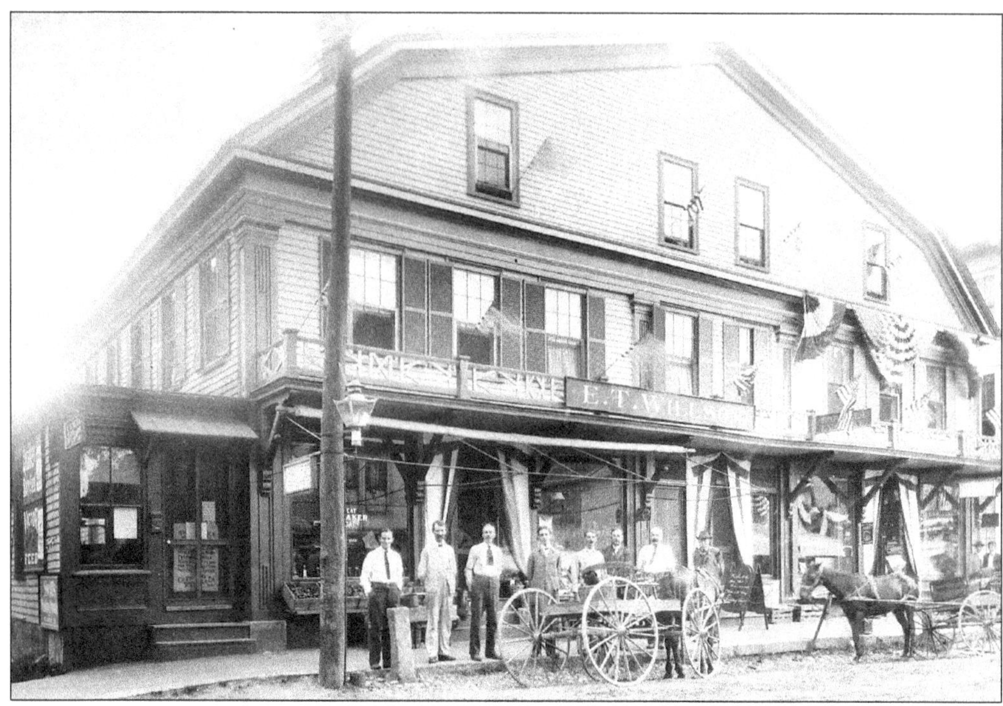

Now the site of the Goodwin Public Library, in 1871 Charles Talpey established a general store in this building. From 1882 until the fire of 1910, this was the Edward T. Willson Store, selling everything but clothing and dry goods.

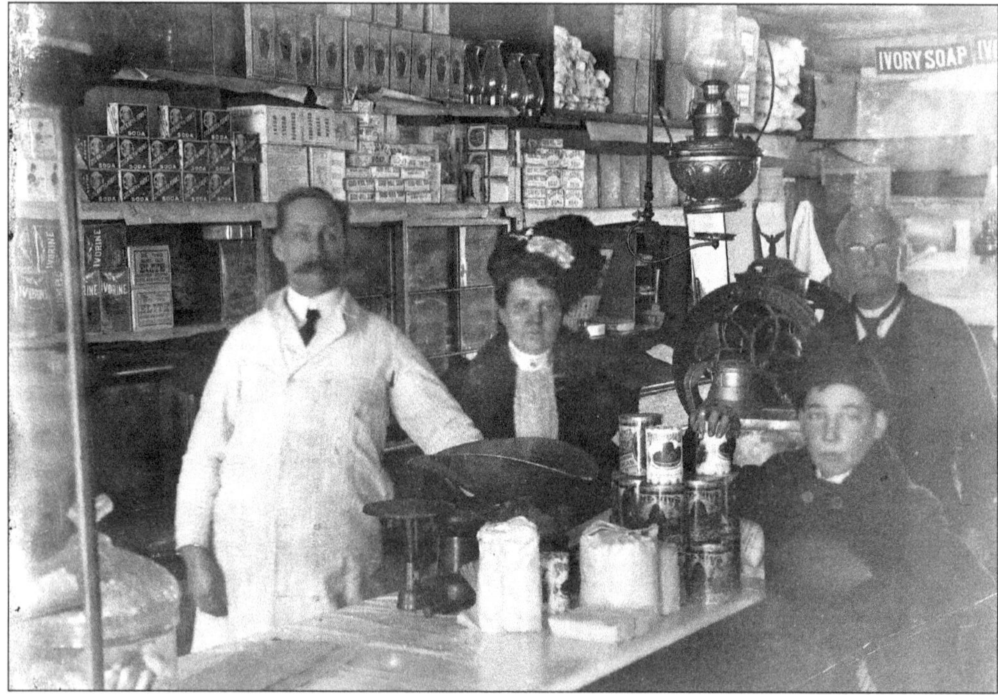

The interior of E.T. Willson's in the era when groceries were wrapped instead of bagged and there was no such thing as self-service.

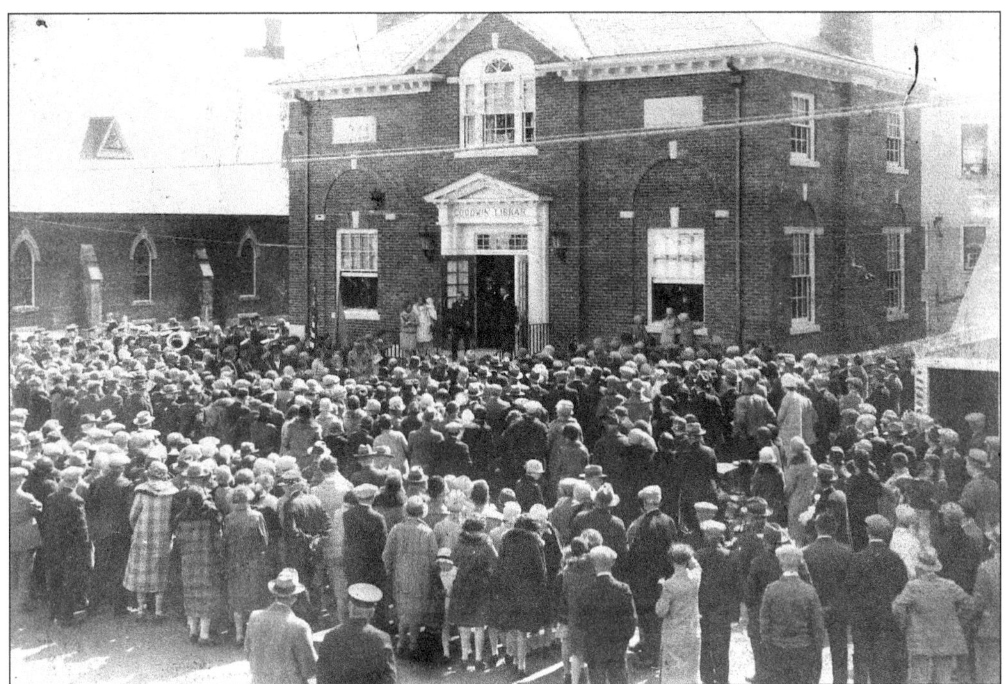

The dedication of the Goodwin Public Library took place on May 10, 1929. The previous library in the Opera House was destroyed by fire in 1928. This was the impetus for a separate library building, and George Goodwin of West Milton agreed to provide funds for its construction.

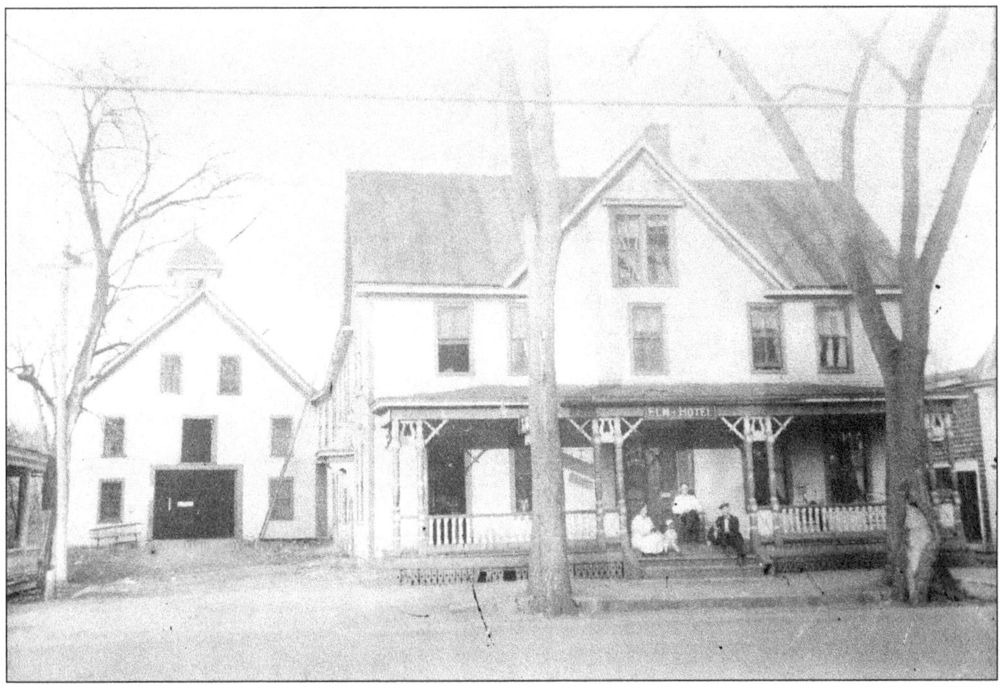

Both its namesake trees and the Elm Hotel are gone now, but this popular stopping place for transients once stood on South Main across from the Congregational church.

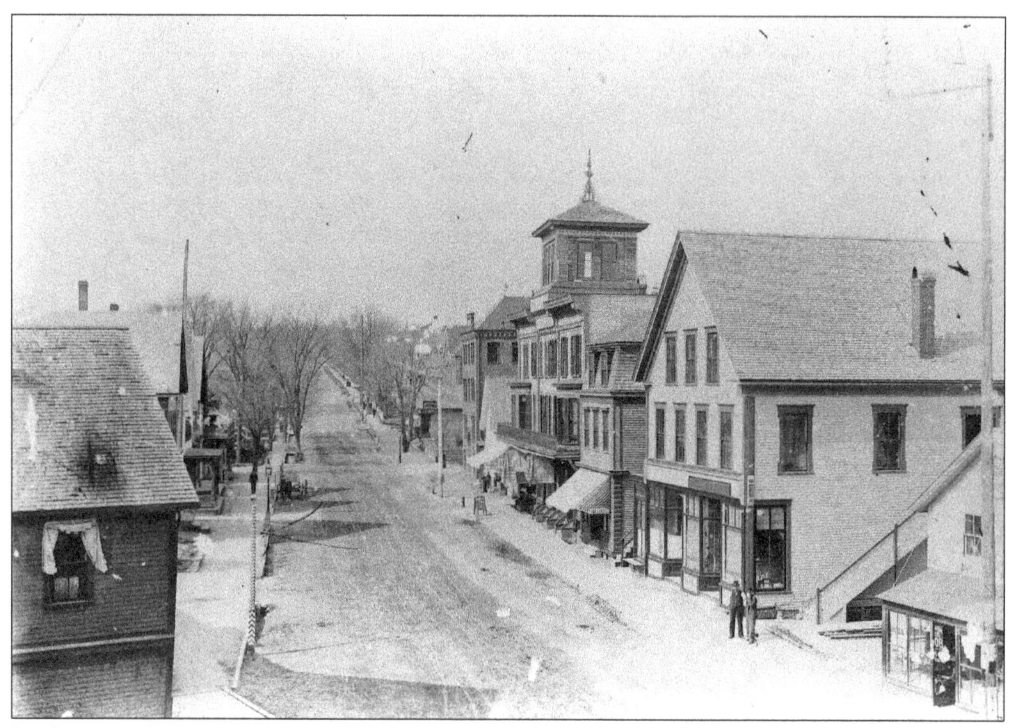

Looking north on Main Street *c.* 1890 prior to construction of the Odd Fellows Block. Note the barber pole and street light on the lower left.

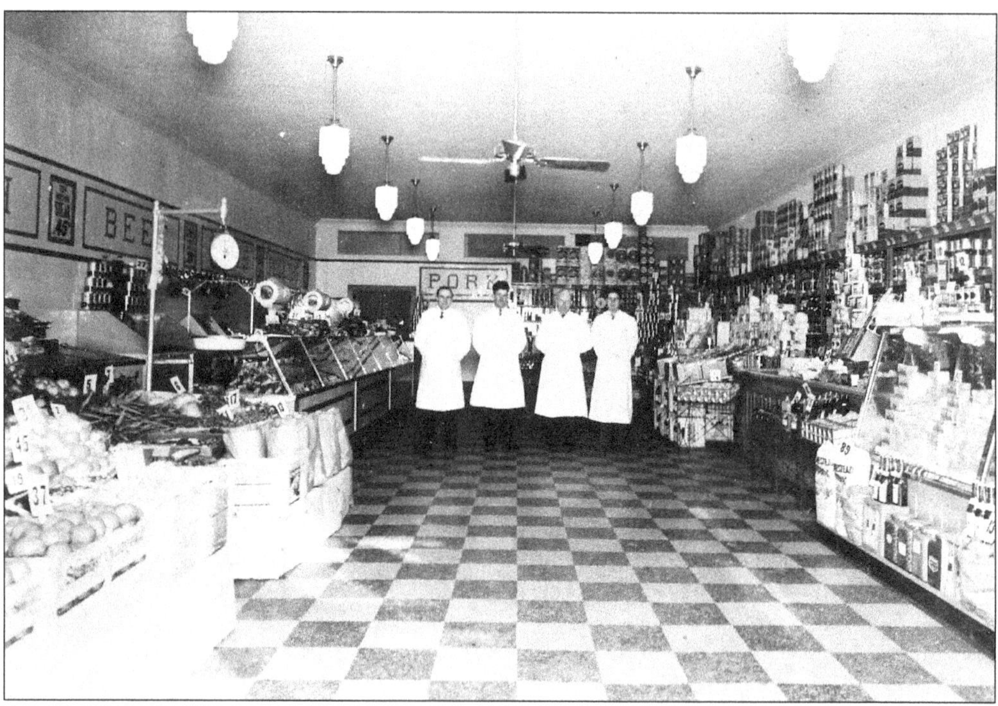

A 1934 photograph of the First National Store with employees Herb Weston, Ray Moreshead, James Hoage, and "Twink" Osgood. Currently a video store and beauty parlor are resident here.

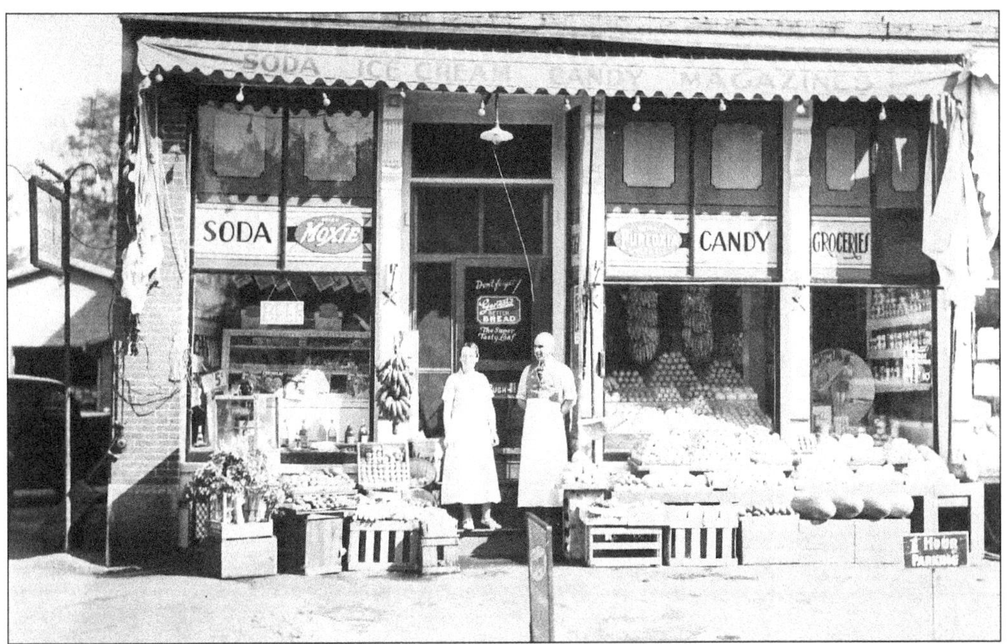

John Brooks and Margarite Furber pose in front of his store on Central Street where the Union Telephone Company is now located.

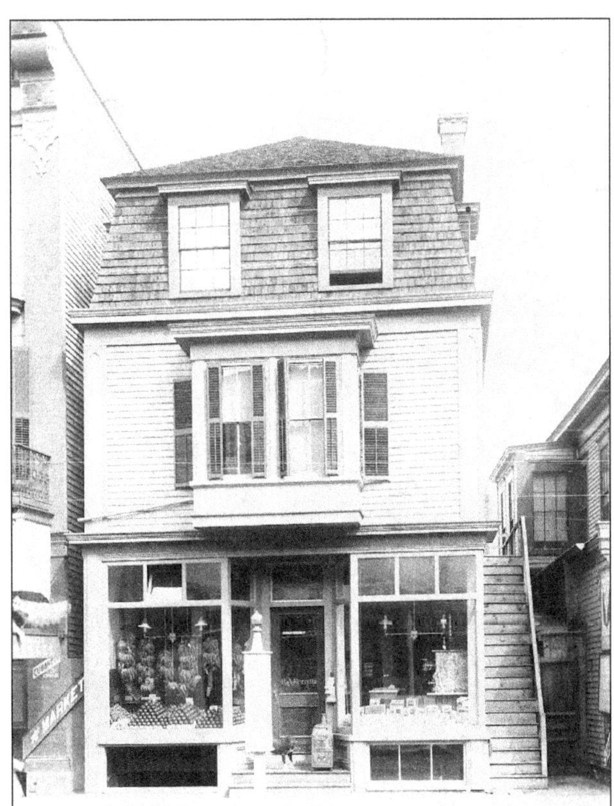

In 1896 Ralph Ferretti opened his fruit and ice cream parlor, advertising "three flavors constantly on hand." You could satisfy your chocolate craving there, at $1.00 per 5-pound box! Gelinas' Market later occupied this site.

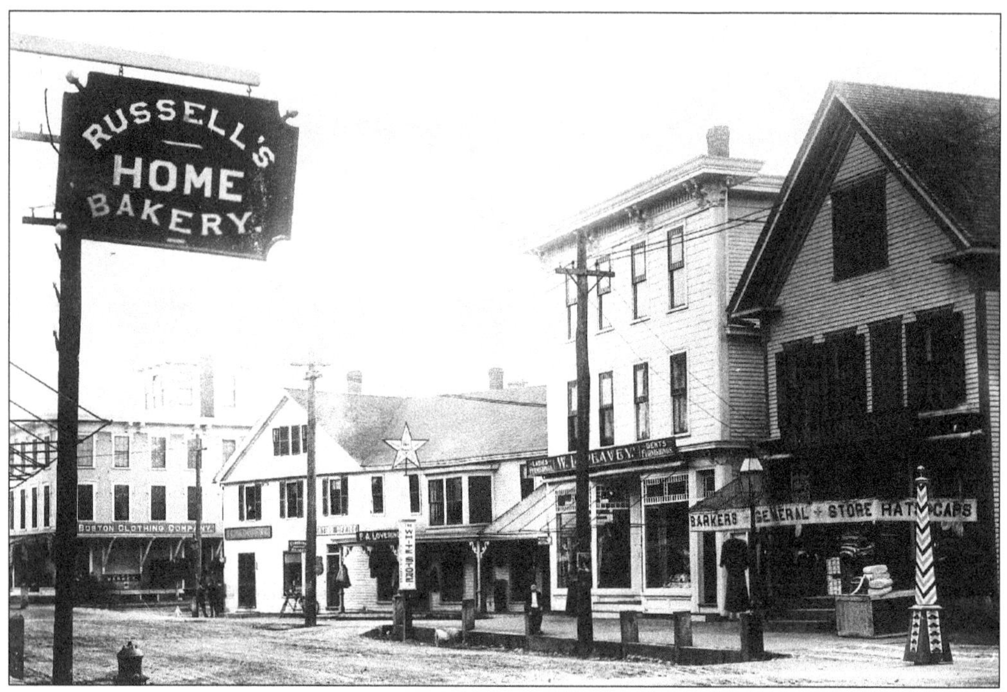

The Masonic Building, with its meeting hall upstairs, had on its first floor The White Store. The 1860 Reed Block next door, which housed John Barker's general merchandise store, burned in 1969.

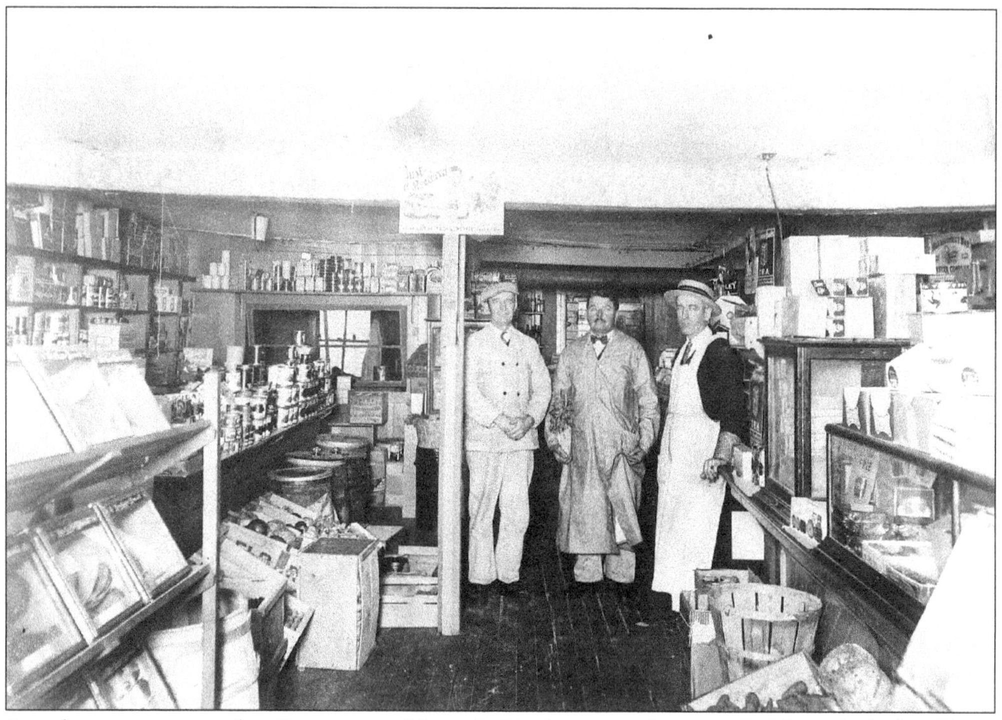

Another grocery on the Square was Nutter's Market, seen here with Harry Pulsifer, Harry Nutter, and Walt Pulsifer.

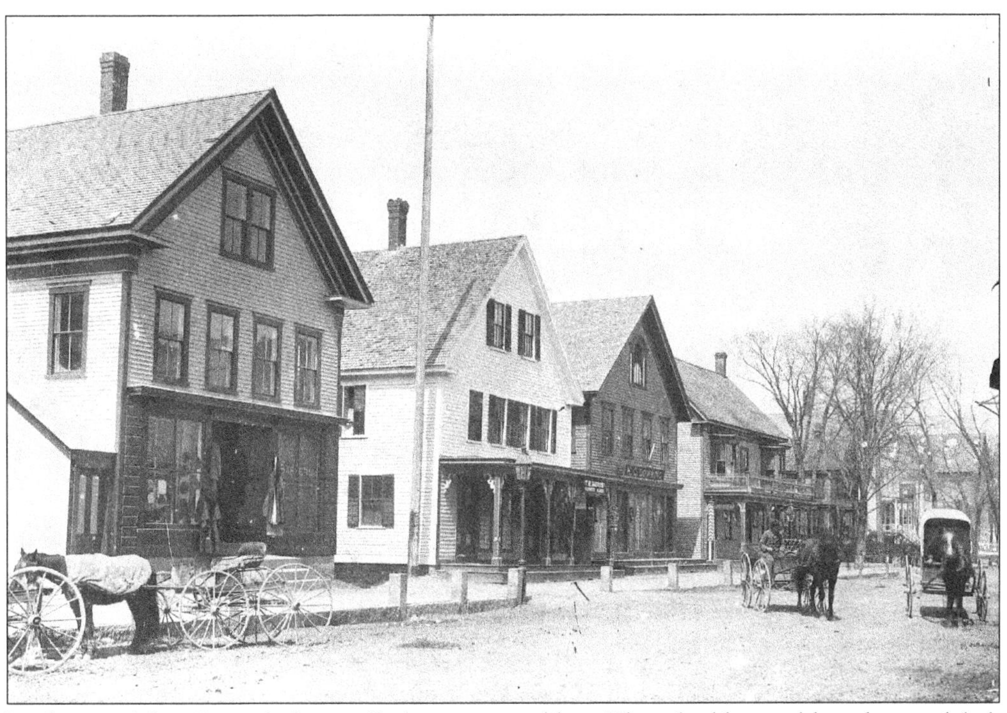
Looking up Main Street before traffic became a problem. These buildings, although remodeled, are still in existence.

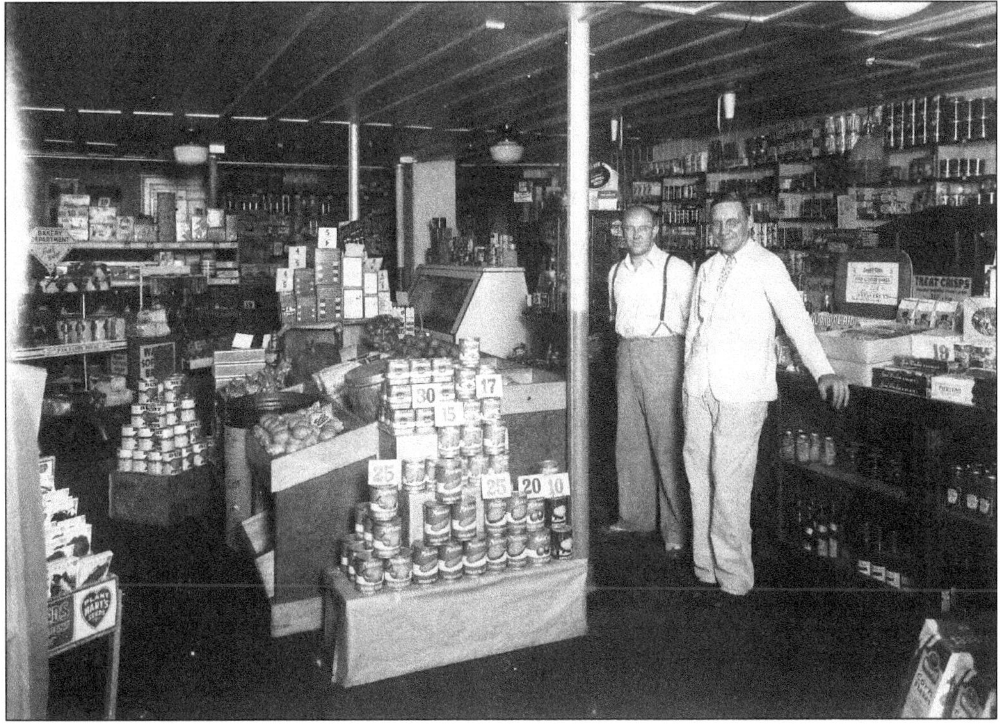

Ernest Kelley, shown here with George Butler, followed in his father's footsteps, establishing his own "Kelley's Grocery" in 1920.

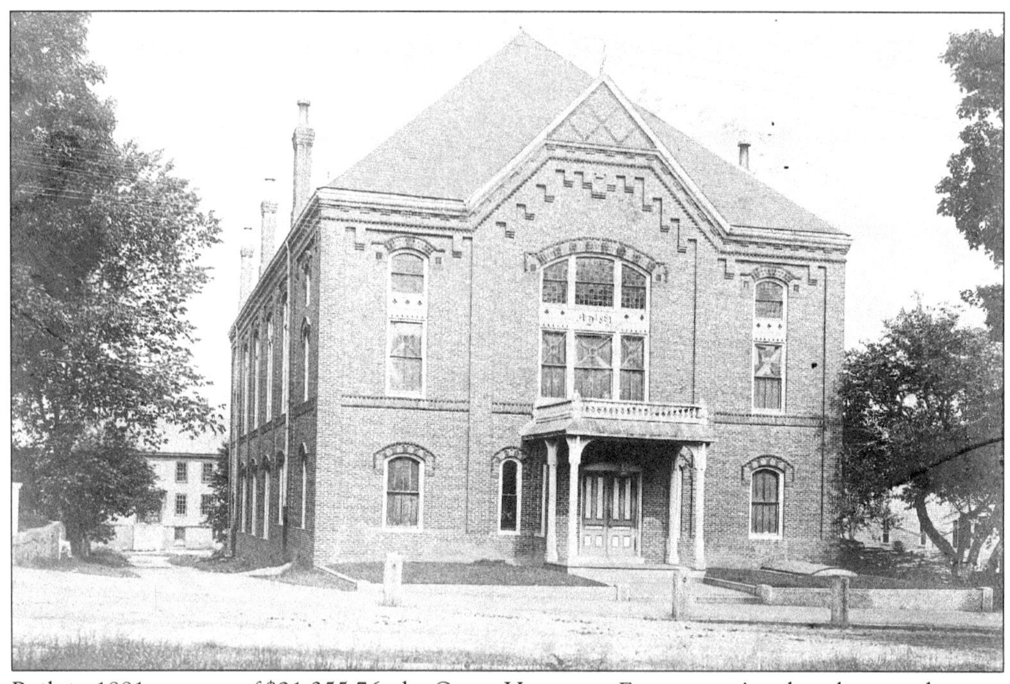

Built in 1881 at a cost of $21,355.76, the Opera House was Farmington's cultural center, hosting plays, dances, and concerts. Since the town offices were located here, its destruction by fire in 1928 caused the irretrievable loss of many town records.

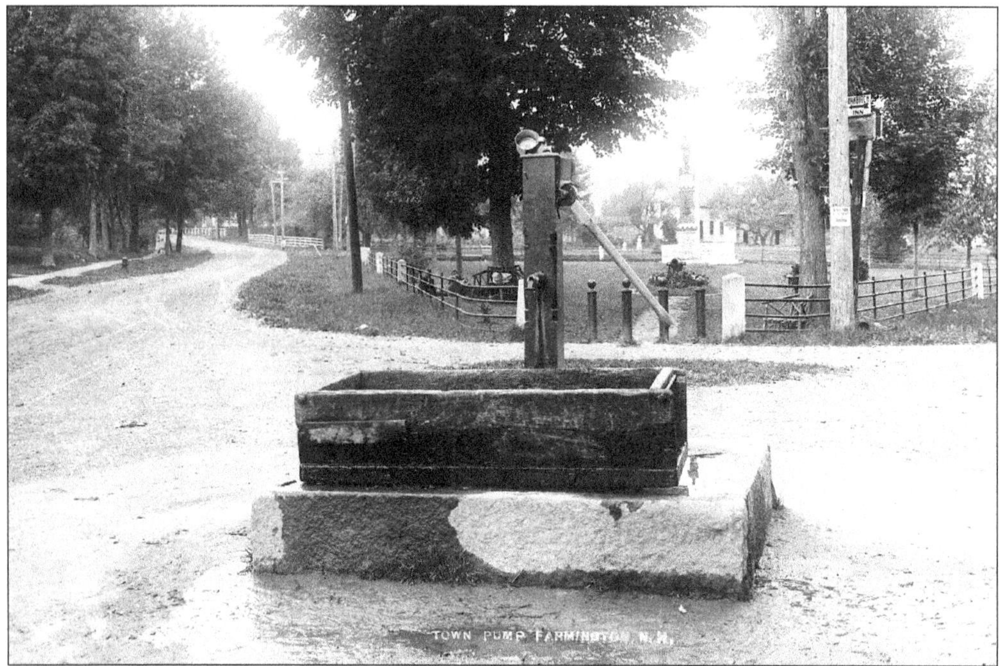

The old town pump with its tin dipper and watering trough stood for sixty years at the intersection of Charles and North Main Streets. After its well was condemned, it was replaced by an artificial pump. Edgerly Park in the background was a gift to the town from James Edgerly in memory of his Civil War comrades.

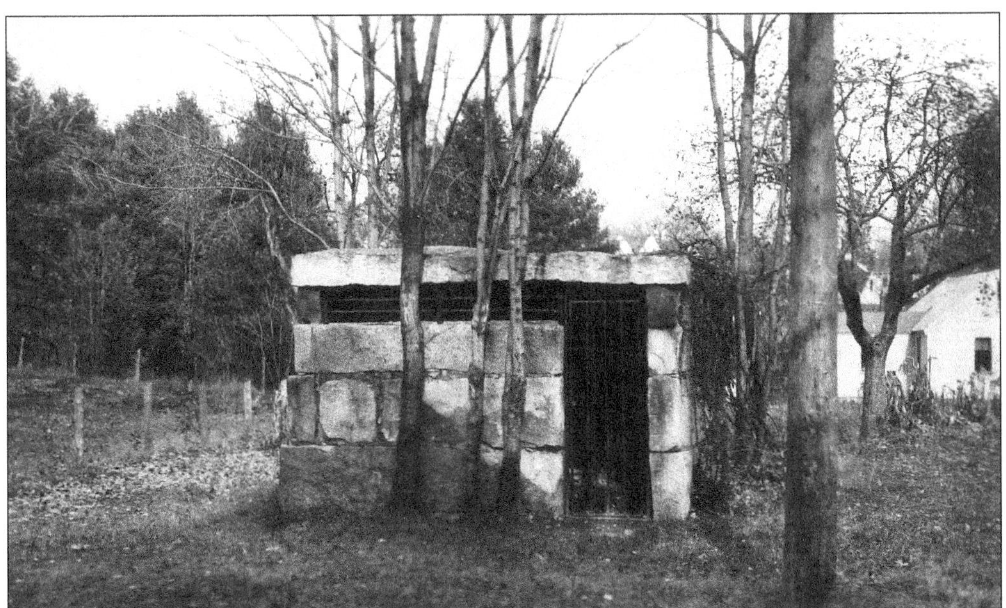

The Stone Lobby, later referred to as "The Lock-Up," was built in 1859 on the corner of Church and Union Streets by William Sampson to confine the lawless element until some legal tribunal pronounced judgment. It was 10 feet long, 10 feet wide, and stood 6.5 feet tall.

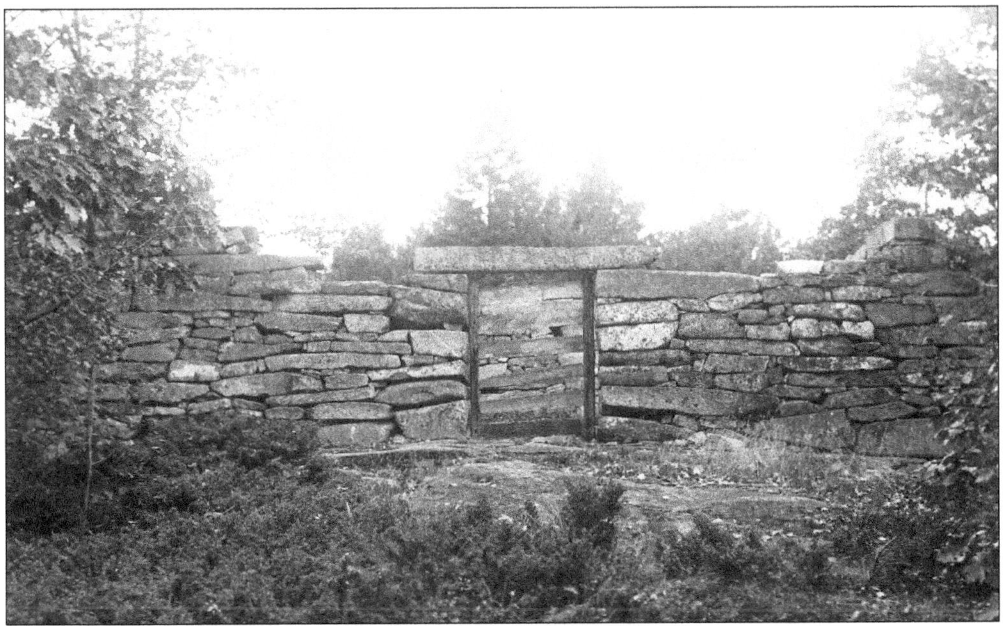

In the early nineteenth century each town was required to maintain an animal pound to restrain strays. Farmington's Town Pound, located on the Pound Road near the geographic center of town, is still an impressive edifice. Constructed in 1823 by Nicholas Colbath, it measures 40 feet square with walls 8 feet high. Due largely to the efforts of Edmund Demers, it was placed on the U.S. Department of the Interior's National Register of Historic Places in 1993.

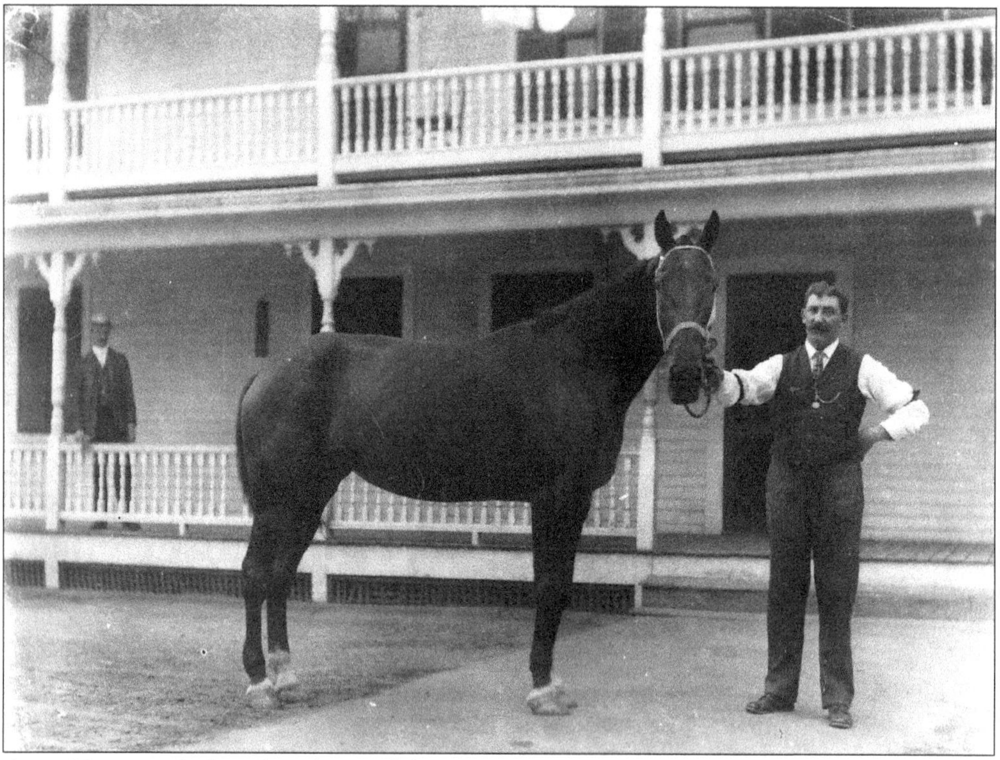

A vital business before the advent of the auto was Locke's Livery on Crowley and Mechanic Streets. Begun in 1889 by J. Wesley Locke, it was here that one could hire or buy horses and carriages.

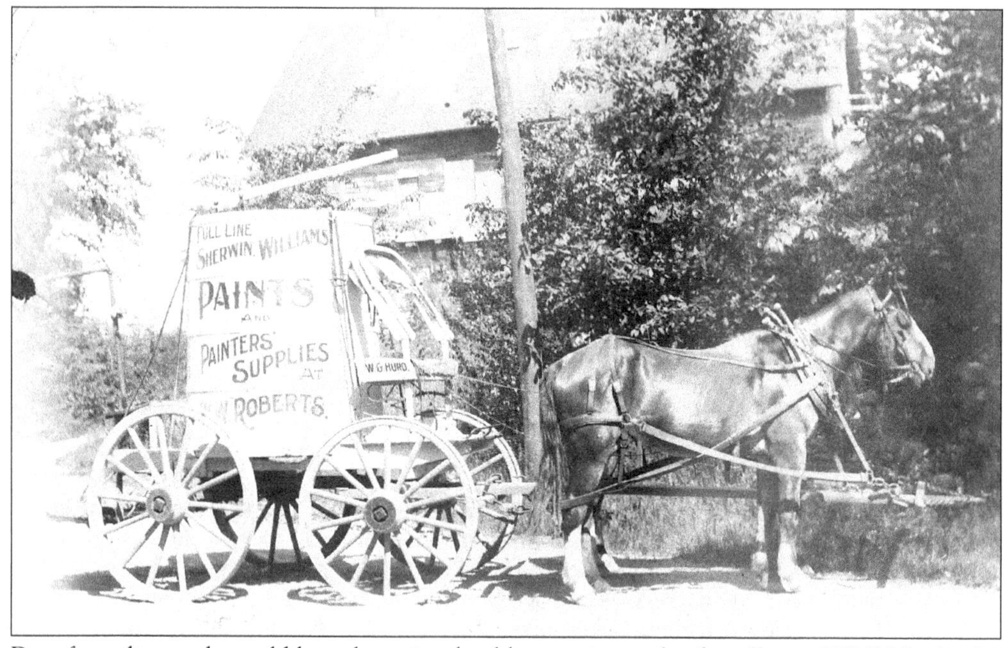

Dust from dirt roads would have been intolerable were it not for the efforts of Will Hurd, who was paid $15.00 weekly by merchants to operate the town sprinkler.

Two

Work: Industry and Agriculture

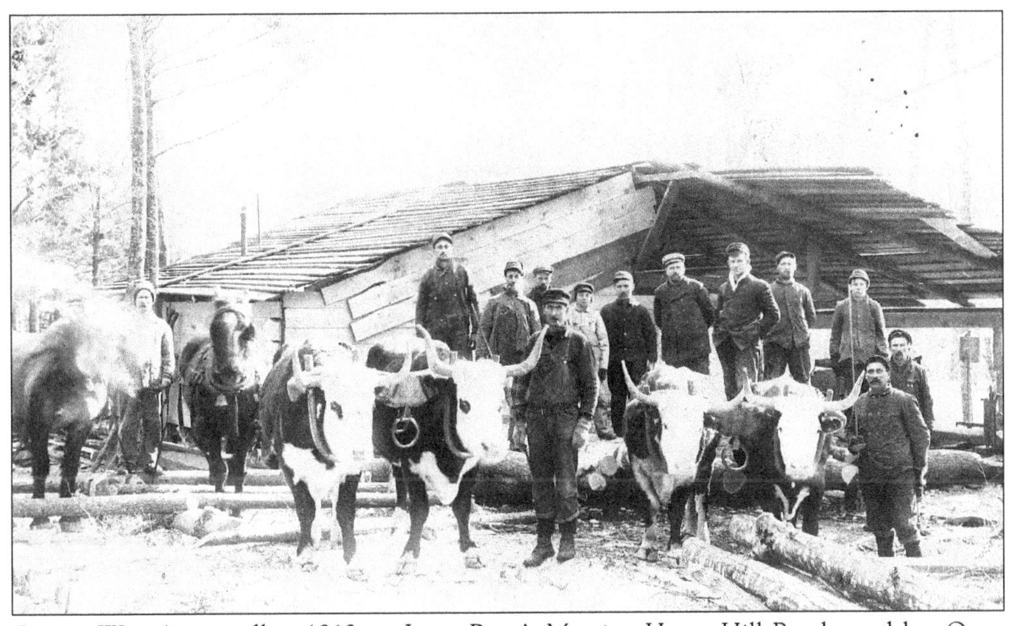

George Wyatt's sawmill *c.* 1913 on Ivory Bean's Meeting House Hill Road wood lot. Oxen teams were the "skidders" in those days.

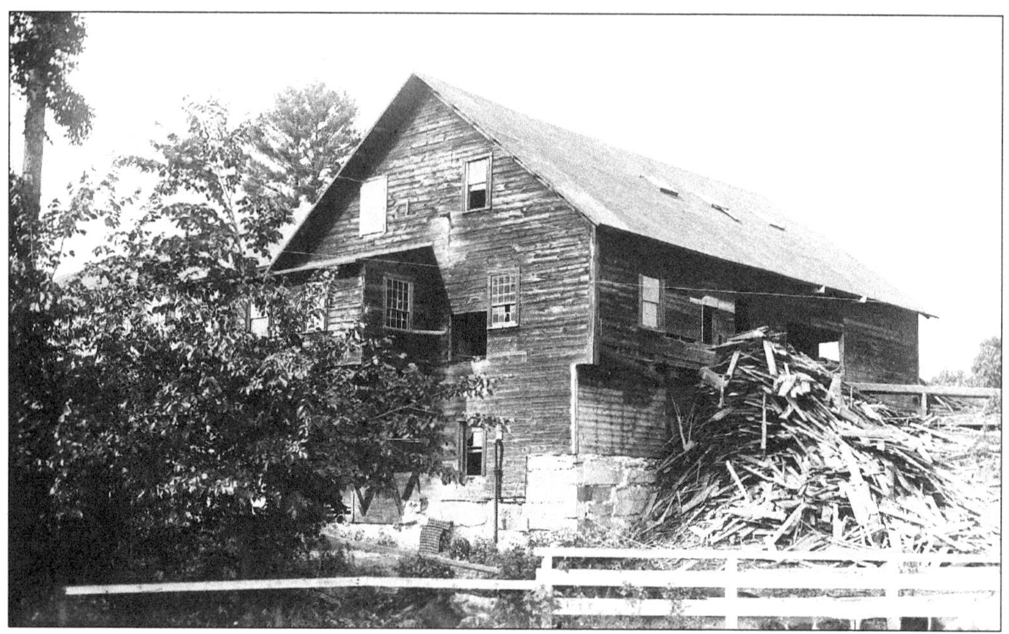

Originally built in the early 1700s on Central Street, the Waldron Mill obtained its power from the Ela River. In later years the mill was replaced by the Electric Light Station, bringing electric street lights to town in 1910.

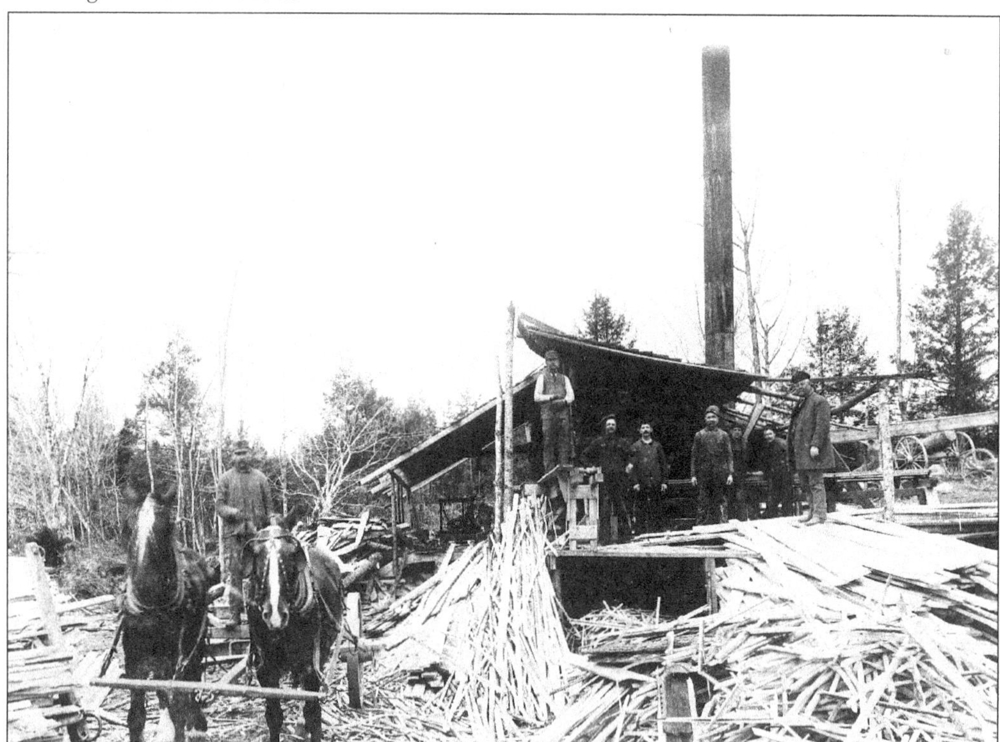

Erected in the mid-1870s by brothers John and Charles Jenness, the Jenness Mill on East Grove Street sawed lumber and manufactured wooden boxes. The bulk of the mill was dismantled in the 1940s, the remainder in 1971.

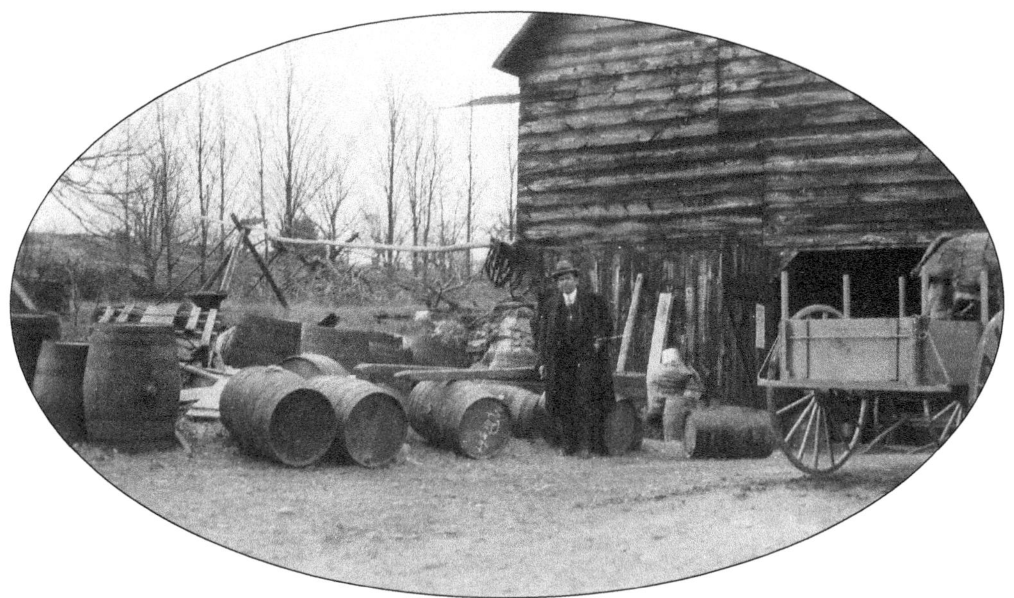

This barrel factory on East Grove Street kept a number of coopers employed, for the wooden barrel was the major container for the storage and sale of items such as flour, sugar, apples, and cider.

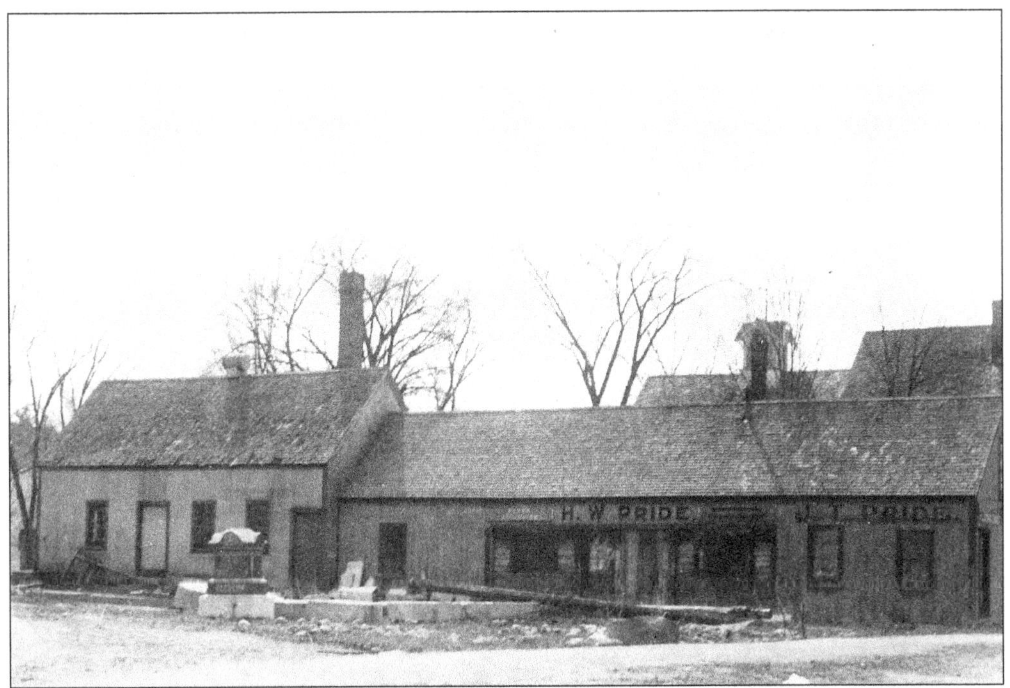

The Pride family operated a stone monument works in the 1880s at the junction of Central and Tappan Streets near where the Catholic church now stands. Many a granite tombstone in Pine Grove Cemetery was manufactured here.

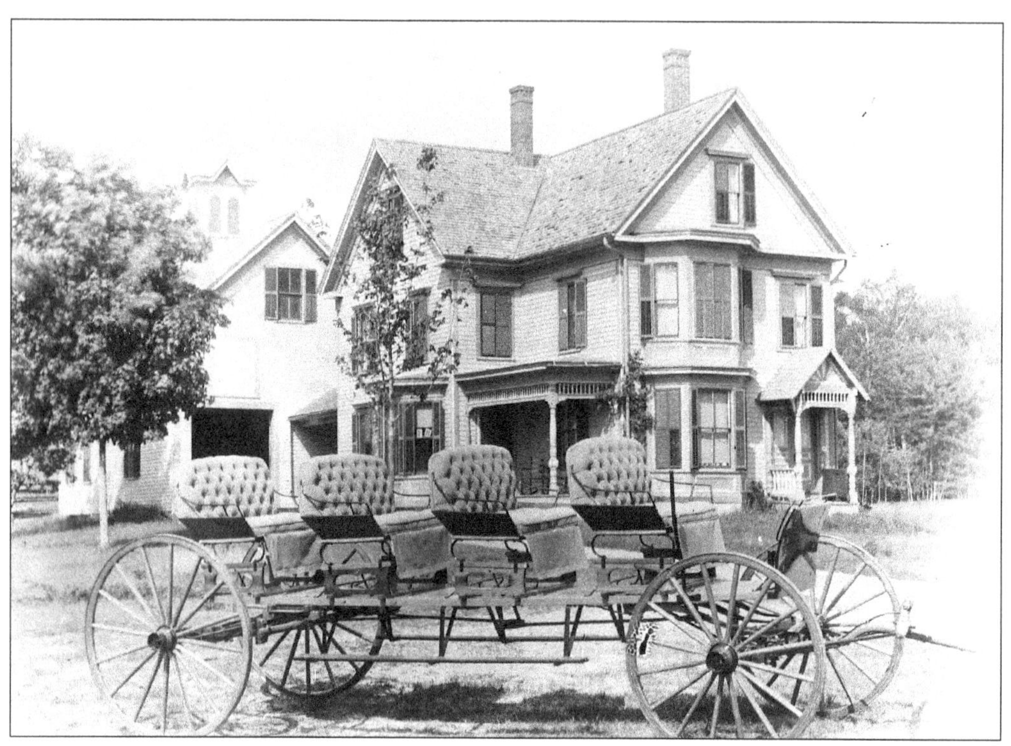

B.F. Perkins located his factory and residence on the banks of the Mad River where High (Route 11) and Central Streets intersect. He built wagons and custom-made vehicles and also served as an undertaker. The house pictured burned in 1910; Cameron's Garden Center today occupies the factory site.

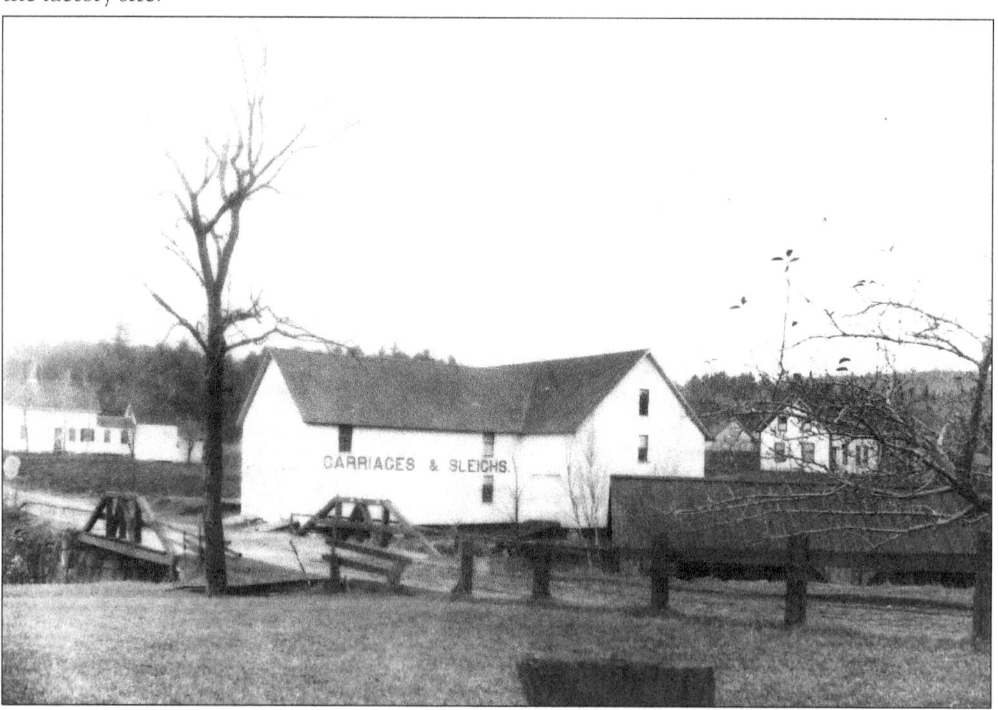

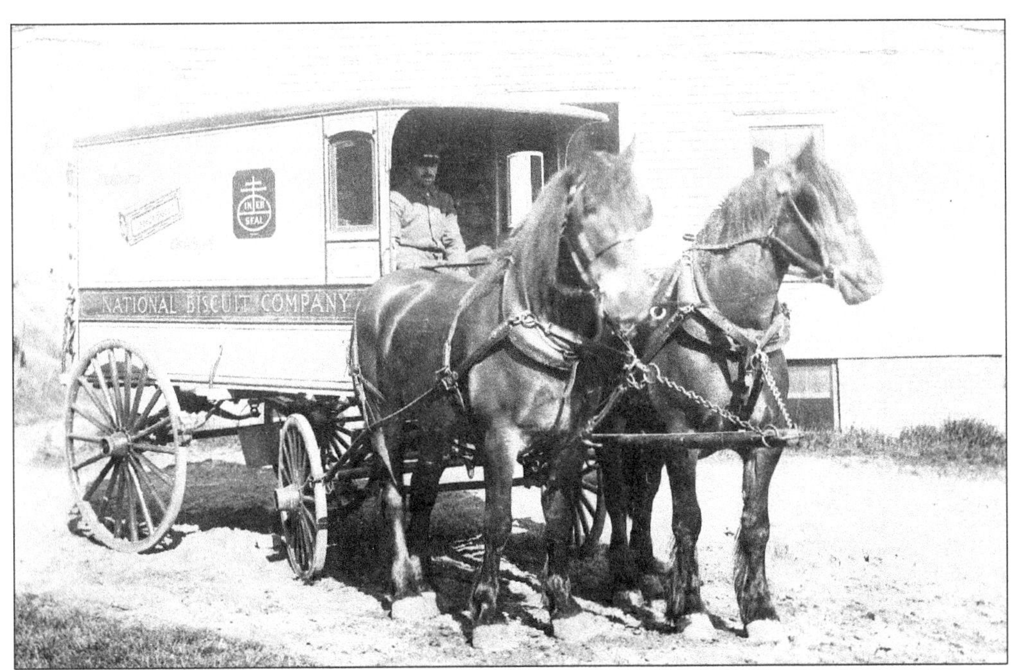

"Cracker" Horne was a local delivery man around 1900 who resided on Lone Star Avenue.

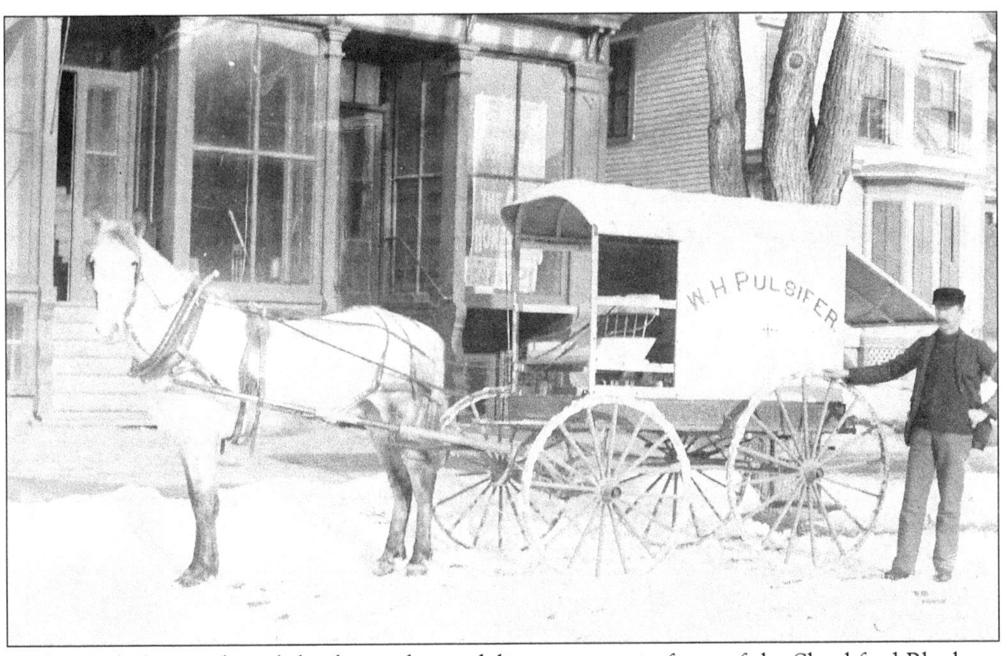

Walter Pulsifer stands with his horse-drawn delivery wagon in front of the Shackford Block on Central Street.

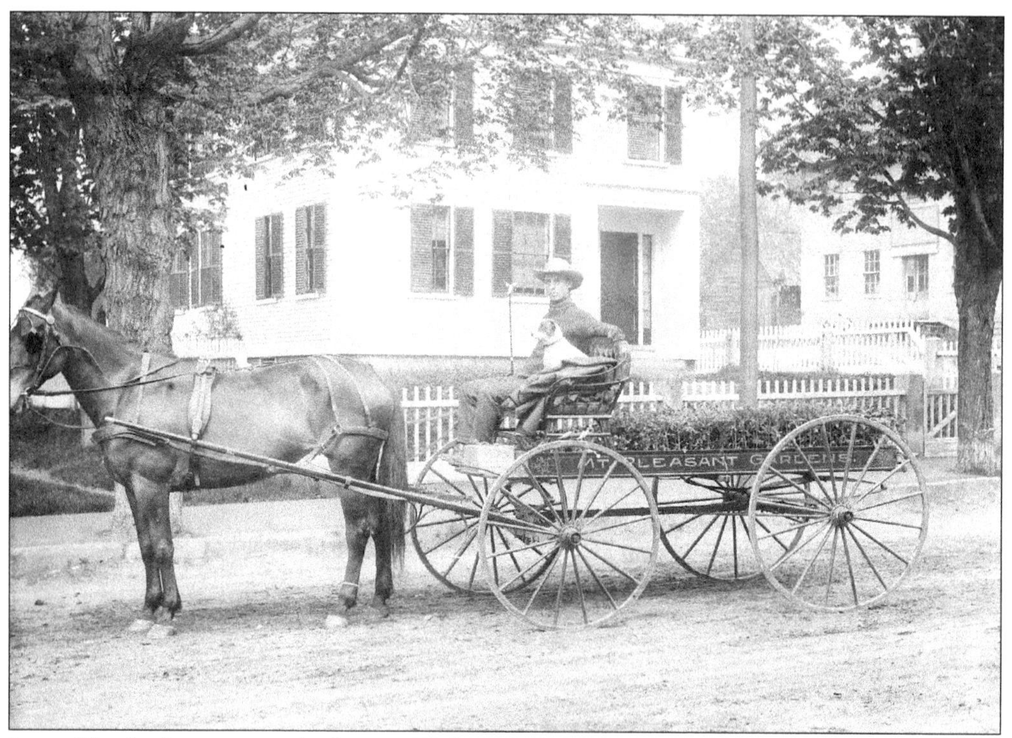

James Fletcher's wagon made frequent deliveries from the greenhouse near his home on Mt. Pleasant Street where he operated a market garden business.

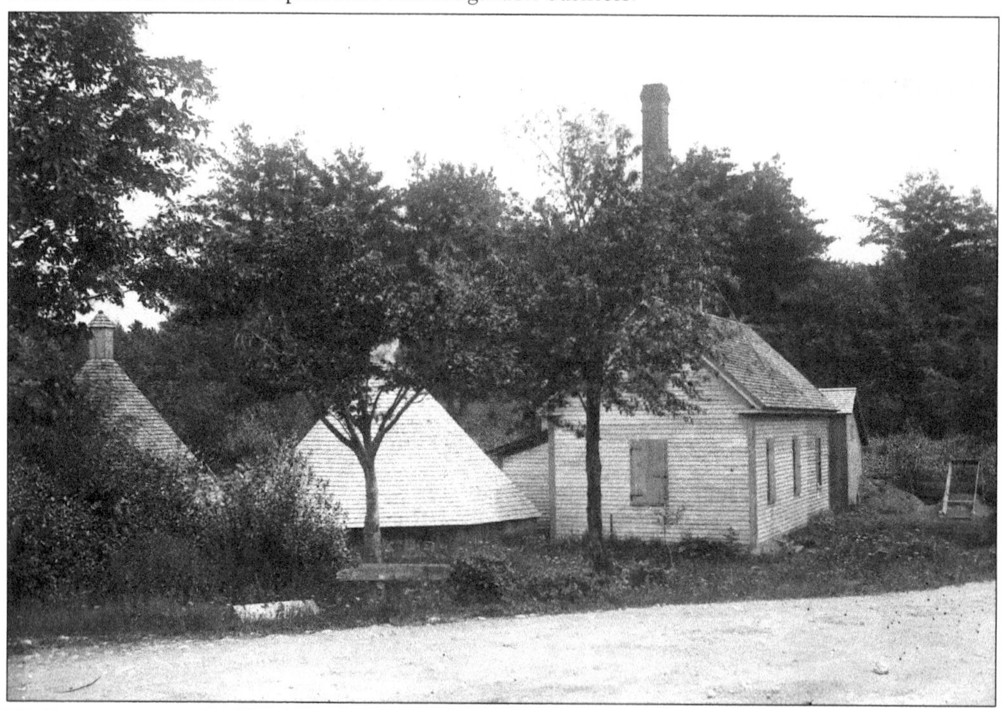

Wells comprising the Fletcher Water Works, which supplied water to residents on the east side of Main Street and beyond, were located on the hill off Mt. Vernon Street.

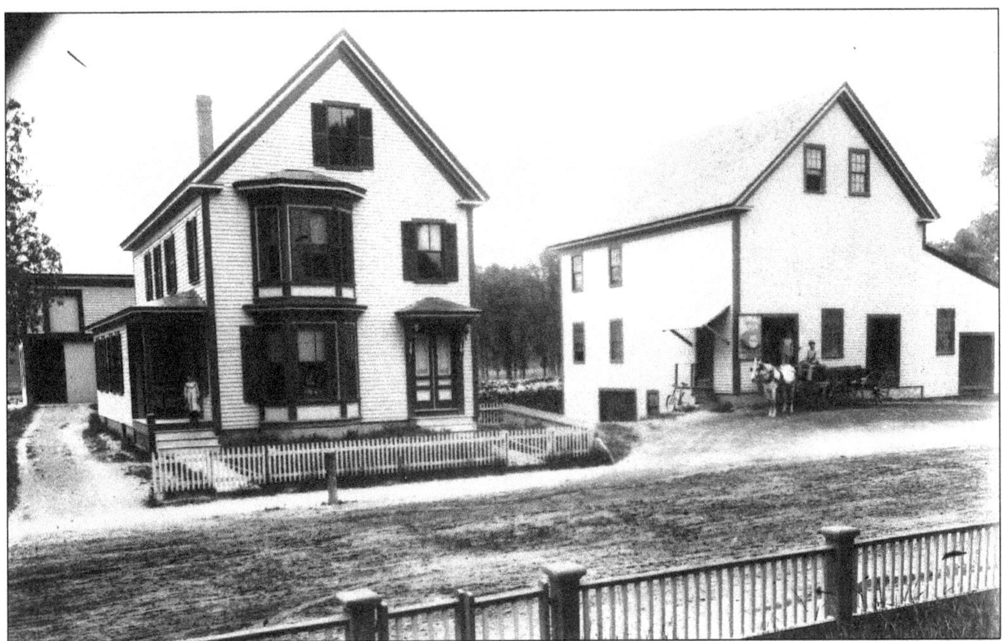

Beginning in 1899 H.W. Roberts operated a gristmill next to his home on Central Street. Using a 25-horsepower steam engine instead of water power to grind grain and flour, he was able to operate his mill year-round.

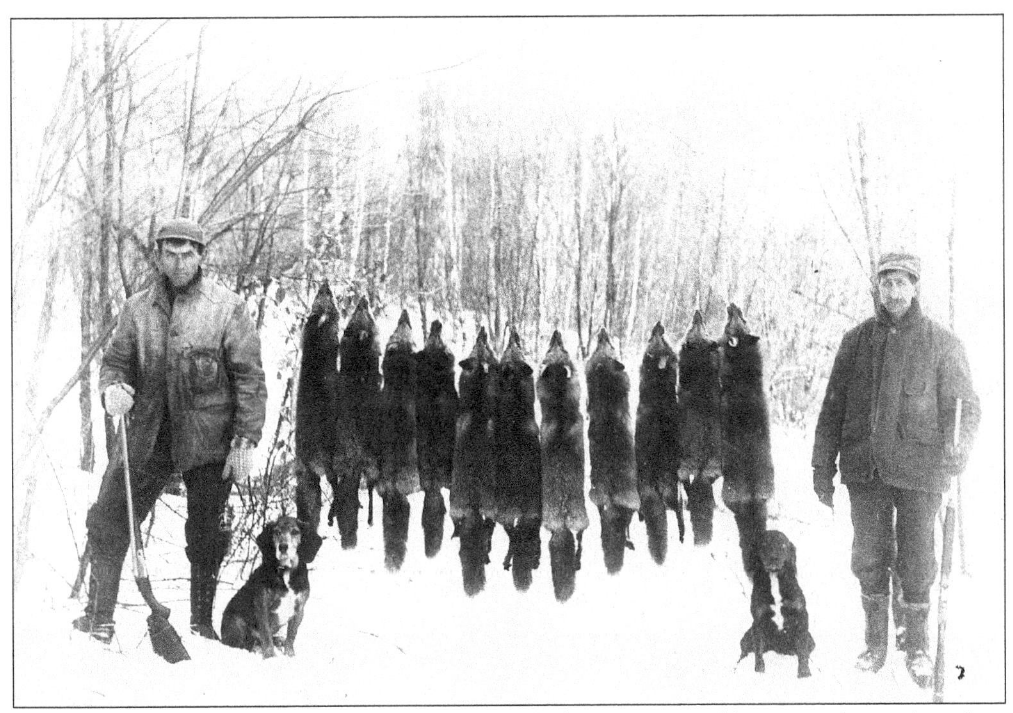

Back when fur coats were a popular item of apparel, the trapping and hunting of animals such as these foxes shot by Charles Wyatt (on right) and friend provided a seasonal means of income.

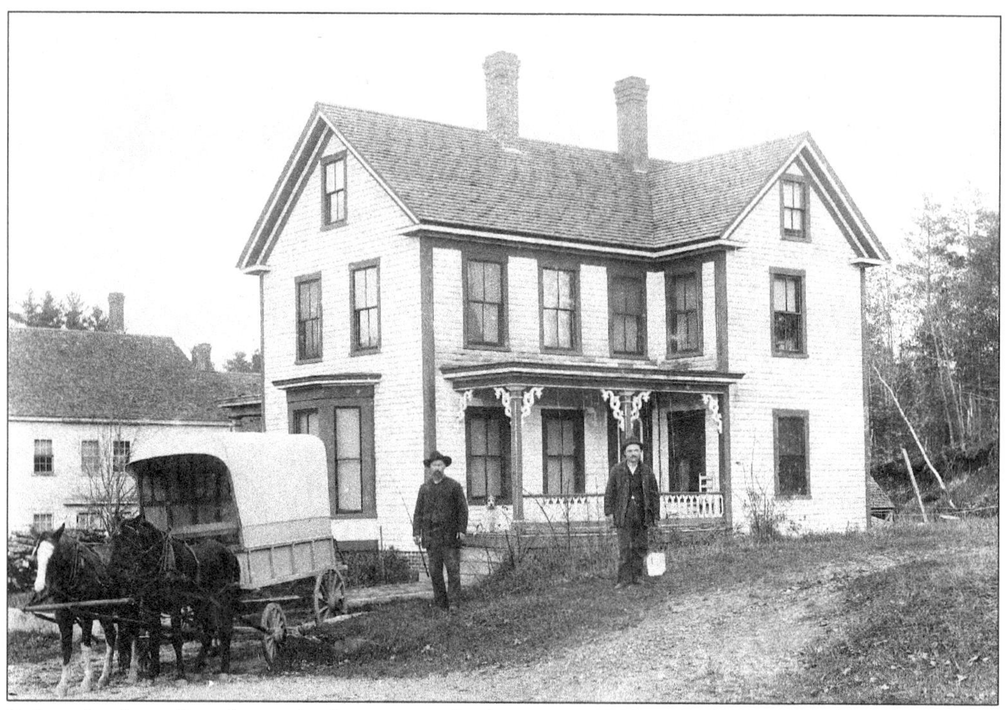

Before the days of mechanical refrigeration, food was preserved in "ice boxes," insulated containers that could hold a large block of ice. In winter, cakes of ice were cut, packed in sawdust, and stored in ice houses to keep all year. Freeman Johnson operated such an ice house on Beaver Pond off Spring Street, and his horse-drawn cart delivered ice to the homes in town.

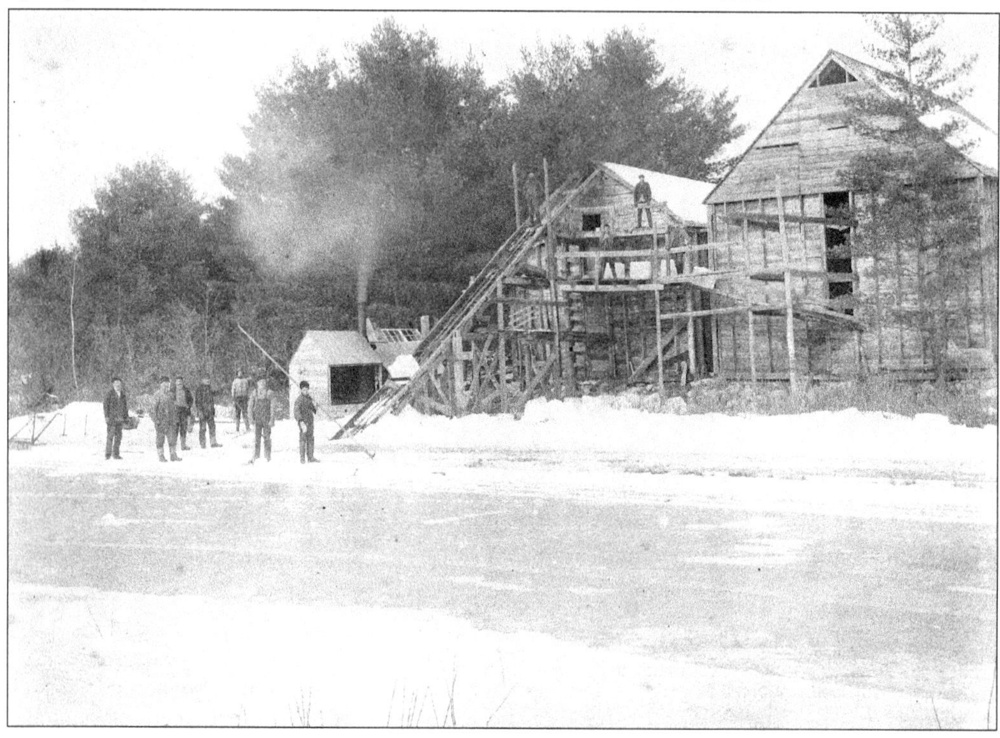

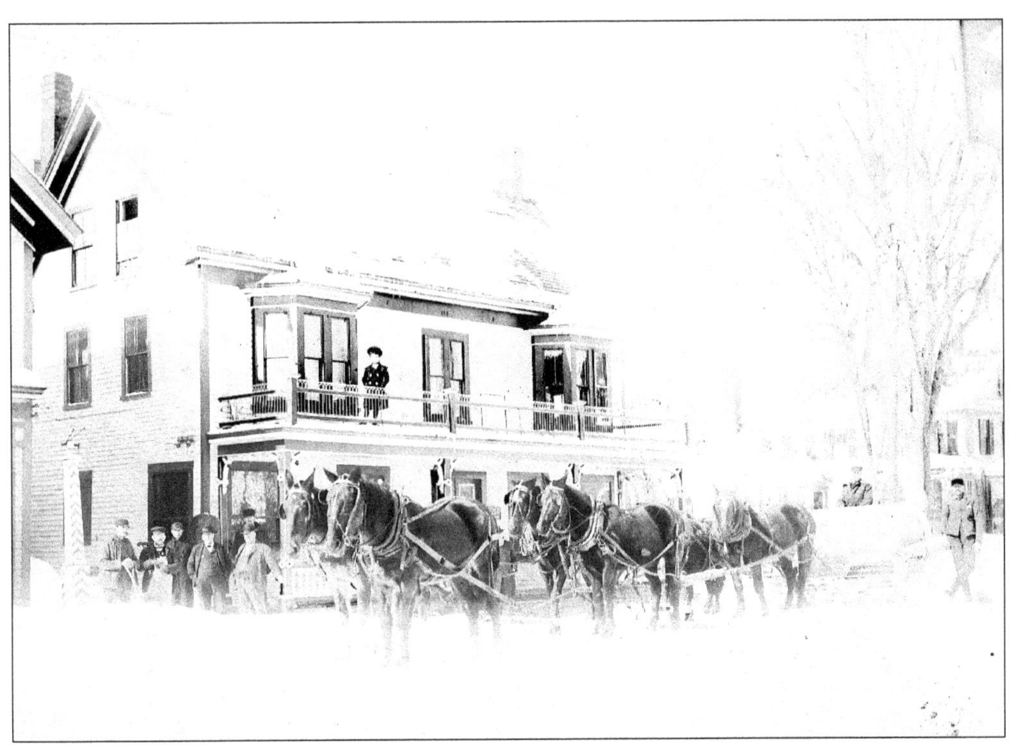

Six of Wes Locke's finest pull a snow roller along Main Street in front of Nutter's Saloon, thus packing down the road for the passage of sleighs, the common mode of winter travel.

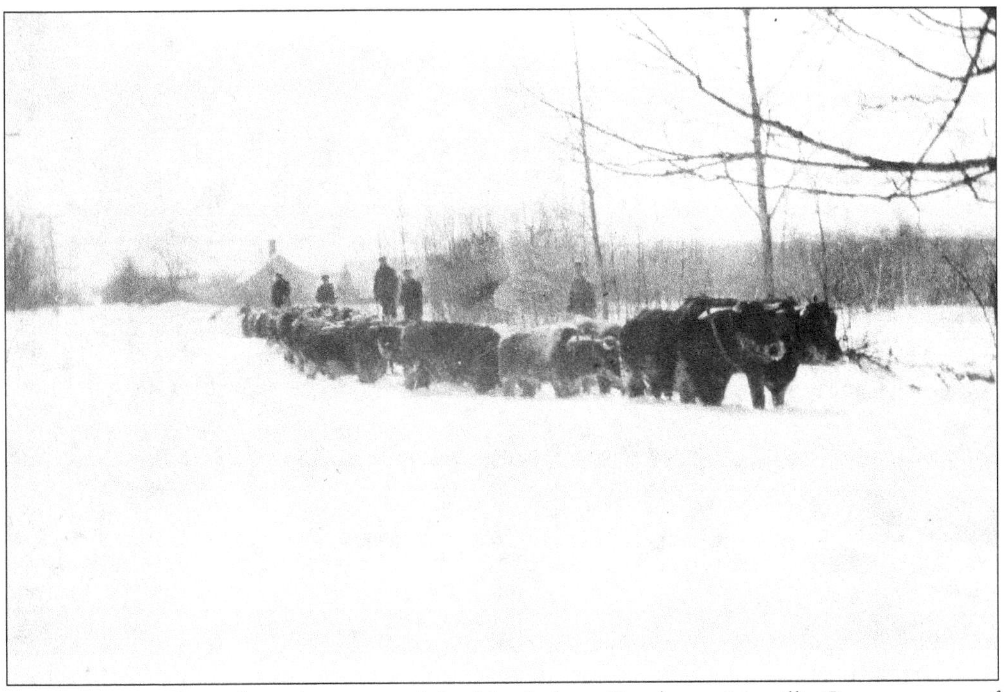

On country roads, such as this scene of the Meaderboro Road near Merrill's Corner, teams of oxen "broke the road" after a deep snowfall so that horses could travel.

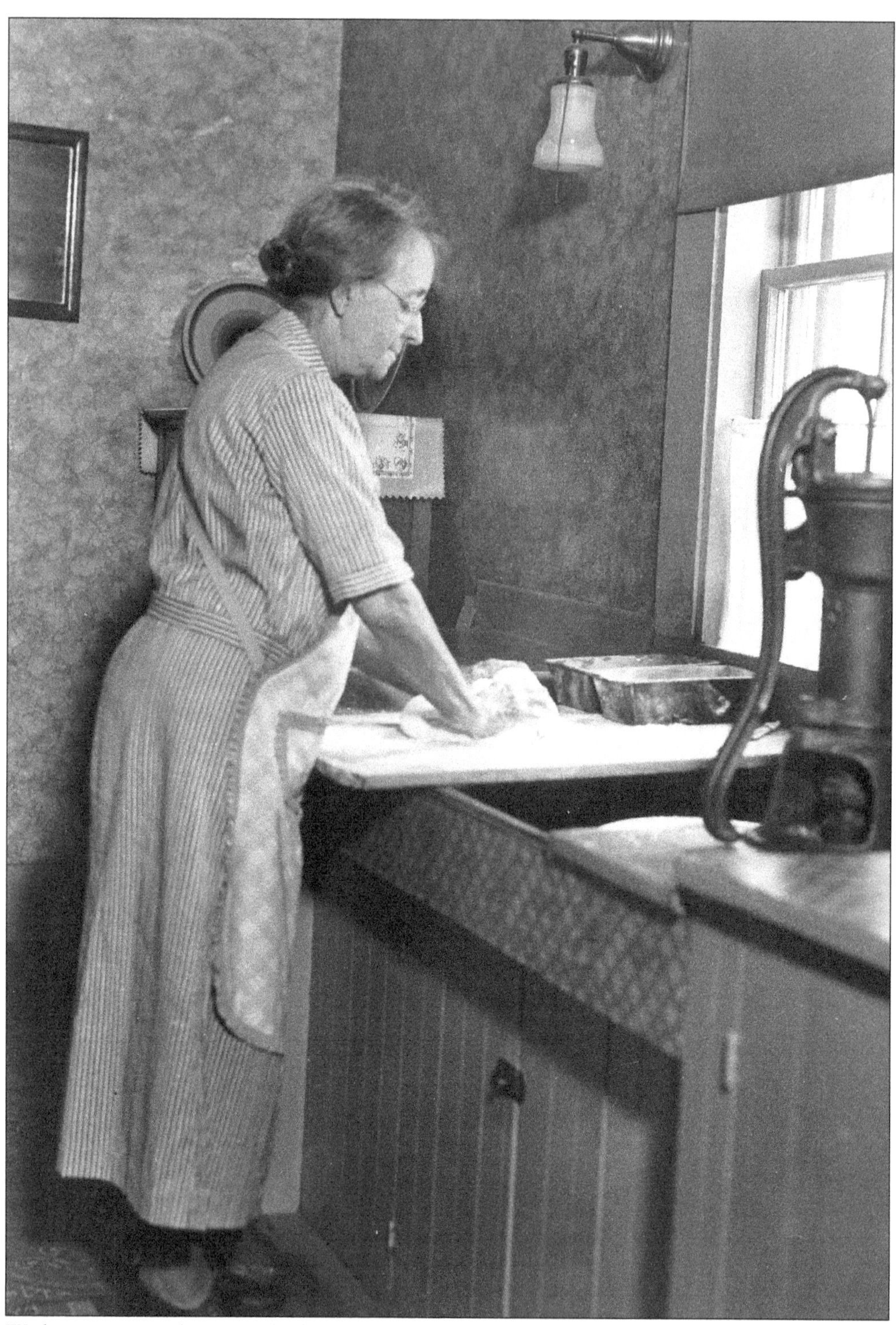

With no supermarkets on which to depend, a woman's work was never truly done in earlier times. Each morning she had to bake bread for the day in a wood-fired stove, no pleasant task in the heat of summer!

Farm women such as Ida Bean raised all their own fruit and vegetables, spending many days canning and drying produce for winter use.

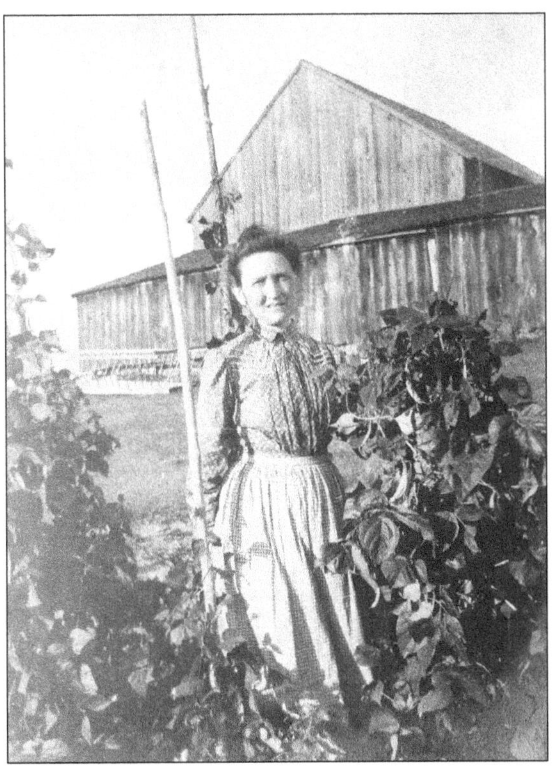

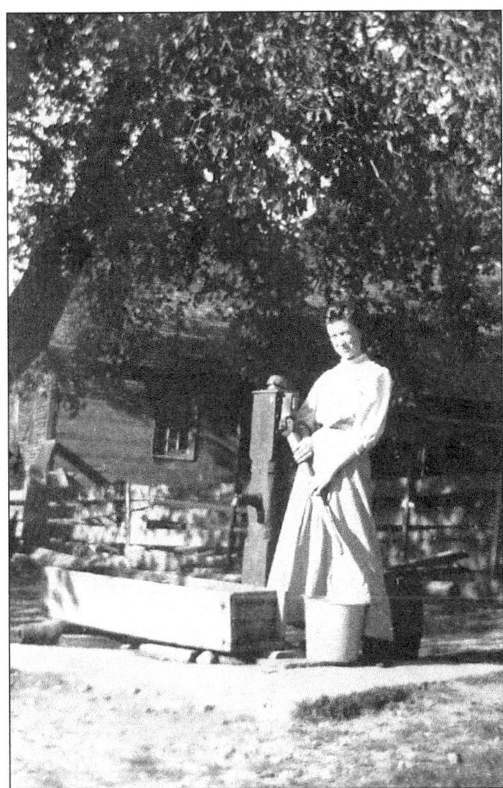

Before the days of running water in the home, a hand pump in the dooryard was a necessity. Beulah Wyatt is shown drawing water on the Demeritt farm from a well which is still operable today.

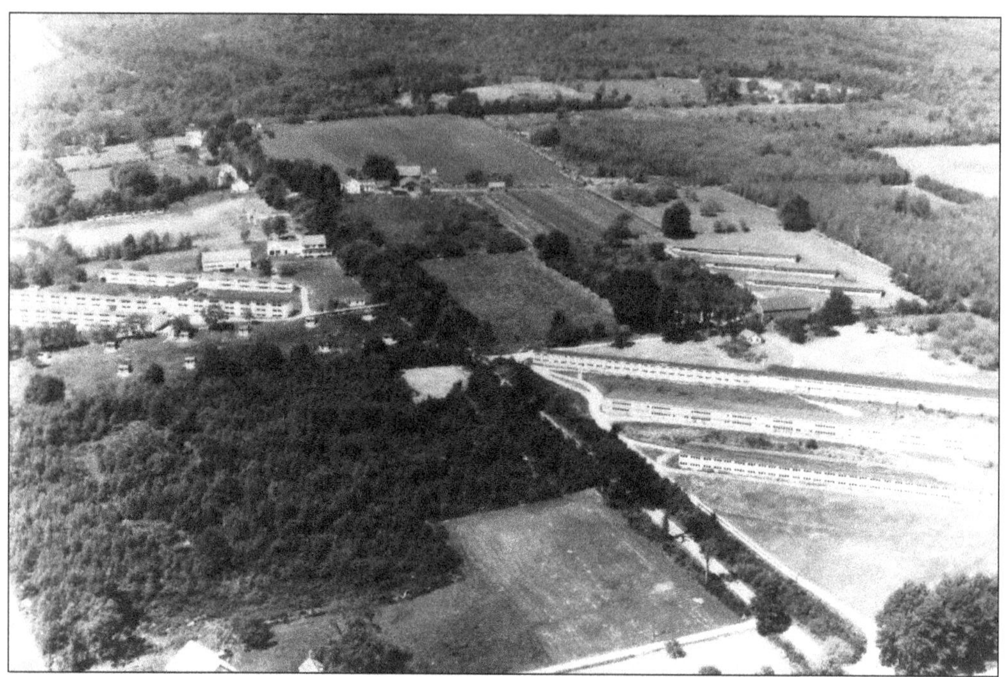

An aerial view of "The Hensnest" on Meaderboro Road. One of the largest privately owned poultry farms east of the Mississippi River, it was operated by Ralph W. Canney from 1926 to 1963. Although enduring fires both in the 1950s and 1960s, some of these buildings remain and are used today.

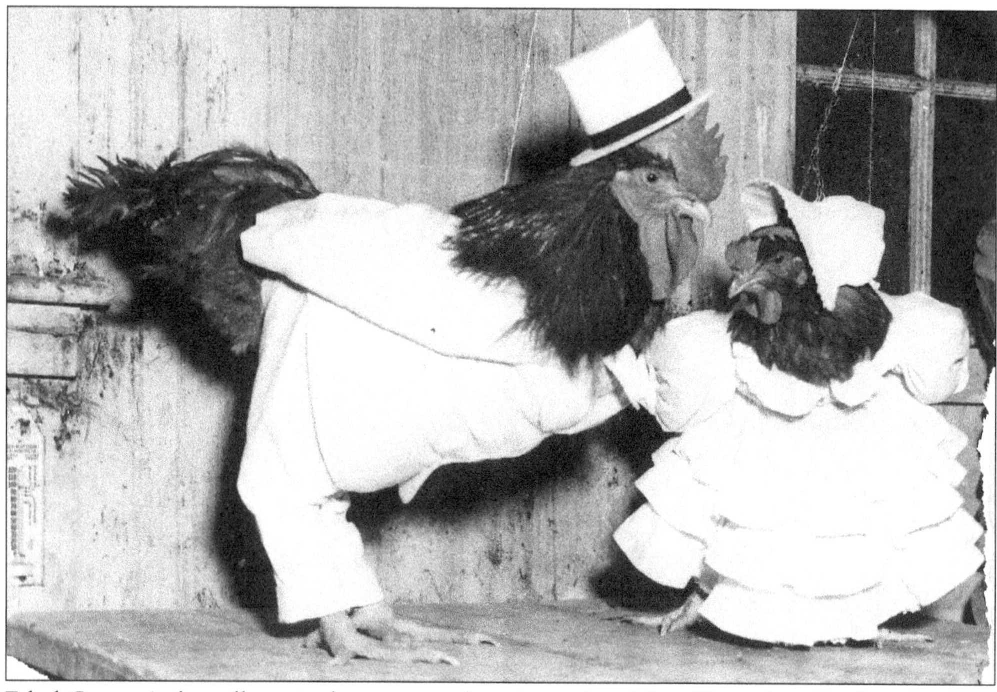

Ethel Canney's formally attired entry was the winner in a New Hampshire Poultry Grower's Association contest for best original idea in "dressed poultry!"

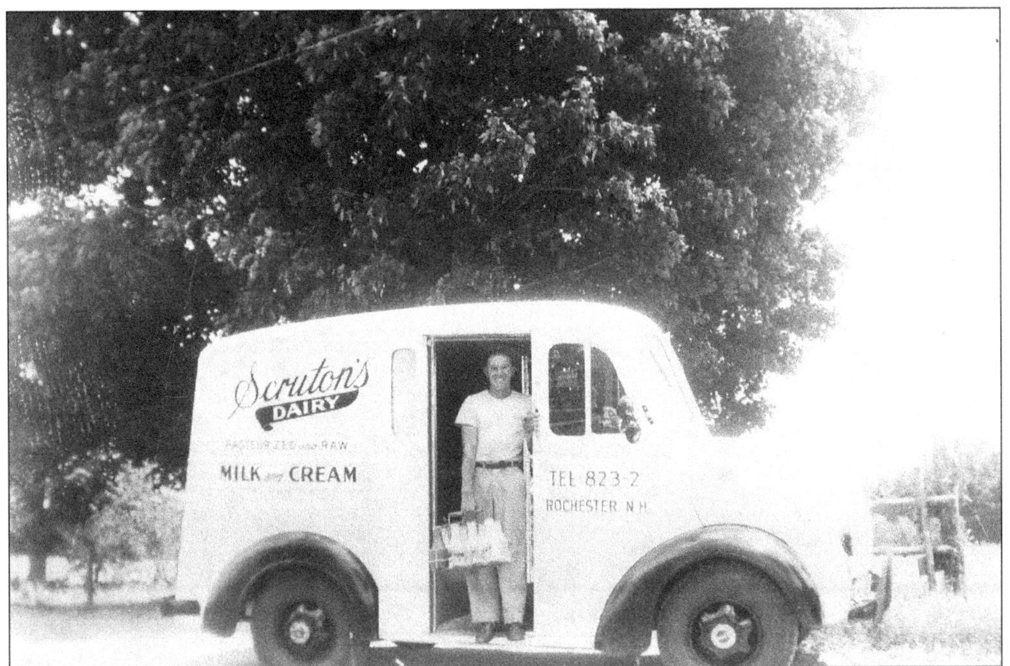

With a herd of over two hundred Holsteins, the Scruton Dairy on Meaderboro Road was the largest and last producer-handler of milk in the state. Established in 1942 by Arthur Scruton and his son Frank (the milkman in the 1948 picture above), the farm still raises and milks prize-winning cows but no longer processes and delivers.

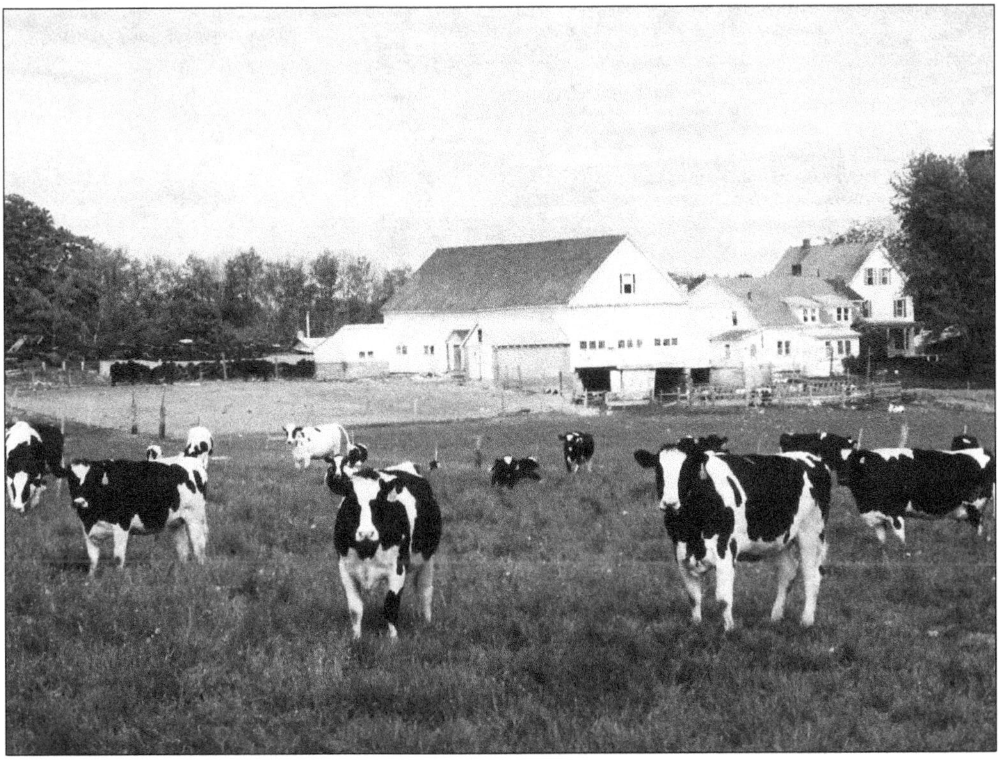

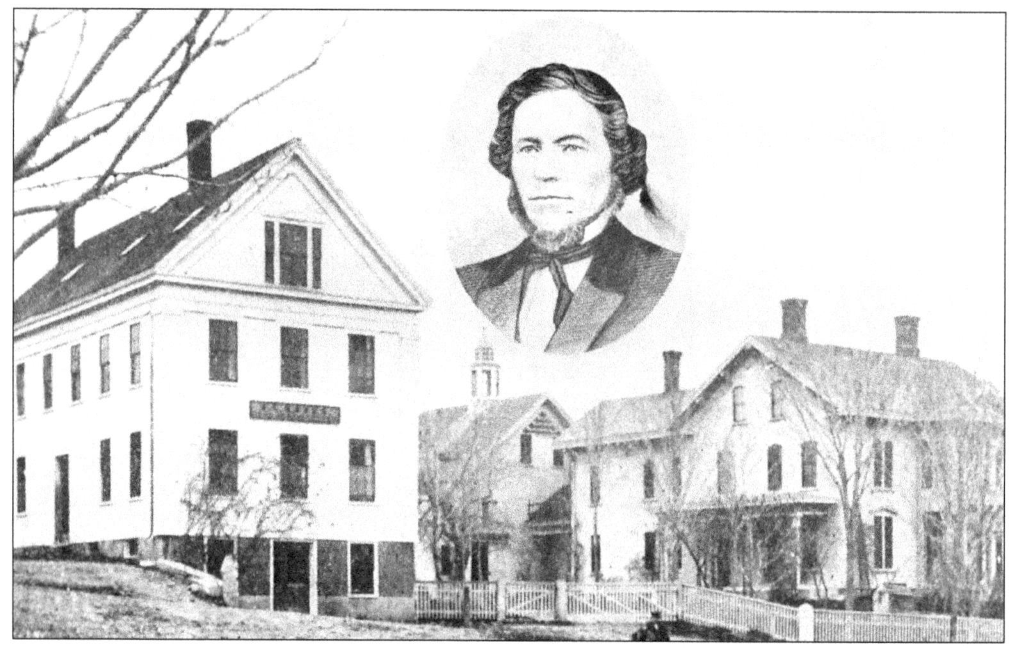

Farmington began its long legacy as a shoe manufacturing center in 1836 when E.H. Badger opened a shoe shop on Spring Street. Martin Luther Hayes soon took over the business and prospered. He is shown here with his enlarged factory and home, both of which still exist, the latter currently the residence of Dr. and Mrs. Quinn.

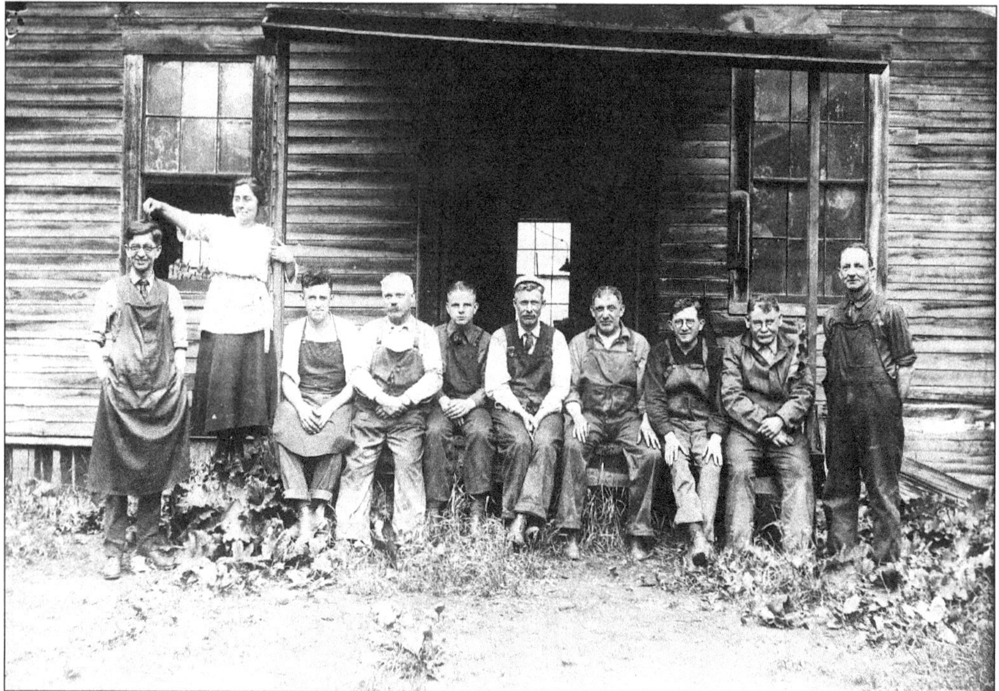

In 1905 the M.L. Hayes factory became the Fred Browne Wire Brush Company, manufacturing twenty-nine types of brushes. Fred Browne stands on the left with his workers. The business remained in the family until 1964; today the building houses an antique shop.

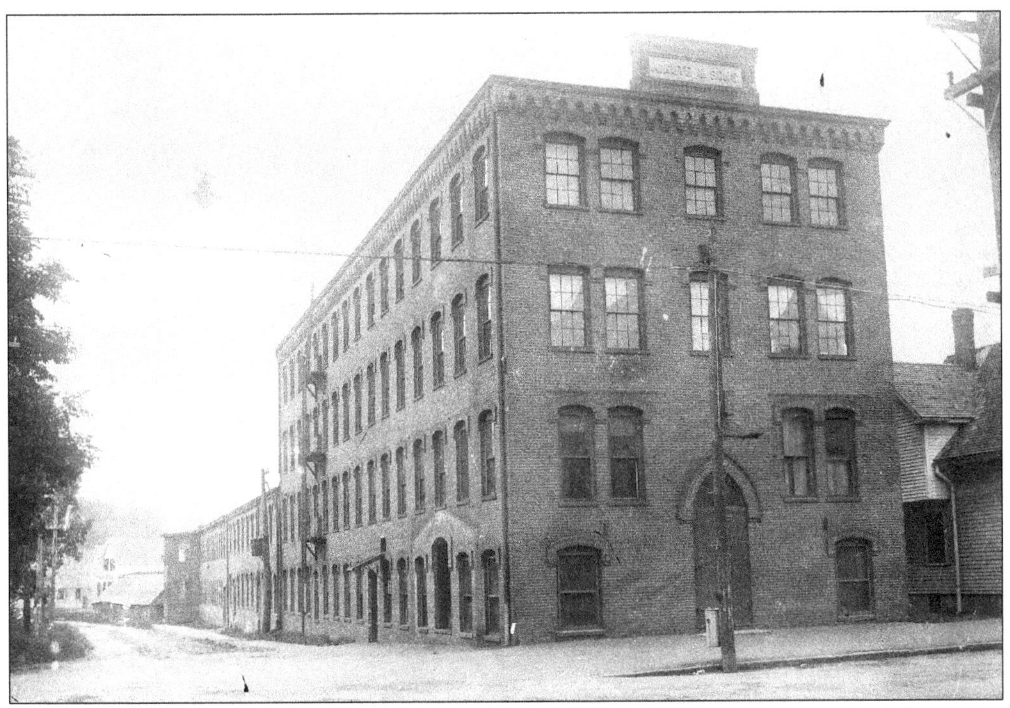

Another pioneer in the shoe business was Alonzo Nute of Milton, who in 1849 located a wooden factory at the corner of Grove and North Main Streets. After a disastrous fire in 1874, the brick building shown here was erected, and it has lasted through the years.

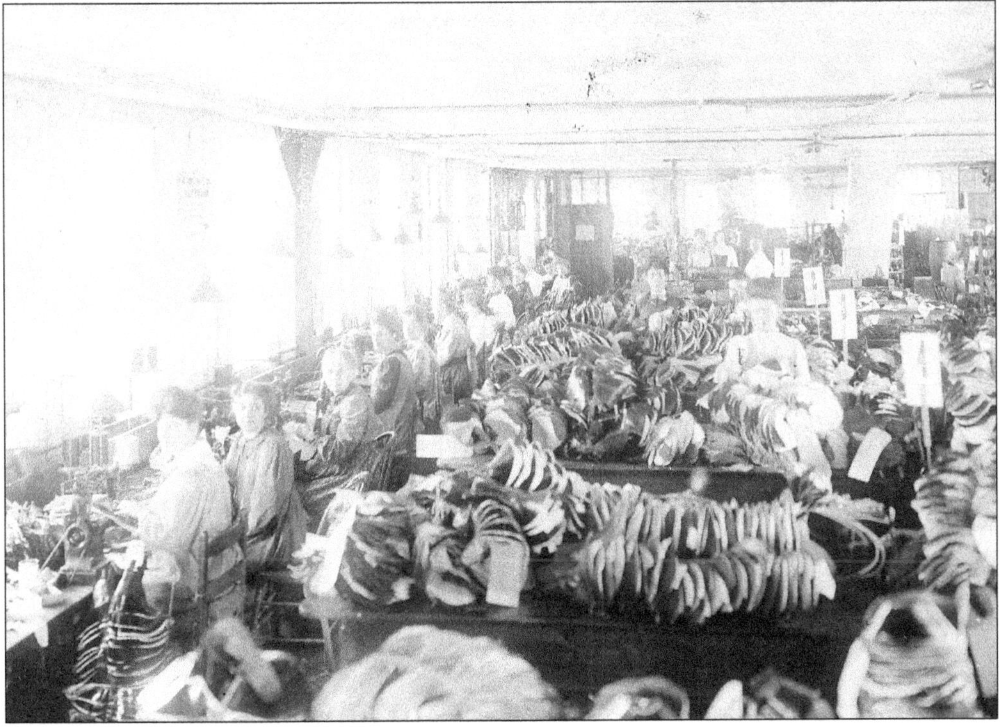

The stitching room of the Nute factory.

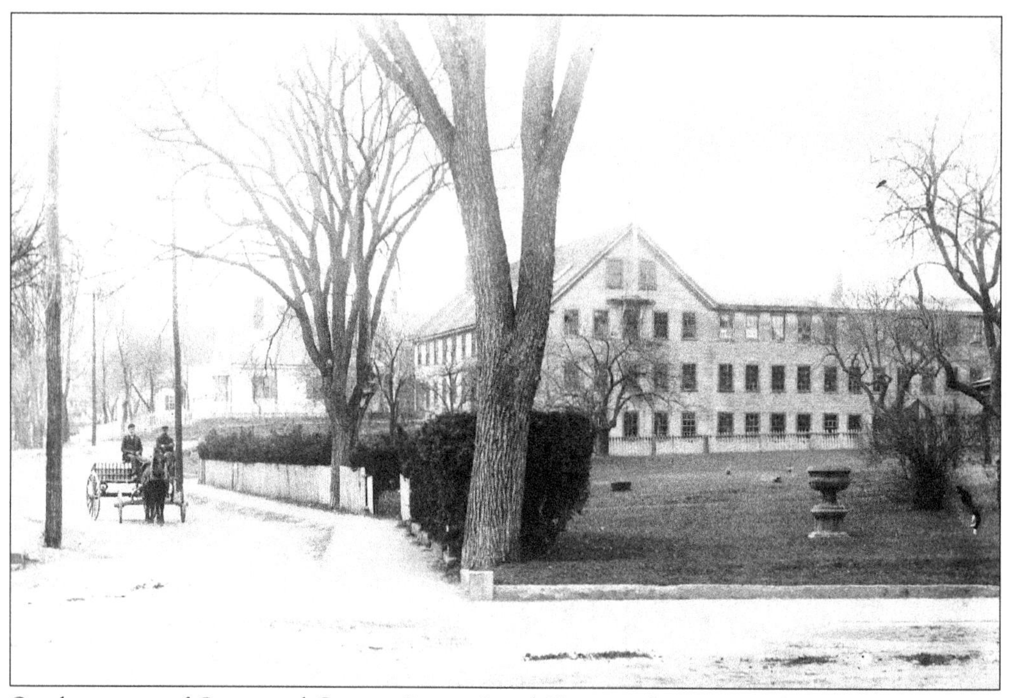

On the corner of Grove and Orange Streets Israel Hayes and sons manufactured shoes in this large factory employing over two hundred people. After the destruction of its rear ell, the building was turned on its foundation and today houses apartments.

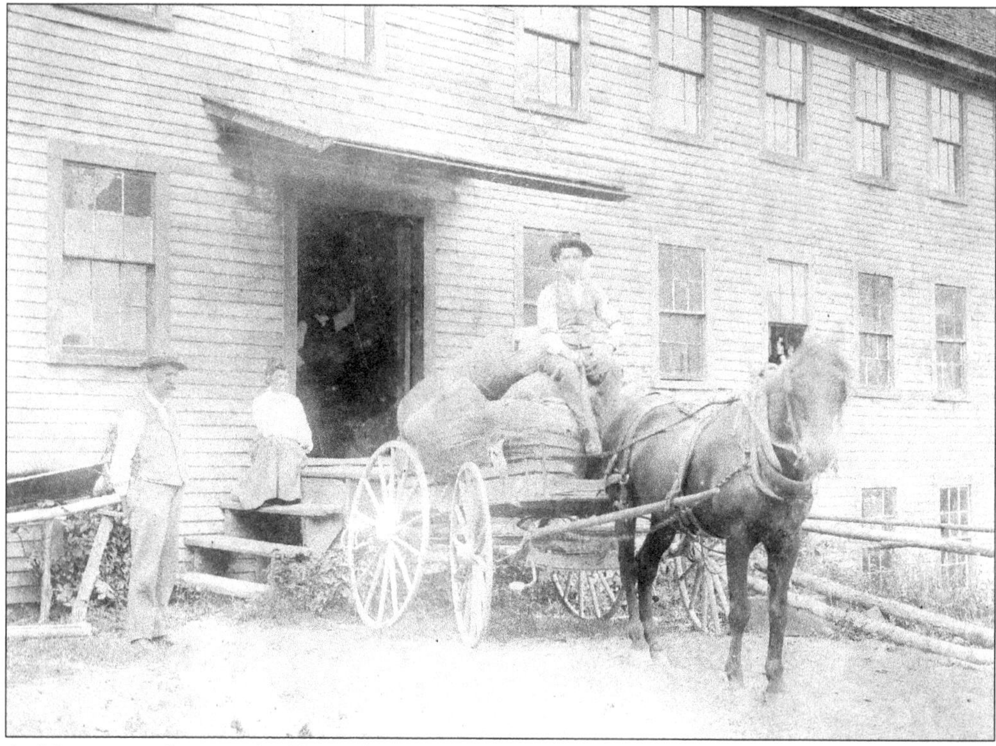

A delivery cart leaving the Hayes factory.

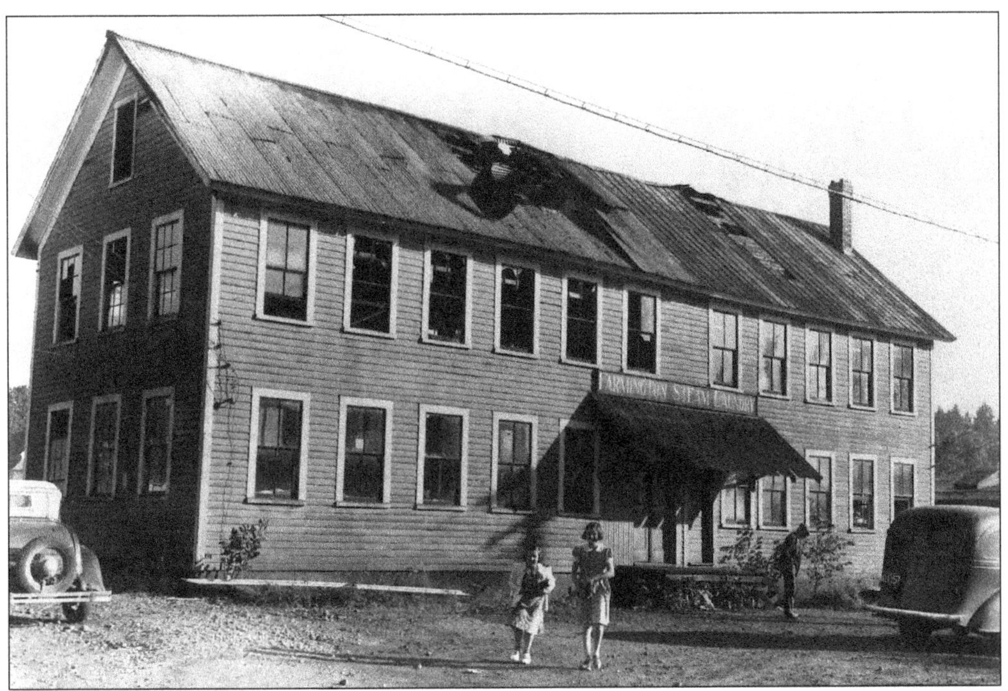

After the shoe last and sole pattern company operated by L.S. Flanders went out of business, its building on East Grove Street became a steam laundry. It is shown here after fire destroyed the interior.

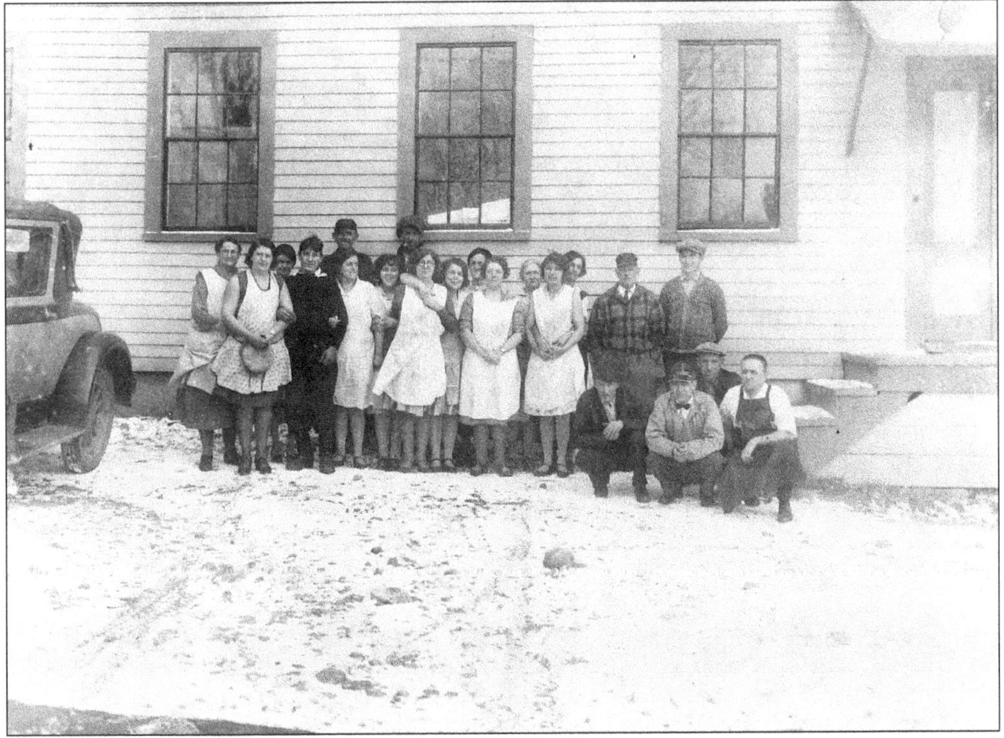

Employees of the steam laundry pose for the photographer on a winter day.

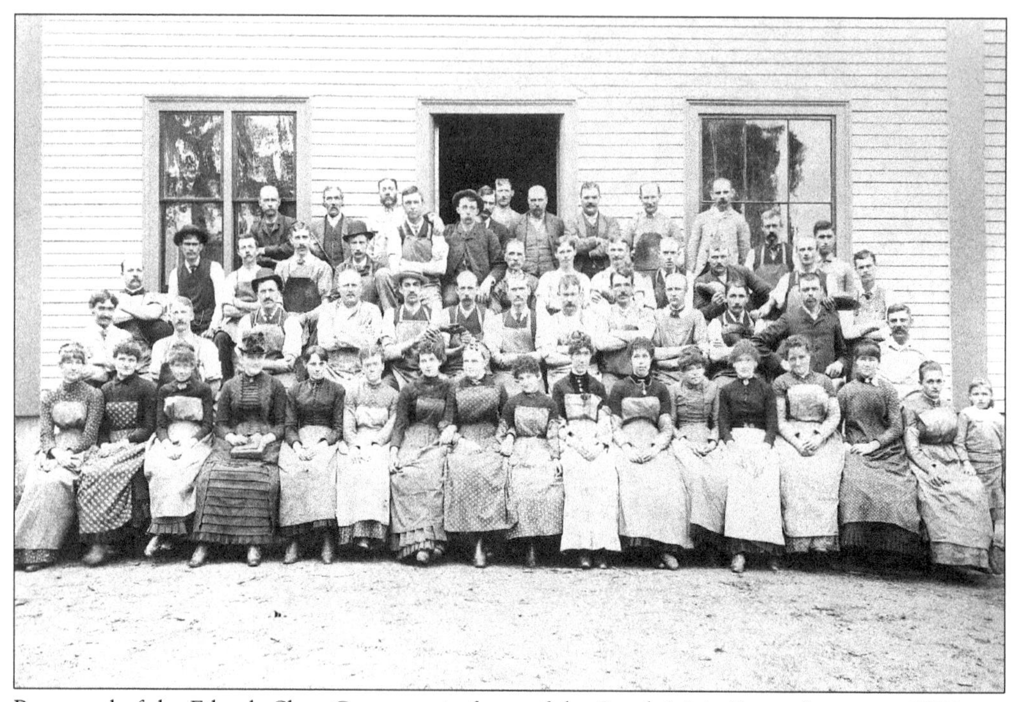

Personnel of the Edgerly Shoe Company in front of the South Main Street factory in 1887.

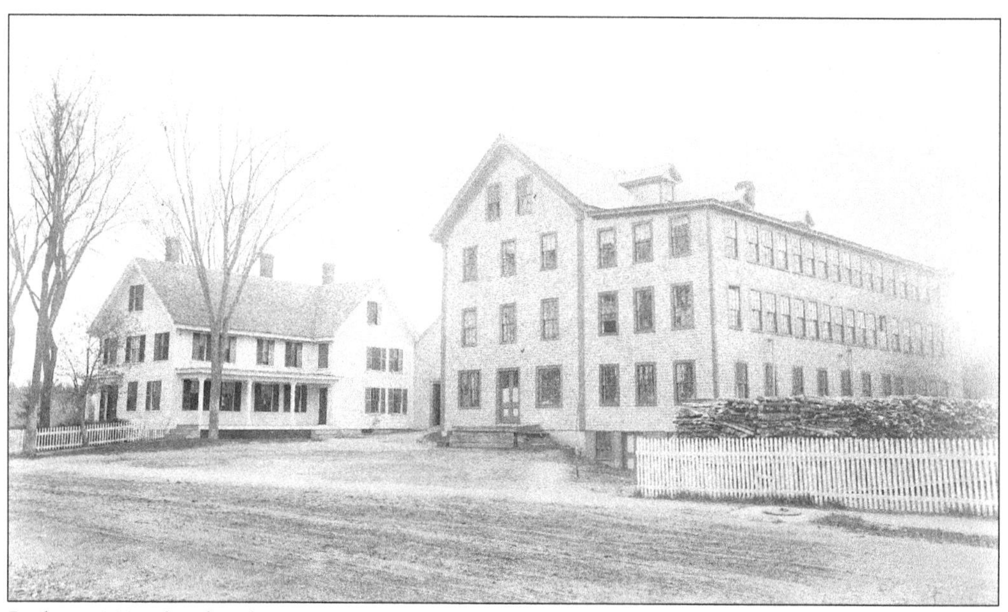

Built in 1880 for the shoe company founded by Hosea B. Edgerly and continued by his son Frank, this building has held many businesses. The adjoining home was later occupied by Frank's daughter, Beatrice E. Ellison, who gave to the town the Summer Street playground.

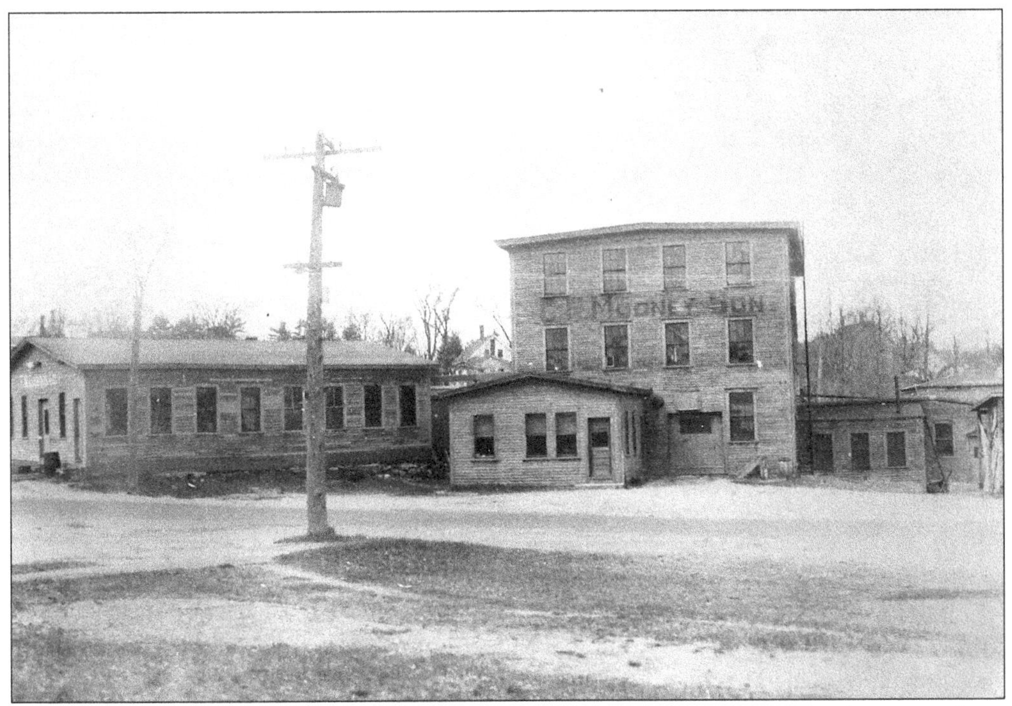

What was originally the William Hayes sawmill became Mooney's Mill, a wood-turning plant, in 1916. Locally it was referred to as the "handle factory," for it produced all sizes and shapes of wooden handles for tools.

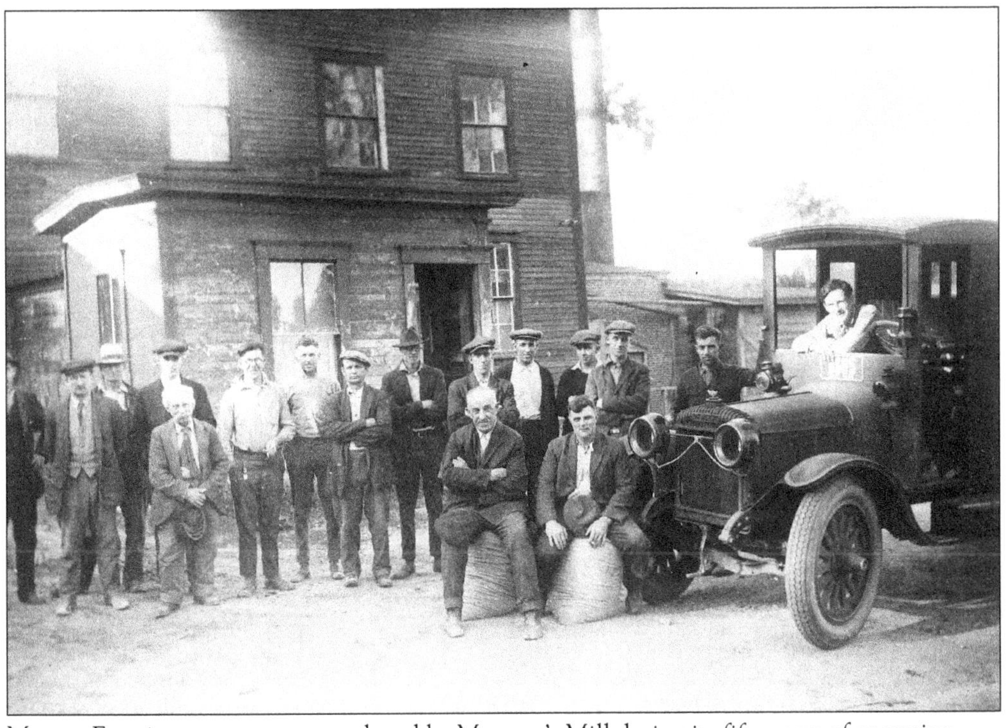

Many a Farmington man was employed by Mooney's Mill during its fifty years of operation.

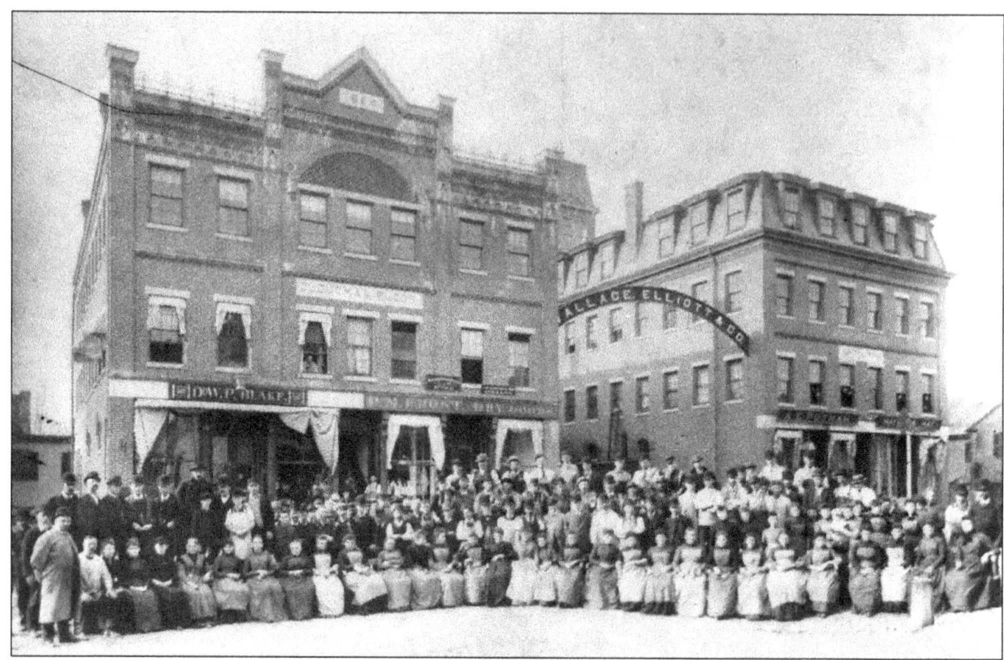

Originally connected by a walkway and always referred to as "The Twin Factories," the Central Block was built in 1877 and the Cloutman in 1884. Wallace, Elliott & Co., manufacturers of fine boots, was an early occupant. Extensively damaged by fire in 1971, one block is now apartments and the other houses the Union Telephone Co.

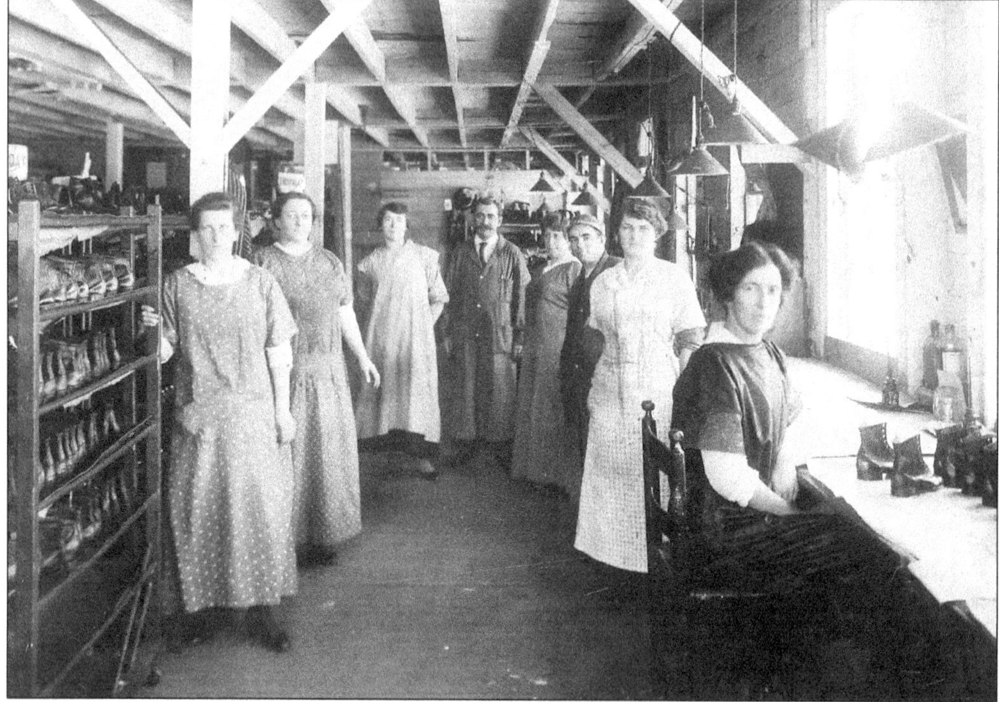

A typical shoe shop interior. Hattie White (on the far right) donated a large collection of town photographs to the library.

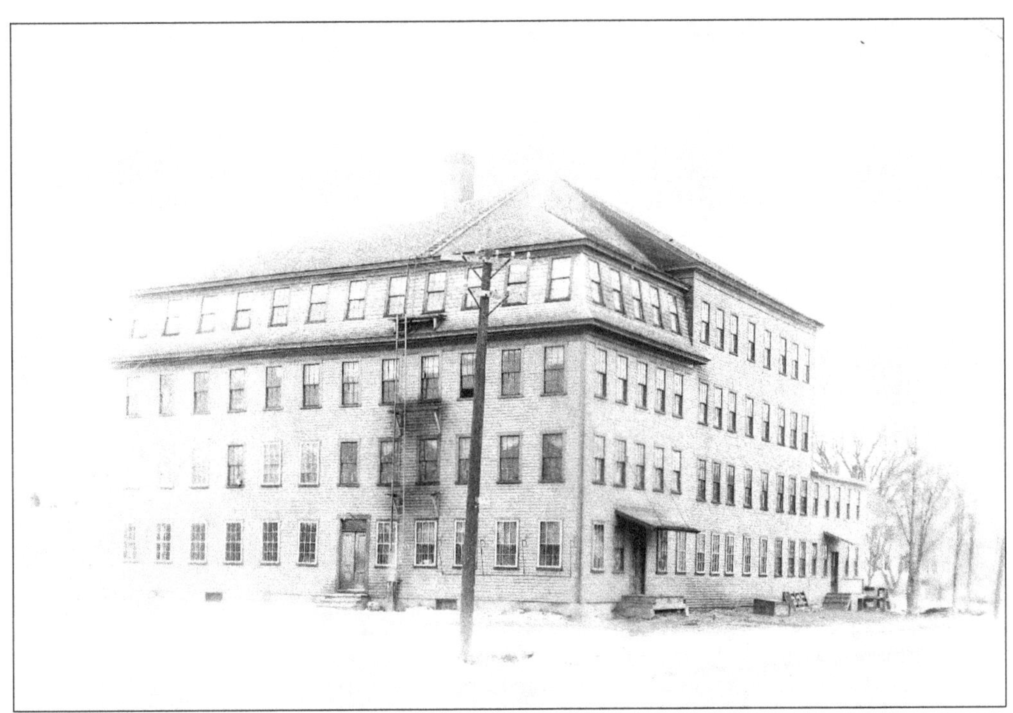

Located opposite the site of Main Street School, this impressive four-story factory for the production of mens and boys shoes was erected in 1873 by Arthur Berry. Purchased by John Cloutman in 1896, it burned to the ground in 1918.

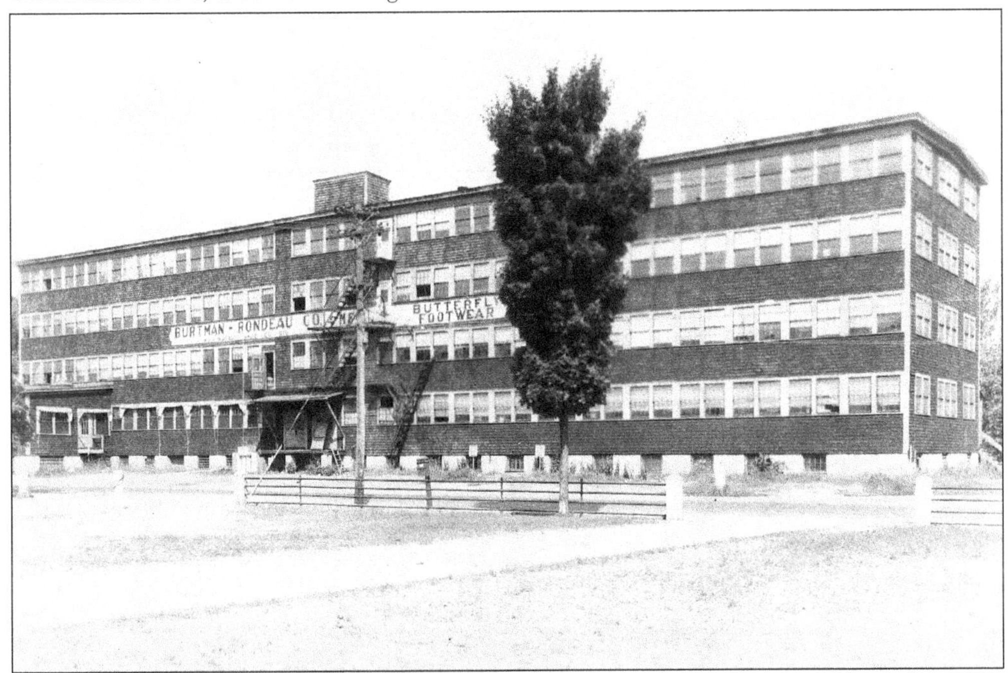

A new Cloutman Factory rose from the ashes of the old and was back in production that same year. Eventually this building became the property of Abe Burtman and Omer Rondeau, philanthropic businessmen who provided funds for the former high school's gymnasium.

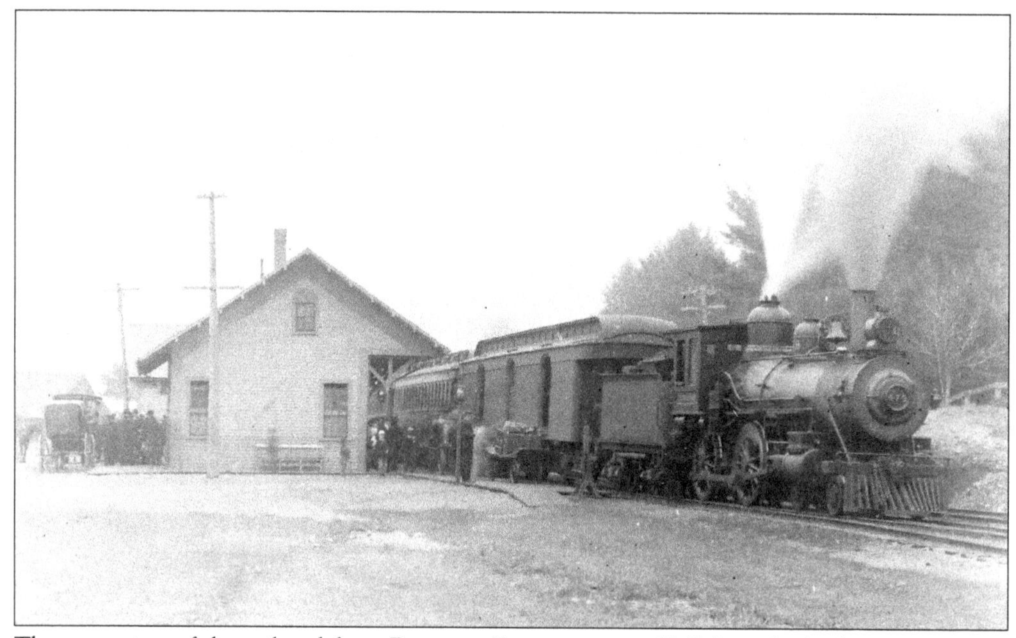
The extension of the railroad from Dover to Farmington in 1849 brought both passenger and freight service. The Boston and Maine Railroad purchased the line in 1892, operating this station until 1953.

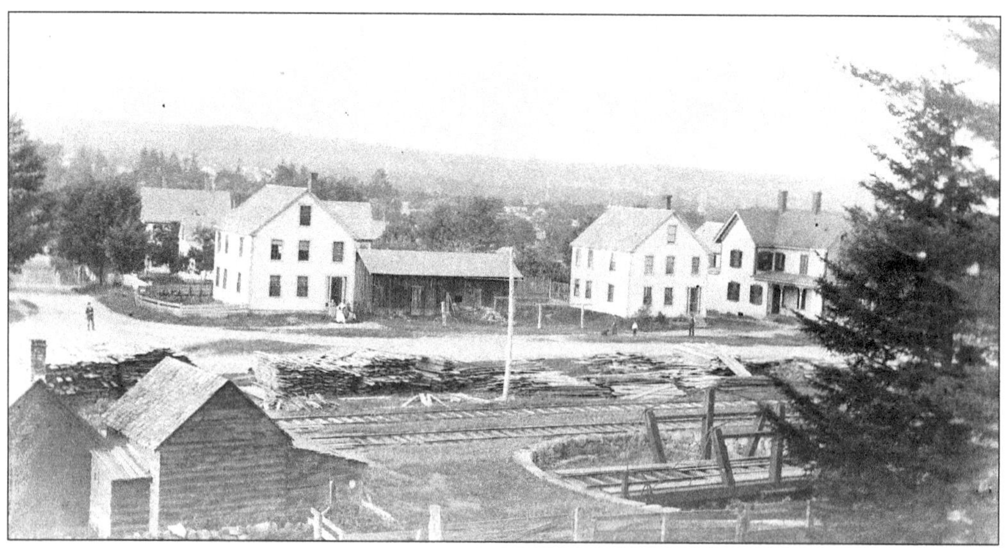
This view of the railroad tracks at the corner of High and Maple Streets shows the turntable used to redirect trains back to Dover.

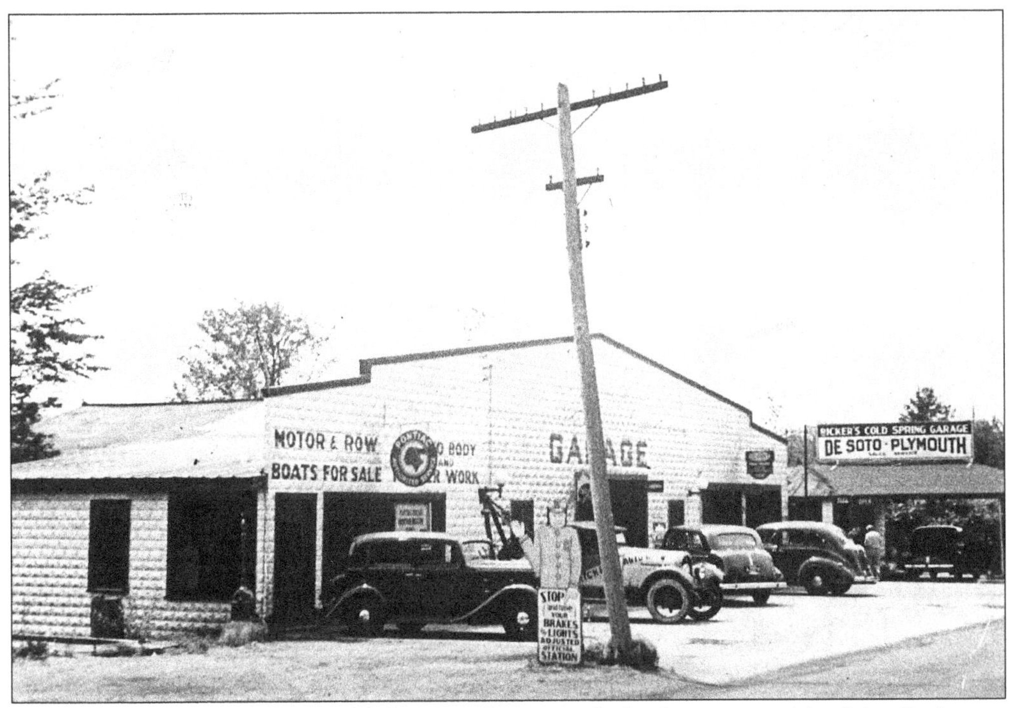

Prosperity arrived with the establishment of an auto dealership operated by John Ricker on Spring Street.

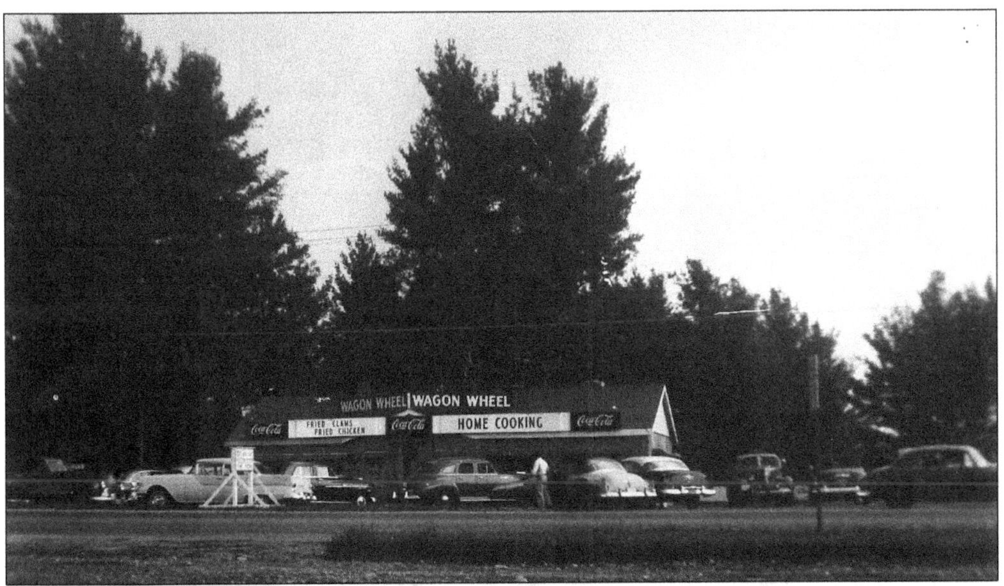

With a "car in every garage," dining out became a common occurrence. A popular place was the Wagon Wheel Restaurant on the Farmington Road. Started in 1930 by Jack and Helen Cardinal, its home cooking was famous for thirty years.

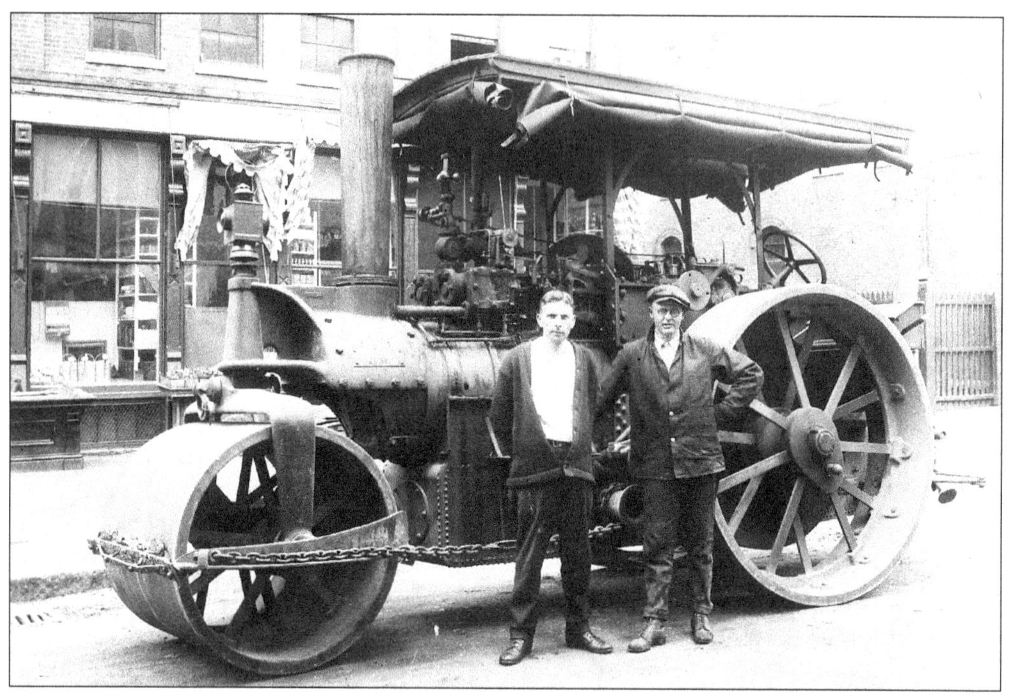

This noisy and cumbersome steam roller used for road maintenance was operated by Harry Knox (in hat).

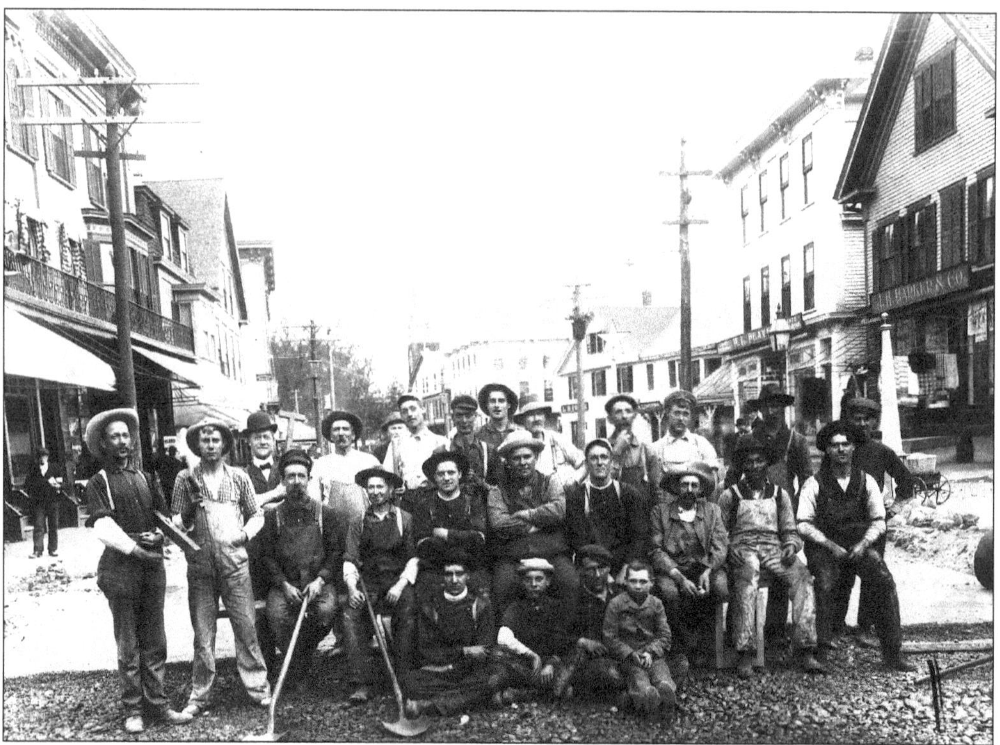

Progress comes to town! Main Street is paved at last by Harry Howard of Rochester and his road crew.

Three

Homes

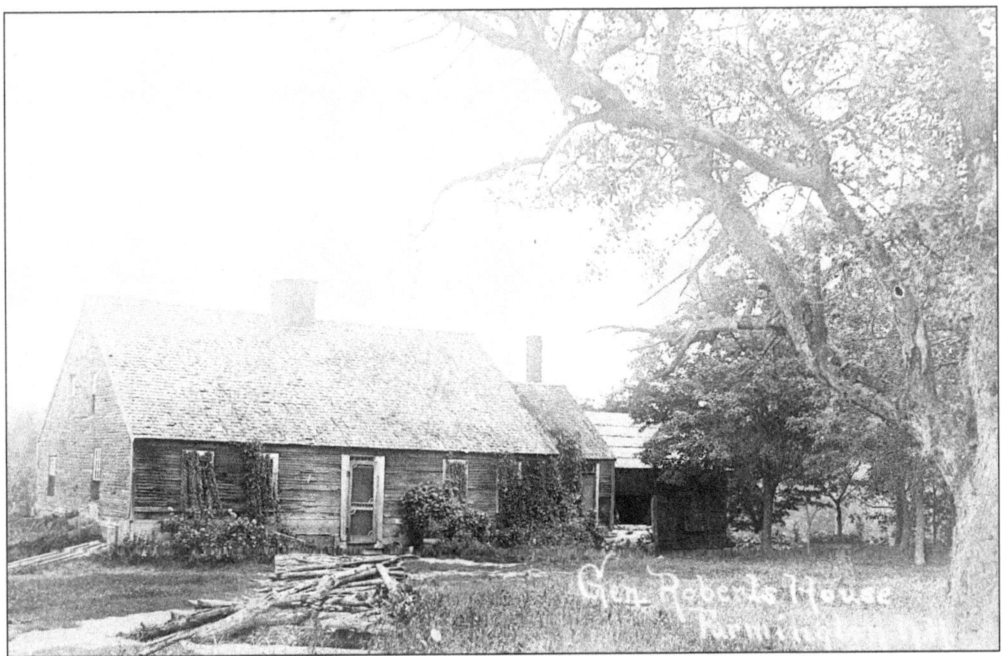

One of the earlier homes, the Roberts House, was located on the Farmington Road near the Rochester line. General Jeremiah Roberts' sawmill on Rattlesnake Brook provided lumber for the construction of many nearby houses.

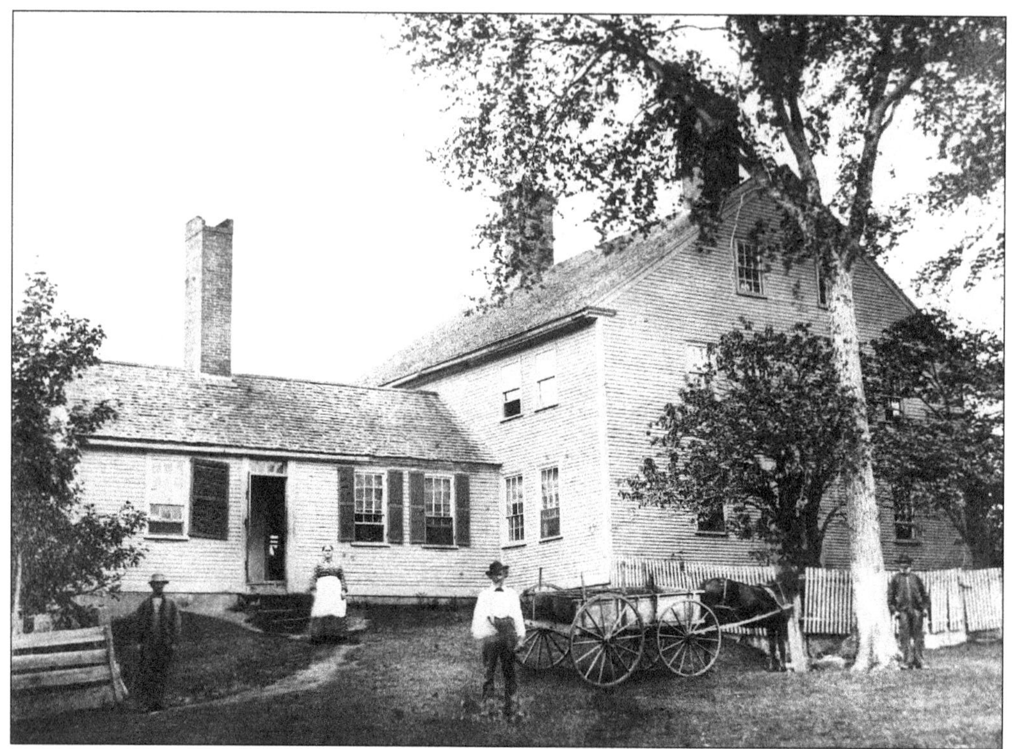

The Demeritt home on Meeting House Hill Road was built in 1818, the third dwelling on this property. The land was settled in 1775 by Paul Demeritt of Madbury, whose grandson Joseph is shown here. Upon Joseph's death in 1915, ownership passed to Ivory U. Bean.

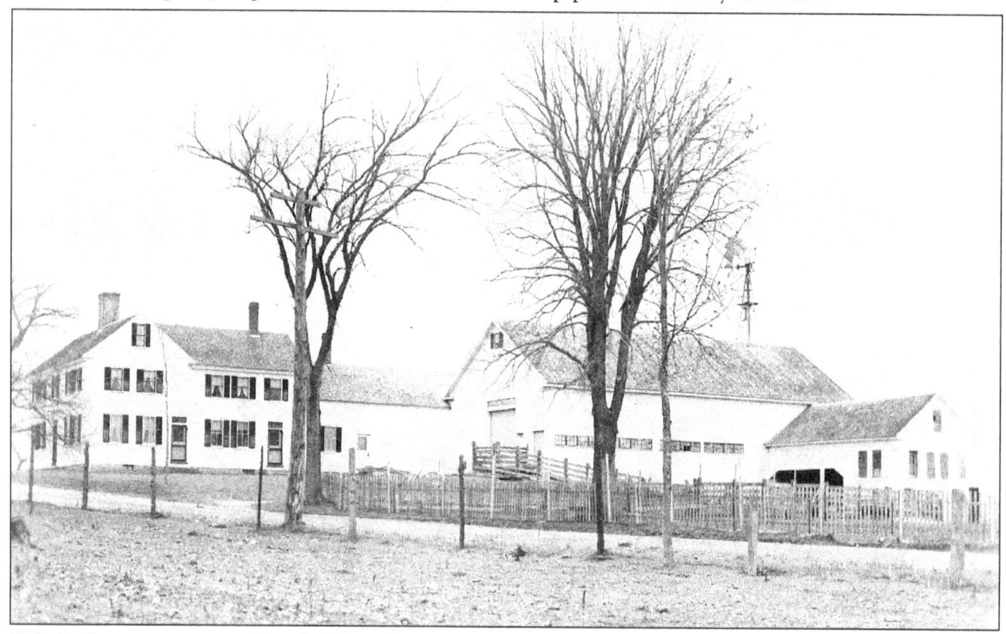

While this property on South Main Street was owned by John W. Knight, it became the scene of Henry Wilson's indenture from 1821 to 1833. The home was purchased by Simon F. Hayes in 1850 and is currently owned by the Gilman family.

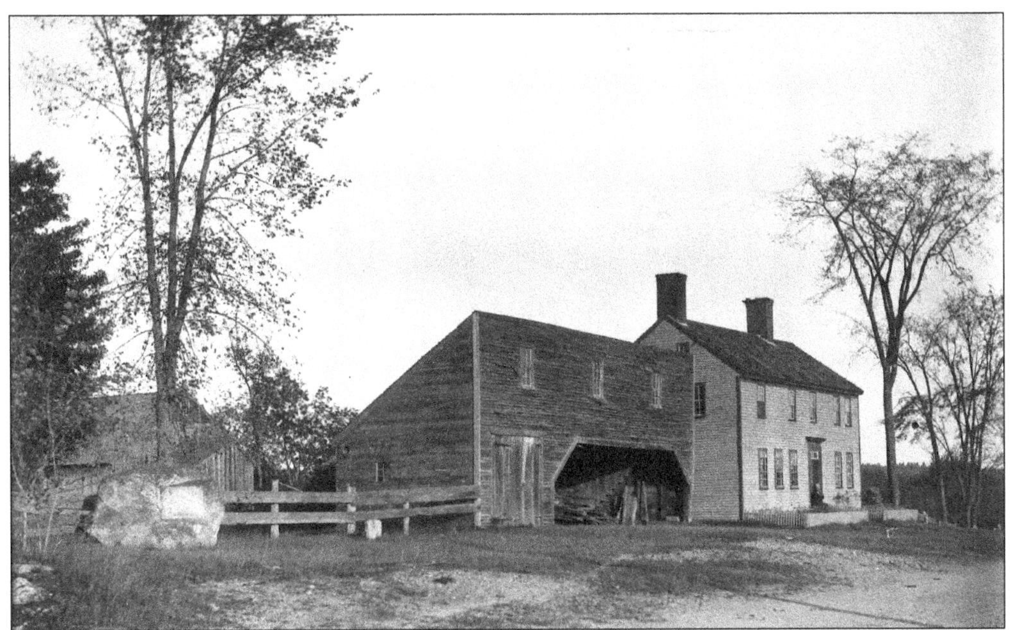

Built by Colonel Anthony Peavey, this dwelling served as both a home for his eleven children and as a tavern on the stagecoach route between Wolfeboro and Portsmouth. In 1924 the property was purchased by the Country Club for a golf course and clubhouse.

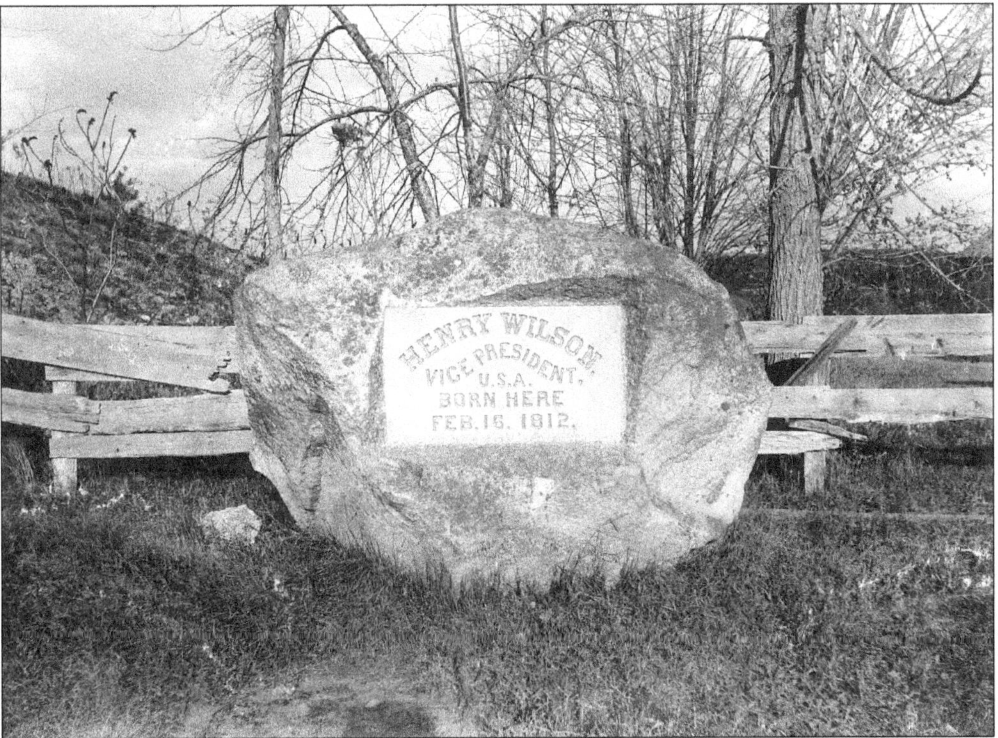

Henry Wilson was born in a modest cottage next to the Peavey home. The property was subsequently deeded to the town by Martin Luther Hayes, Wilson's lifelong friend, who marked the site with this 12-ton boulder.

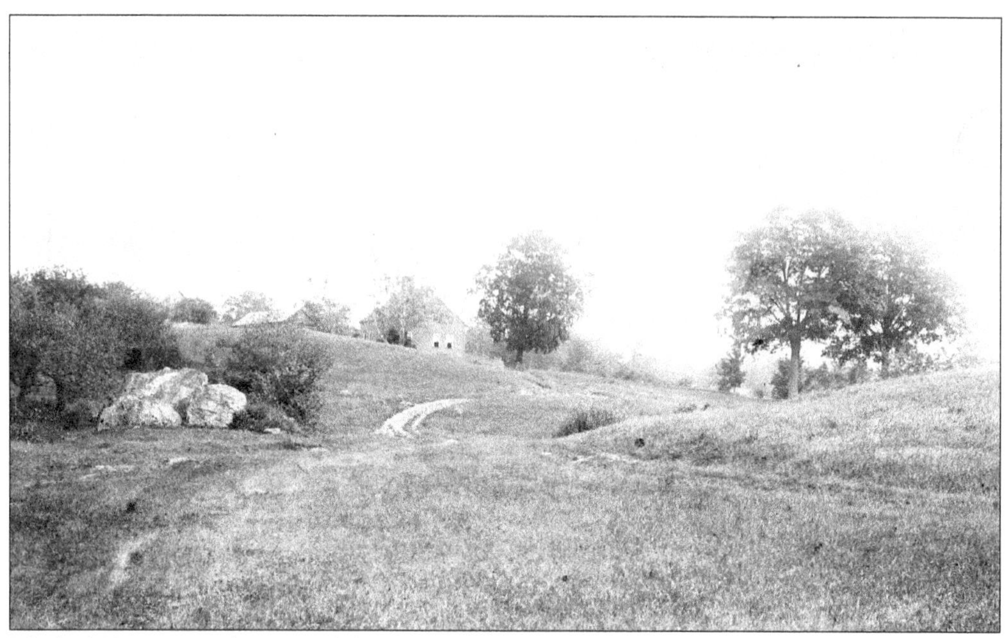

Ichabod Hayes served as one of the first three Farmington selectmen elected in 1799. Prior to the Revolution he built this house on the Chestnut Hill Road, and it remained in the Hayes family for 110 years.

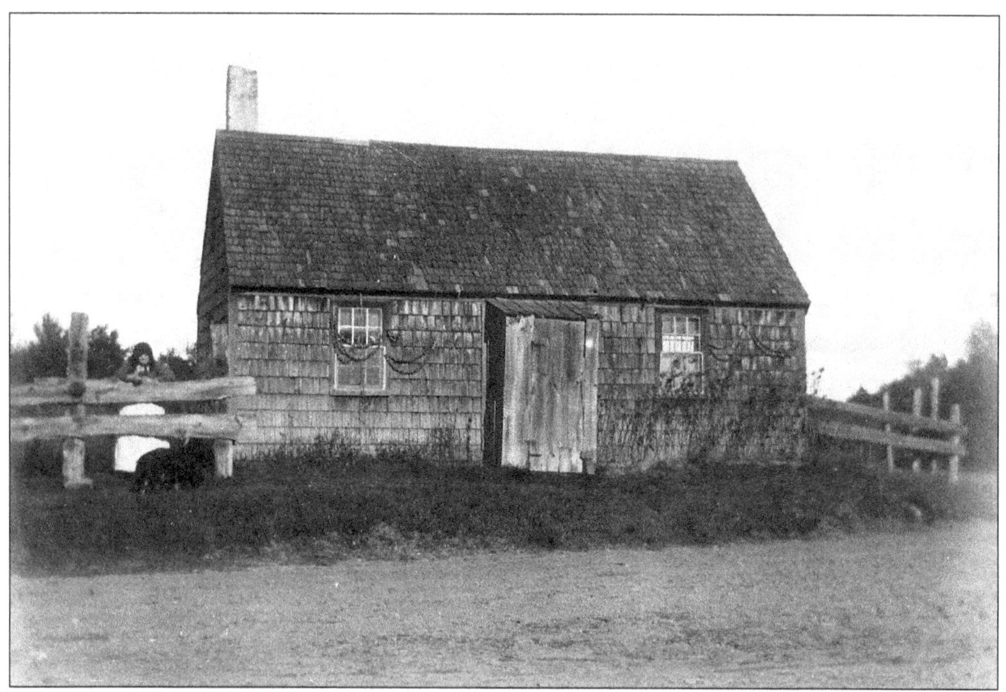

The Watson farm bordered the Cocheco River two miles south of the town. It lives in memory today as "Watson Corner."

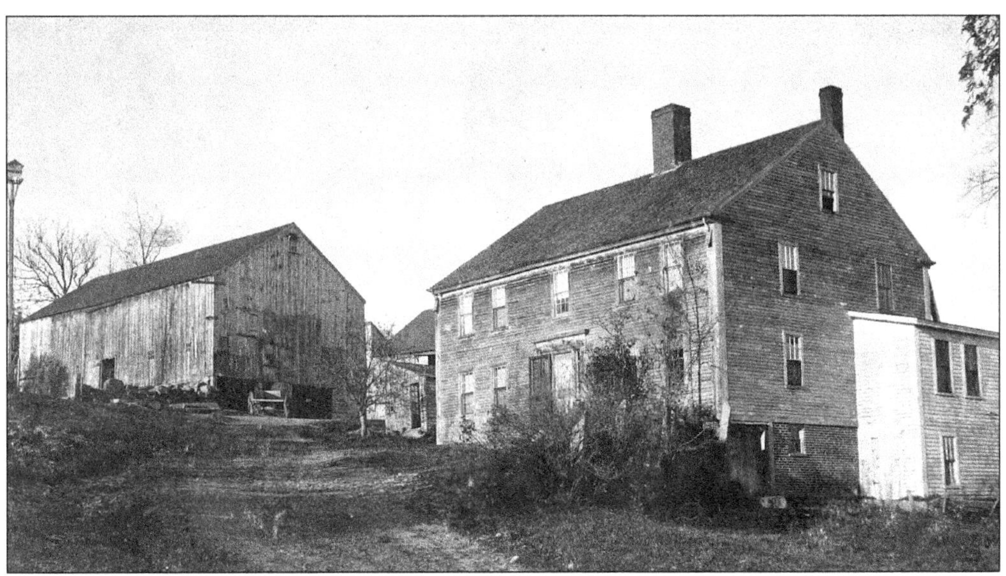

This large 1793 farmhouse situated on Cardinal Hill, once owned by Harley White, now belongs to the Littlefields.

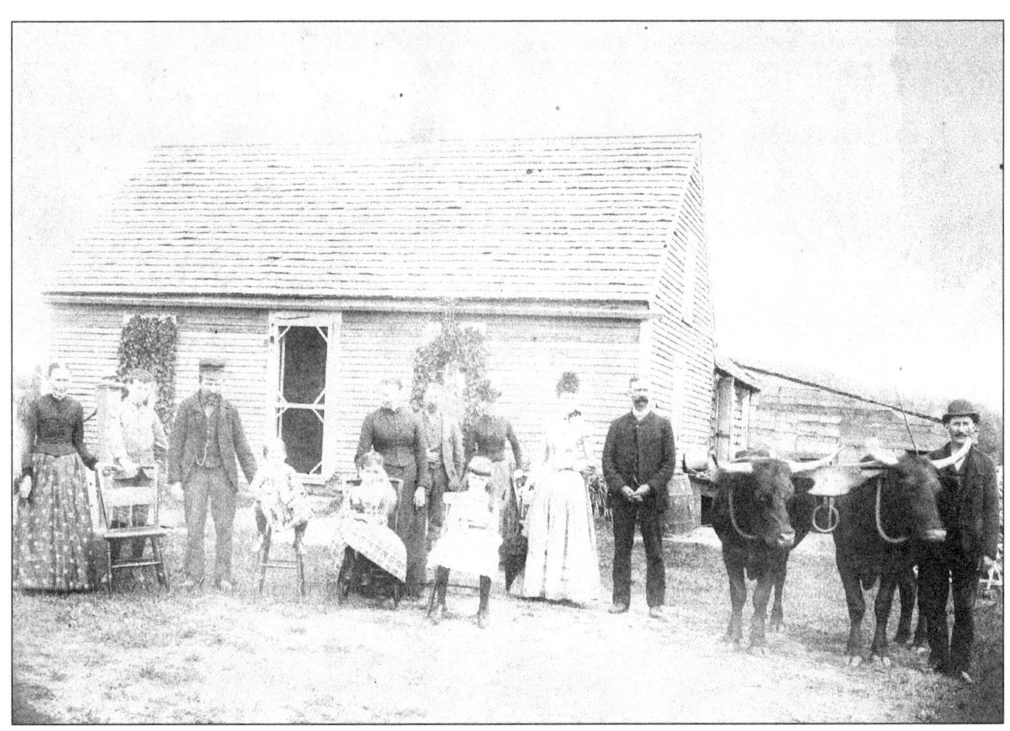

The camera recorded a visit by the C.B. Ricker family of Farmington to the Flanders home. Obviously, oxen were considered a valuable part of the family!

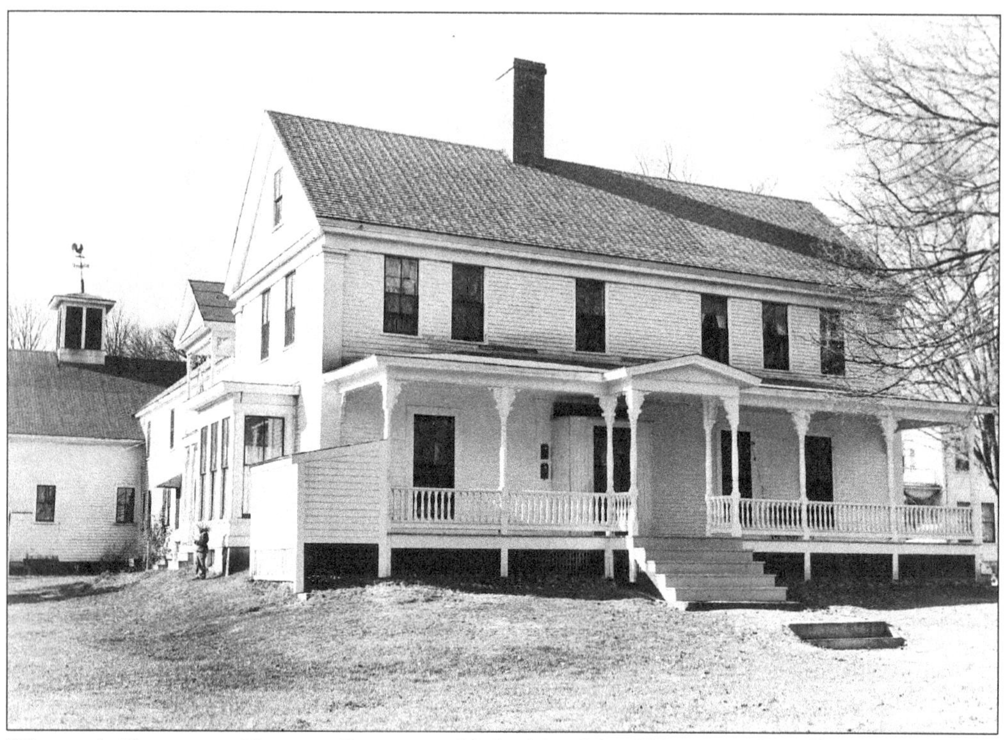

Wingate's Tavern on Pleasant Street, established by John Wingate of Madbury in the early 1800s, was located just behind his blacksmith shop on Main Street. It recently was demolished to provide a site for the new post office.

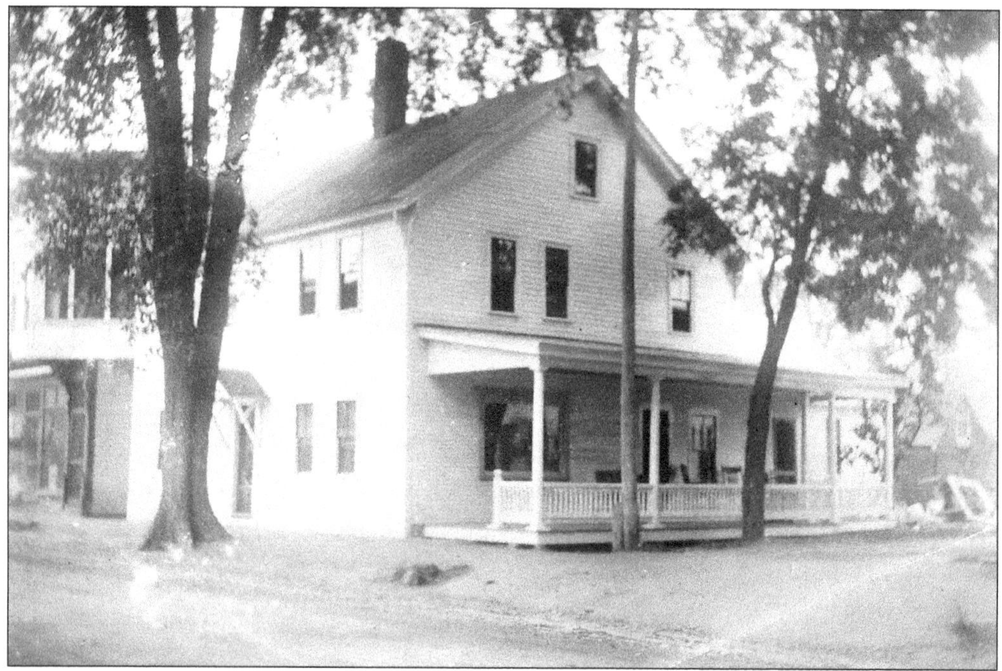

The large Freeman Nutter home on South Main Street, though greatly modified, still stands and currently houses a florist shop.

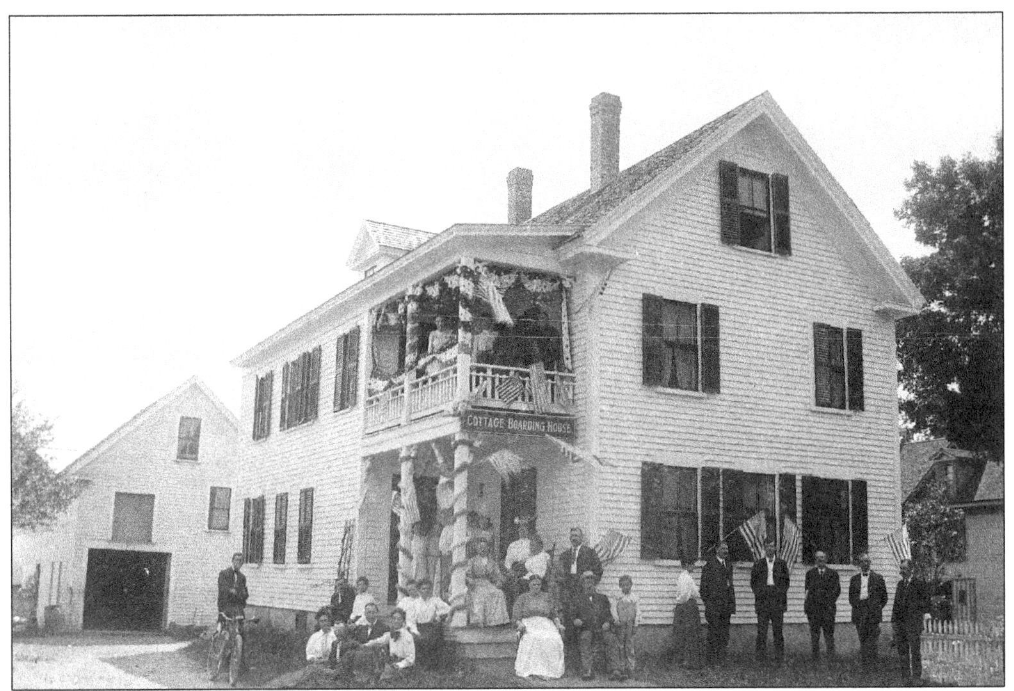

With so many factories operating in town, workers from outlying areas needed housing during the week. Hence the establishment of places such as this Cottage Boarding House on Central Street.

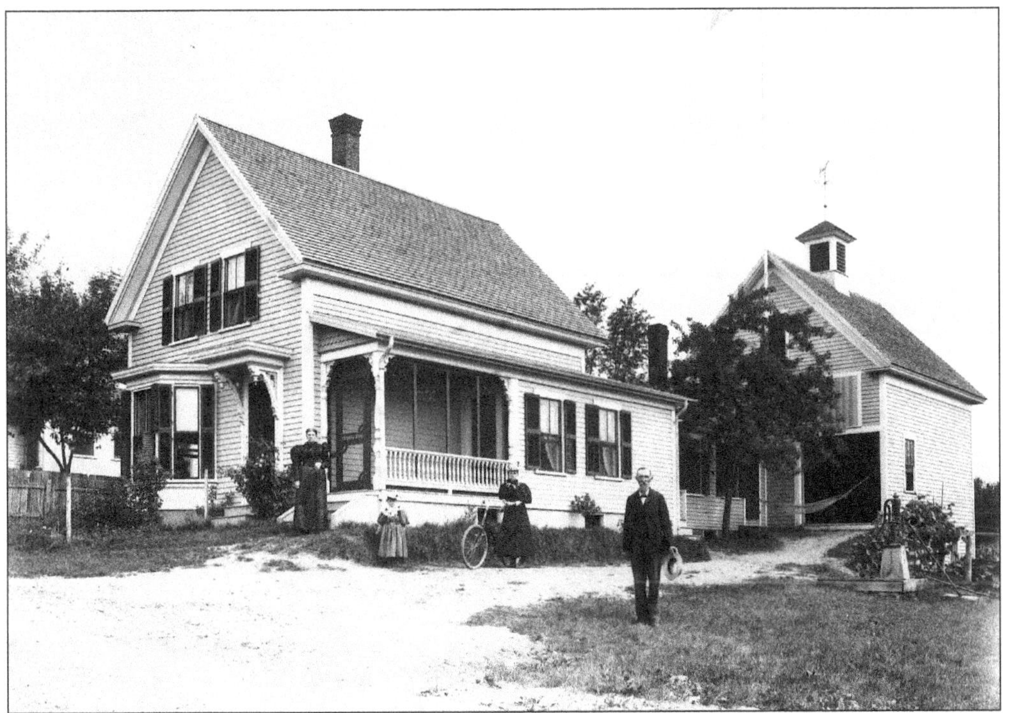

Mr. and Mrs. James Fletcher, with daughter Kitty and granddaughter Iva, are shown in front of their home on Mt. Pleasant Street.

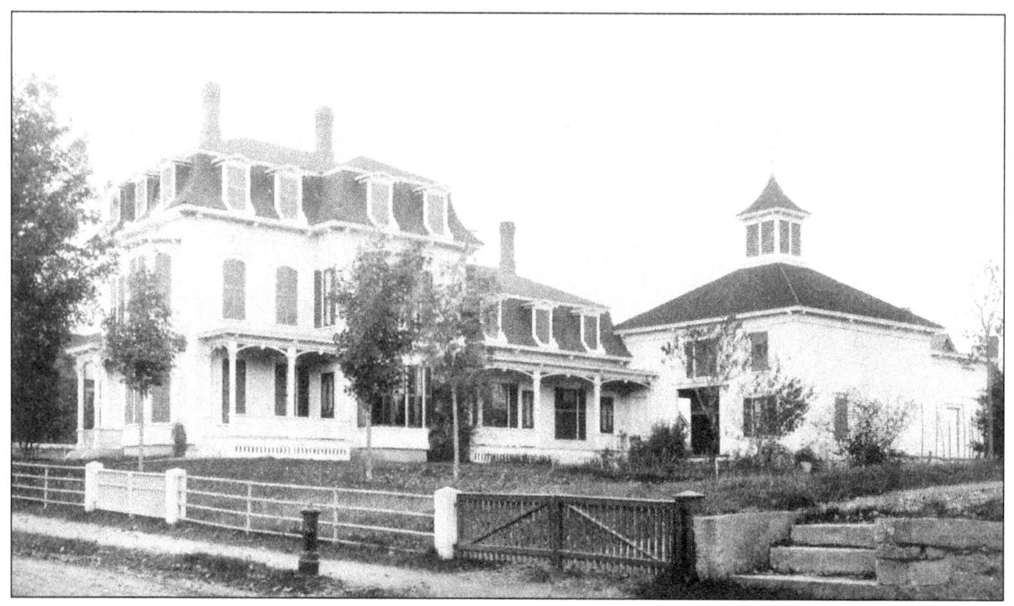
This lovely home on North Main Street was the residence of shoe manufacturer George A. Jones. He was one of the twelve businessmen who laid out the town's first water supply.

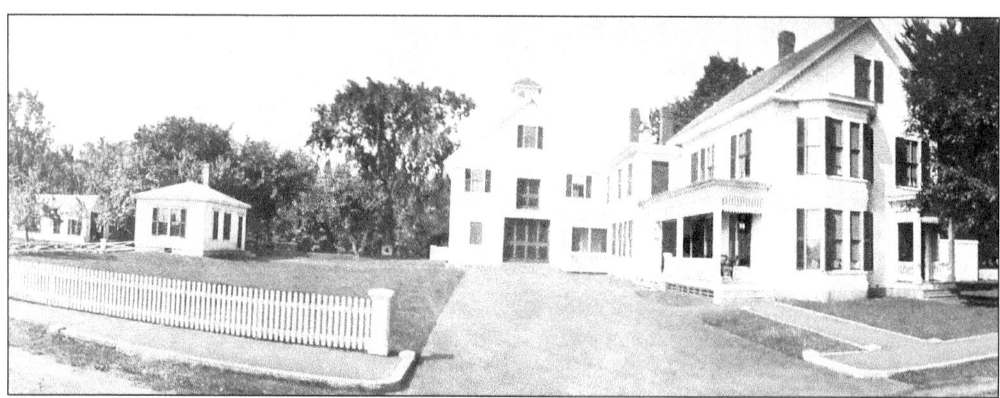
The Barker House was the residence of Hiram Barker, a banker and dealer in lumber and real estate who was one of Farmington's first millionaires. Located on Summer Street, it was built in 1800 by John Wingate. Known for many years as Riverside Manor, it is now the Spurwink School.

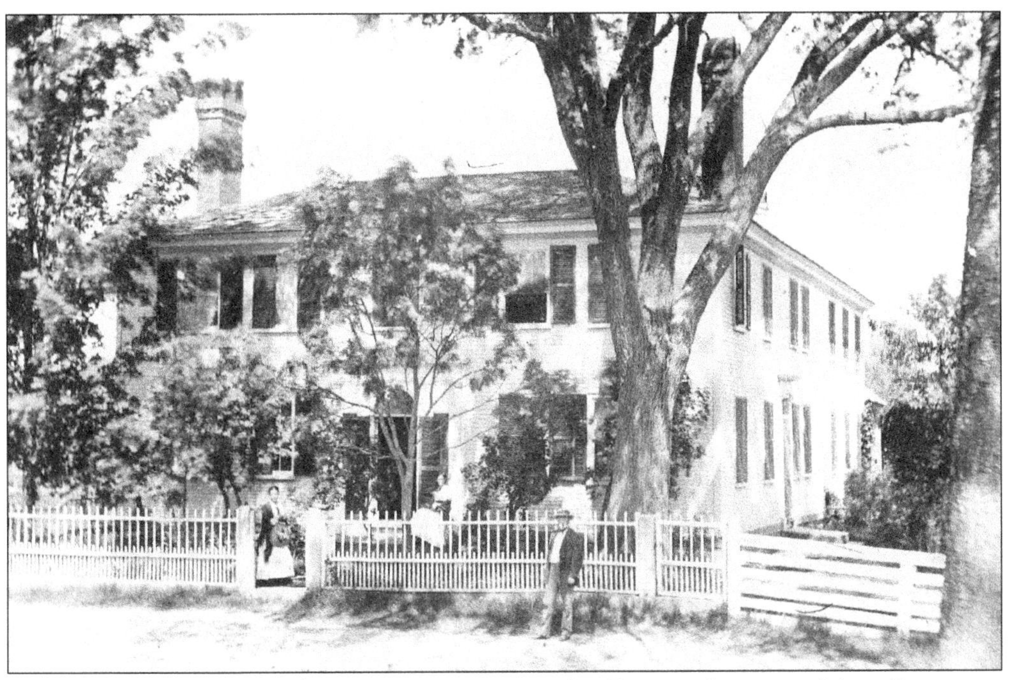

One of the more elegant houses in Farmington, the Eastman home on Main Street was constructed by ship carpenters in 1813 for lawyer Nehemiah Eastman. An unproved but oft repeated tale has the son of Indian chief Paugus buried where the house now stands.

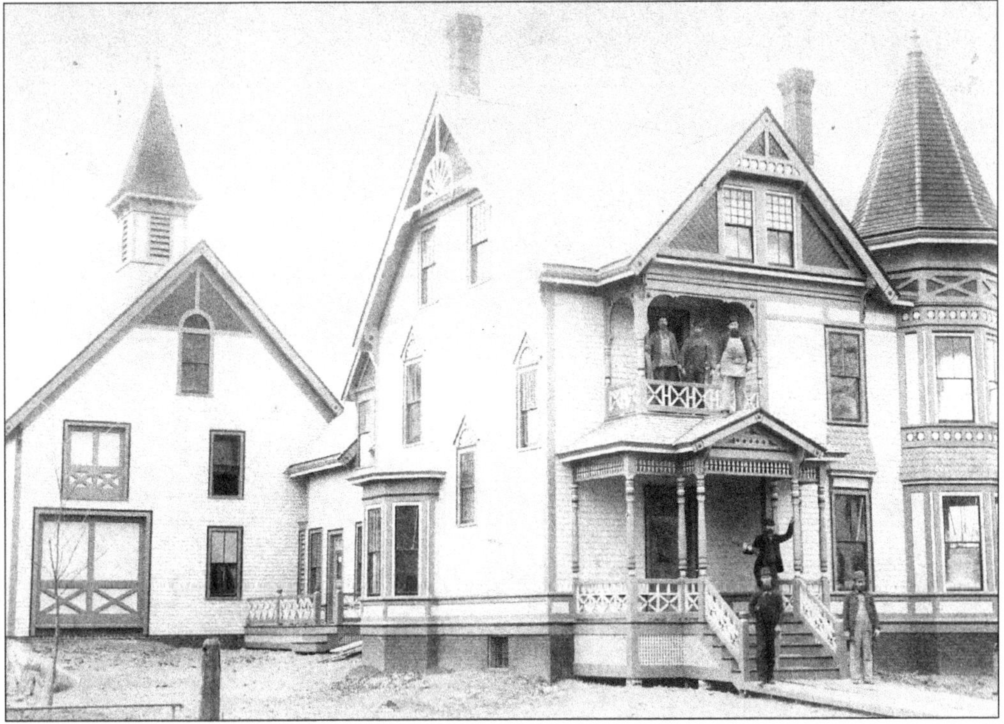

Obviously the workmen took pride in the construction of this fine 1893 Victorian home which was built for F.E. Edgerly at 33 South Main Street.

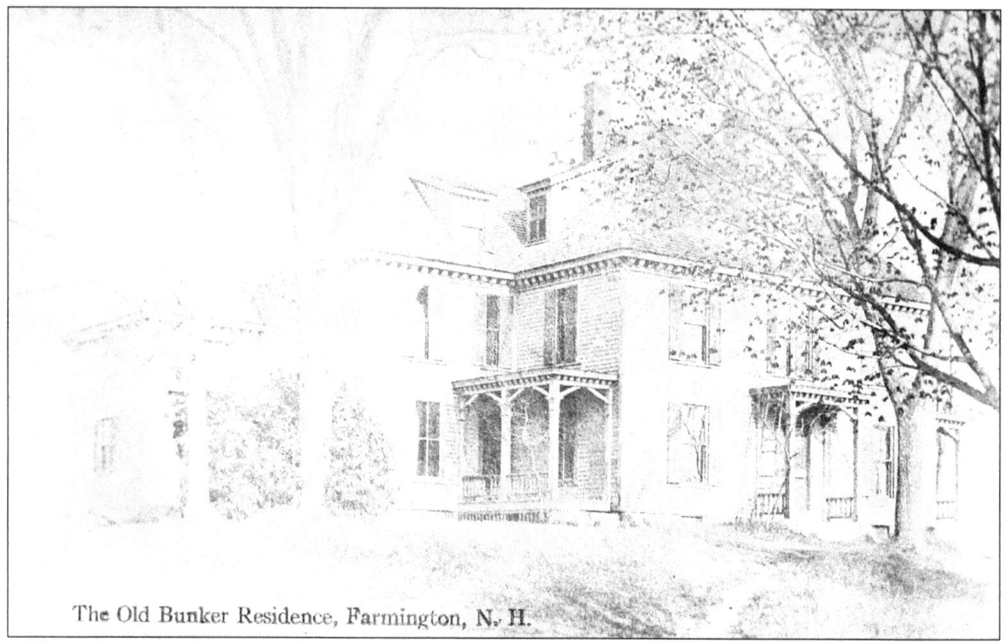

The Bunker House on North Main Street was constructed in 1883 on land inherited by Mary Ann (Ham) Bunker from her grandfather, John Ham. In 1913 the house was purchased by Mr. and Mrs. Elmer Thayer.

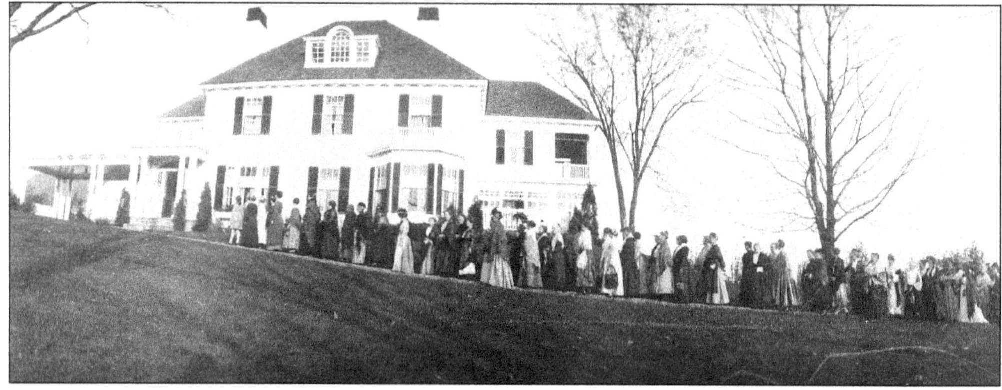

Mrs. Annie Thayer was hostess to the Farmington ladies at a costume tea party in her home. The Thayers had extensively remodeled the house since purchasing it from the Bunker estate.

Four

Notable Natives

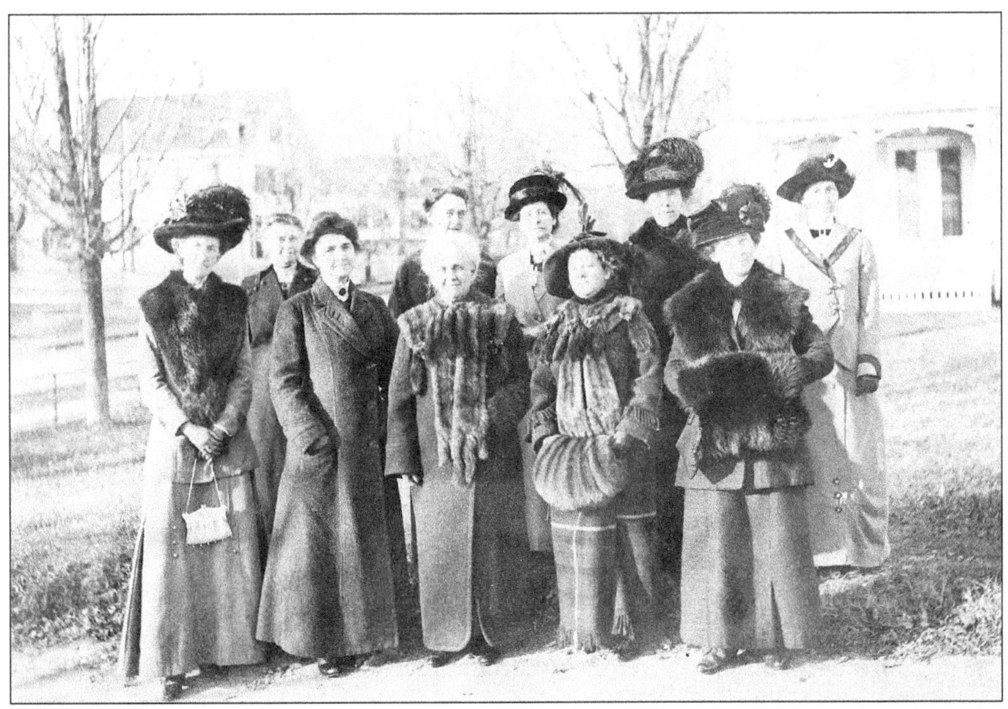

Some members of early Farmington society are shown. In the front row are Lizzie Emerson, Alta McDuffee, Lucia Gordon, Annie Thayer, and Jessie Willson; the back row is composed of Mrs. Goodwin, Nina Greeley, Nellie Allen, Jessie Sargent, and Susie Otis.

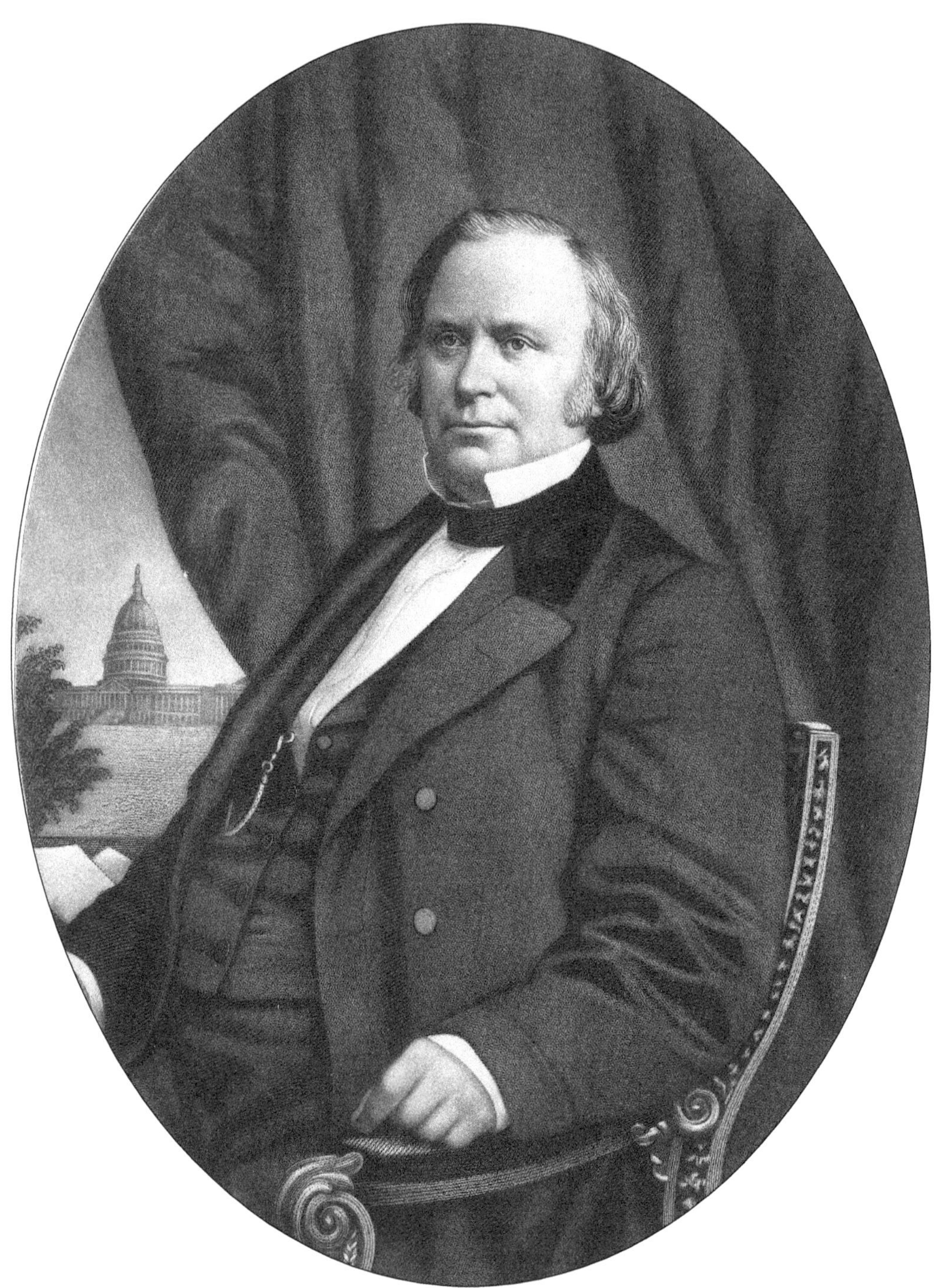

Henry Wilson, who was born Jeremiah Jones Colbath on February 16, 1812, in Farmington, rose from a childhood of abject poverty and indentured servitude to being Vice President of the United States under Ulysses S. Grant.

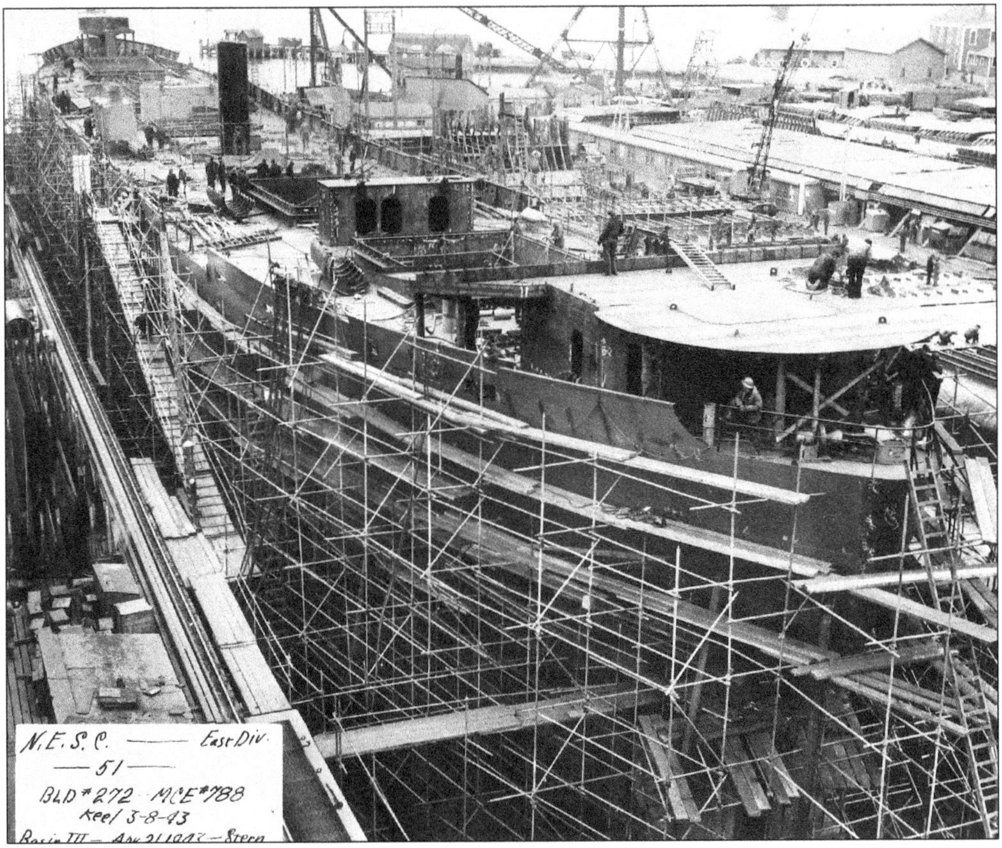

During World War II a cargo vessel, patriotically called a Liberty Ship, was named for Henry Wilson. The above photograph of April 21, 1943, shows the *Henry Wilson* under construction in South Portland, Maine. The launching, seen below, took place on May 3, 1943. The vessel was in use until being scrapped in May 1962. (Photographs courtesy of the Maine Maritime Museum, Bath, ME.)

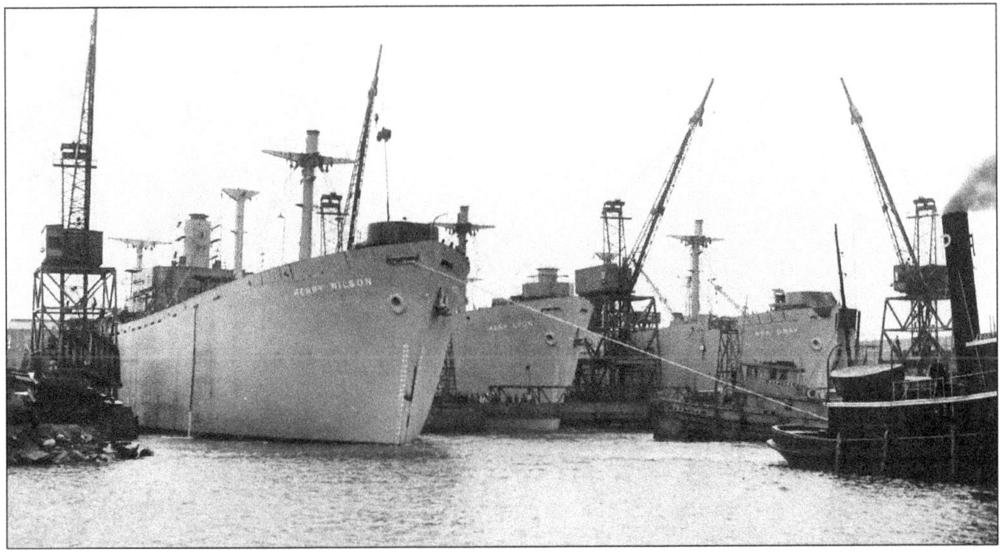

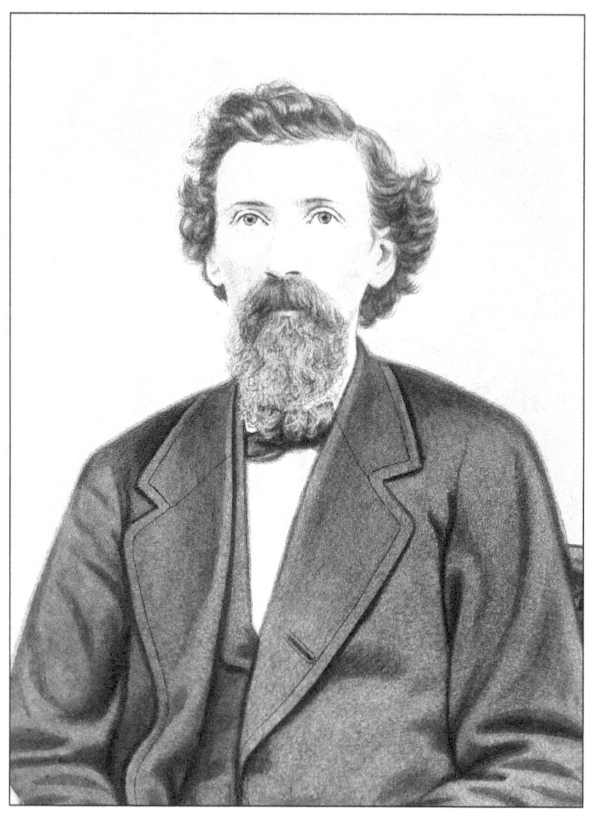

We are indebted to James E. Fernald for much that is known about early life in Farmington, for he founded and published, with his son George, The Farmington News, the paper of record for over seventy-five years.

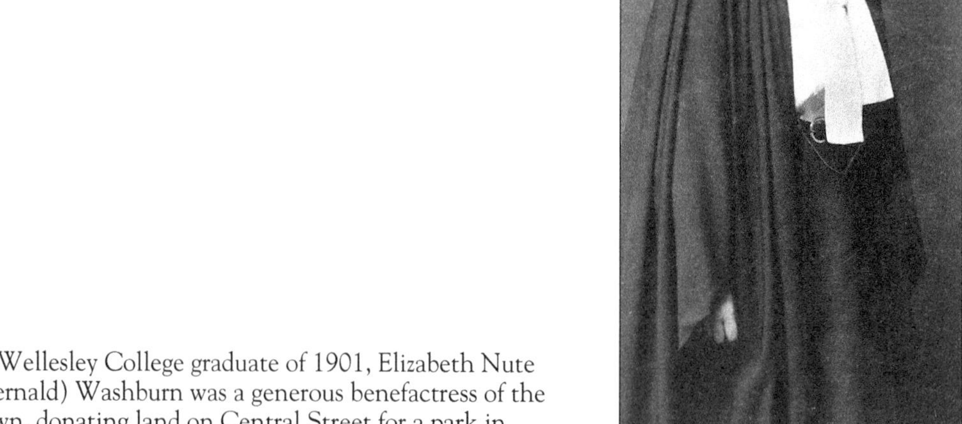

A Wellesley College graduate of 1901, Elizabeth Nute (Fernald) Washburn was a generous benefactress of the town, donating land on Central Street for a park in memory of her father, George Fernald.

Along with being a licensed embalmer and funeral director for fifty-six years, Norman L. Otis also served forty-one years on the Pine Grove Cemetery Board and was town clerk for over two decades.

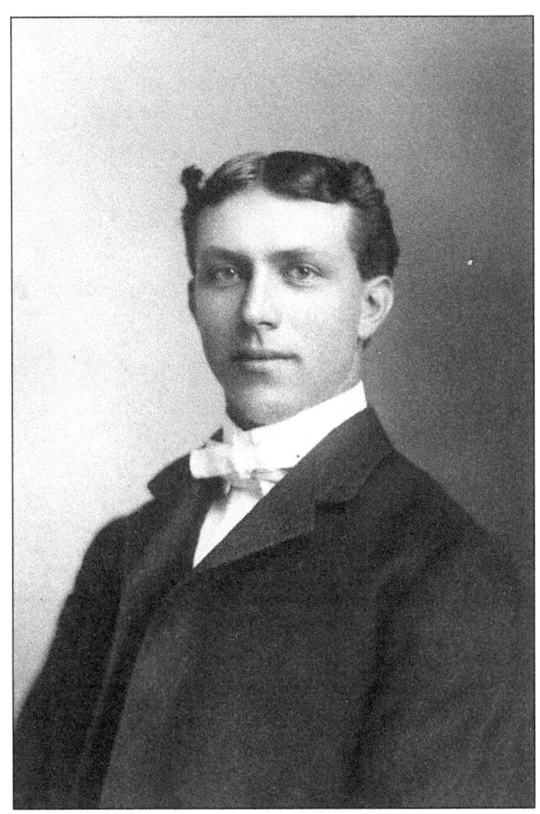

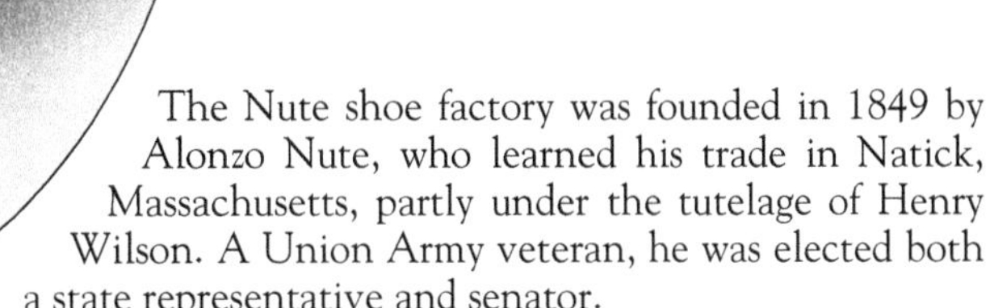

The Nute shoe factory was founded in 1849 by Alonzo Nute, who learned his trade in Natick, Massachusetts, partly under the tutelage of Henry Wilson. A Union Army veteran, he was elected both a state representative and senator.

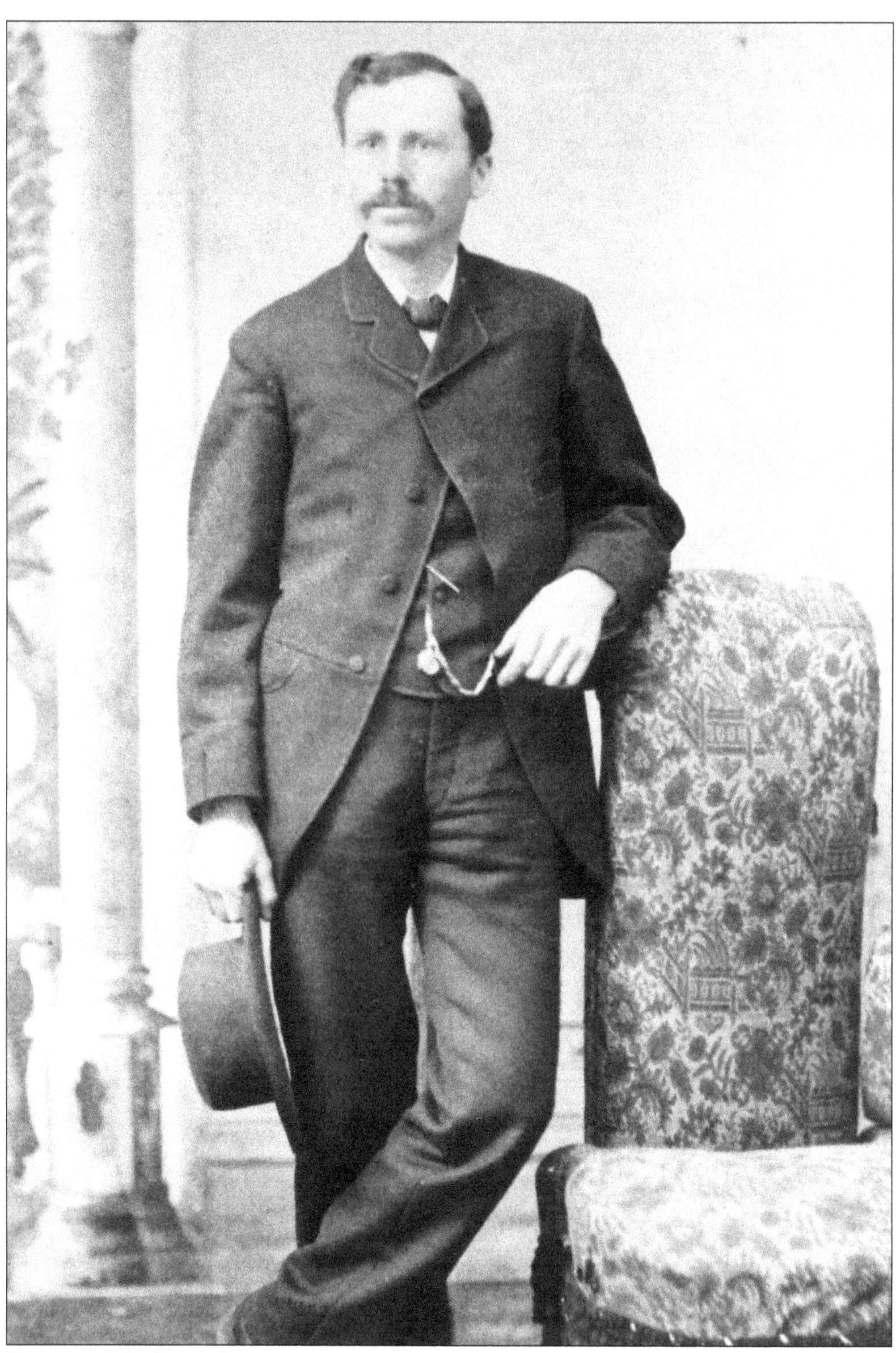

Benjamin F. Perkins, who came to Farmington from Strafford in 1880, was a noted carriage and sleigh manufacturer. A number of his vehicles are still in existence.

Dr. Raymond Pearl (1879–1940) was a Farmington native who earned international fame as a biologist, doing much of his work at Johns Hopkins University. He was also the organizer of the first Dartmouth College band.

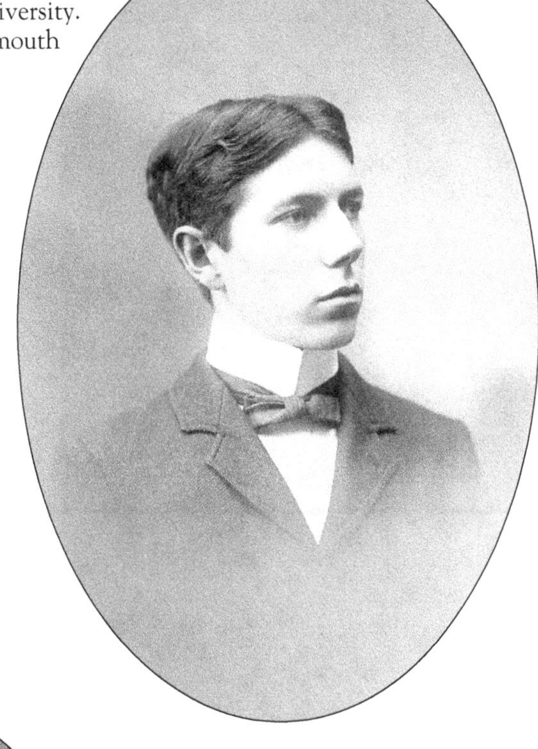

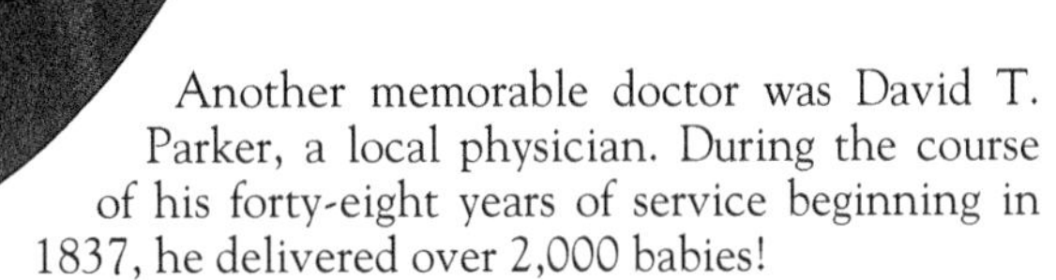

Another memorable doctor was David T. Parker, a local physician. During the course of his forty-eight years of service beginning in 1837, he delivered over 2,000 babies!

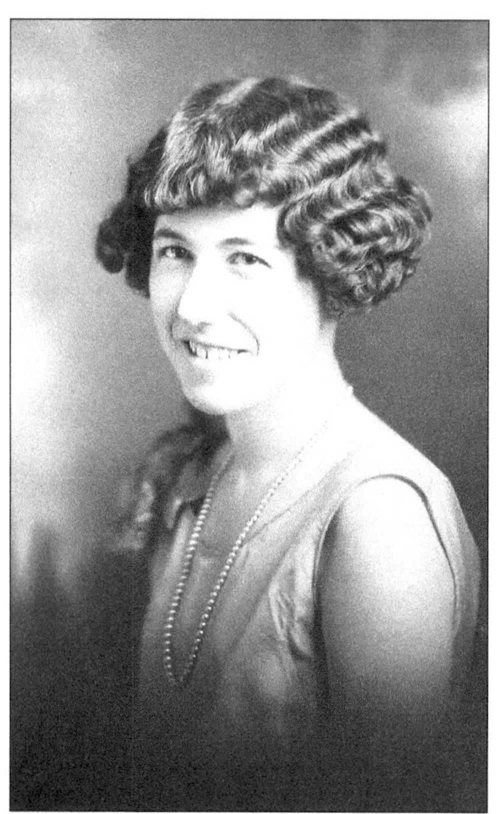

The most notable writer to originate in the town was Shirley Barker. Authoress of nine novels, two books of poetry, and three books for young people, she helped found the N.H. Writers Conference. Her untimely death at age fifty-four in 1965 was ruled a suicide.

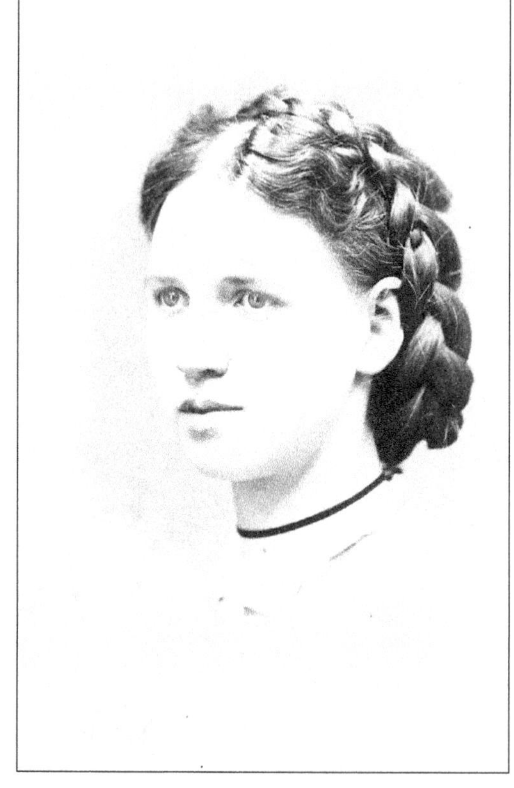

Martha A. (Hayes) Safford developed her artistic talents as a student of Benjamin Champney. Signing her paintings "M.A.S.," she worked in oils and crayon, with studios in Farmington and Rochester.

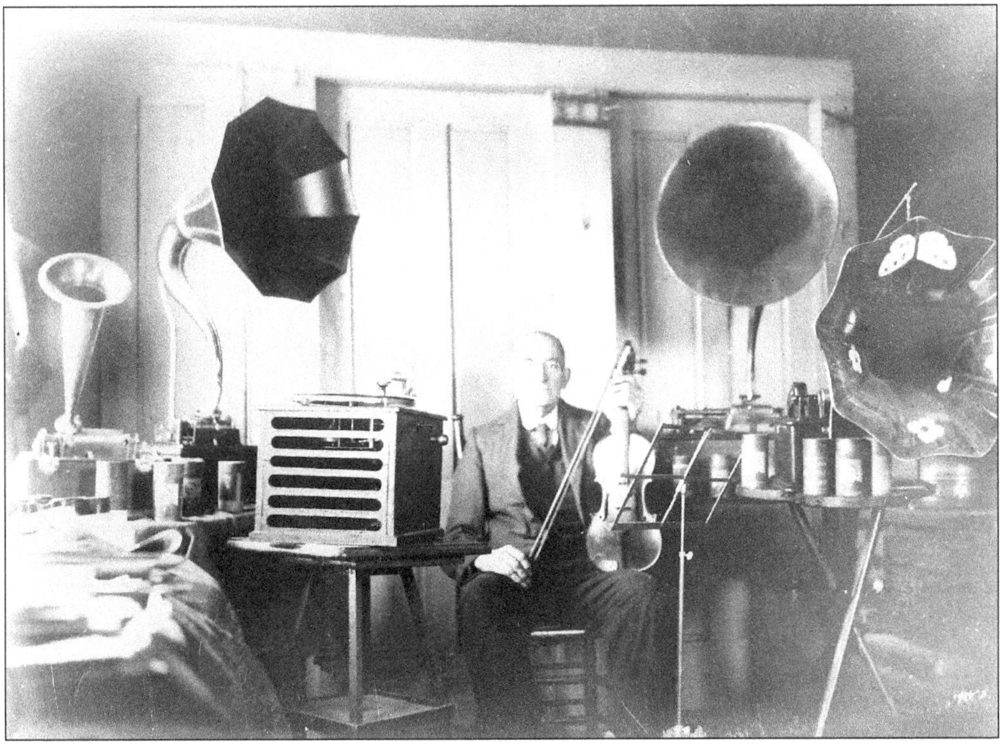

Everett Bailey of Glen Street must have been one of the town's greatest music lovers!

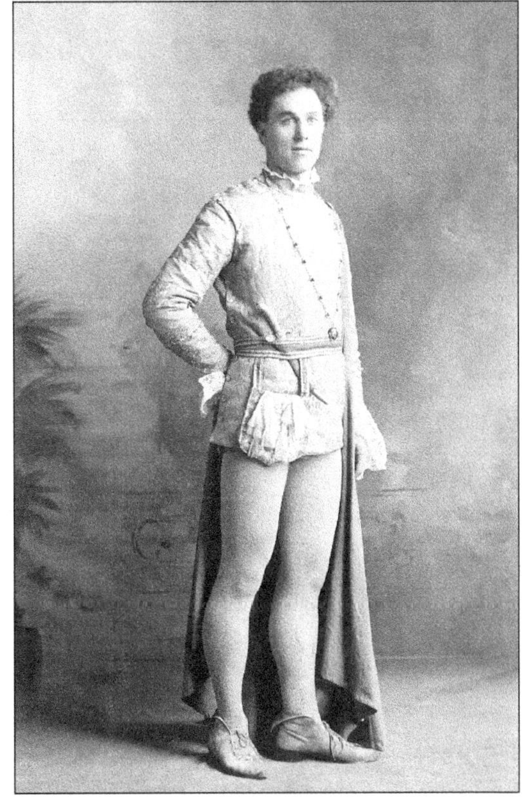

A civic-minded man of many talents, Herbert D. Browne toured with a Shakespearean theatrical company. Returning home, he was employed for over fifty years by Roberts Drug Store.

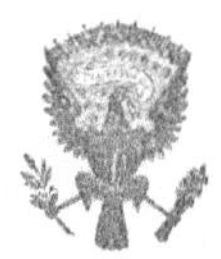

The President and Mrs. Roosevelt
request the pleasure of the company of
Gen. and Mrs. Edgerly
at a reception to be held at
The White House
Thursday evening, February the twentieth
nineteen hundred and eight
from nine to half after ten o'clock

Brigadier General Winfield Scott Edgerly, a West Point graduate and Farmington native, distinguished himself as an Indian fighter and was in command of the 7th Cavalry's rescue company for General Custer's men at Little Big Horn. He is shown here with President Theodore Roosevelt.

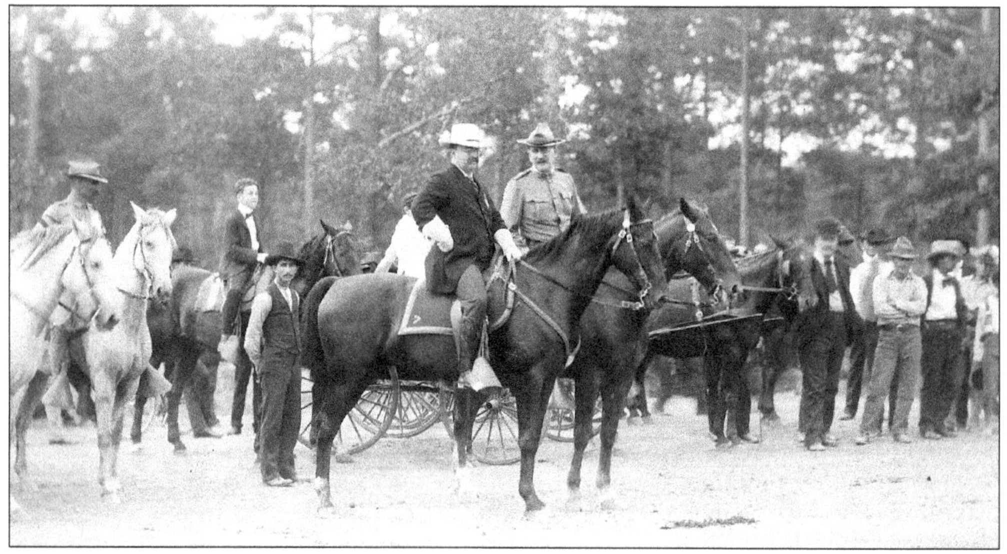

Five

Disasters

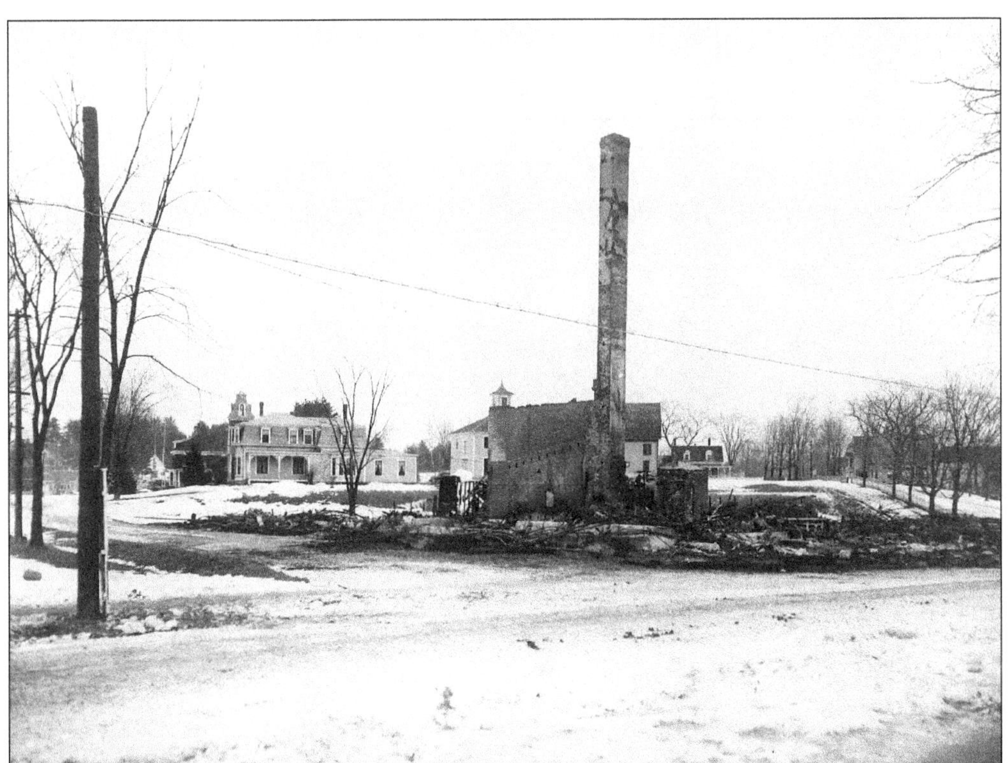

Farmington's largest industrial fire claimed the J.F. Cloutman Shoe Co. on February 14, 1918, resulting in the temporary unemployment of 228 people. Mr. Cloutman's home on Garfield Street was saved and may be seen in the background of this picture.

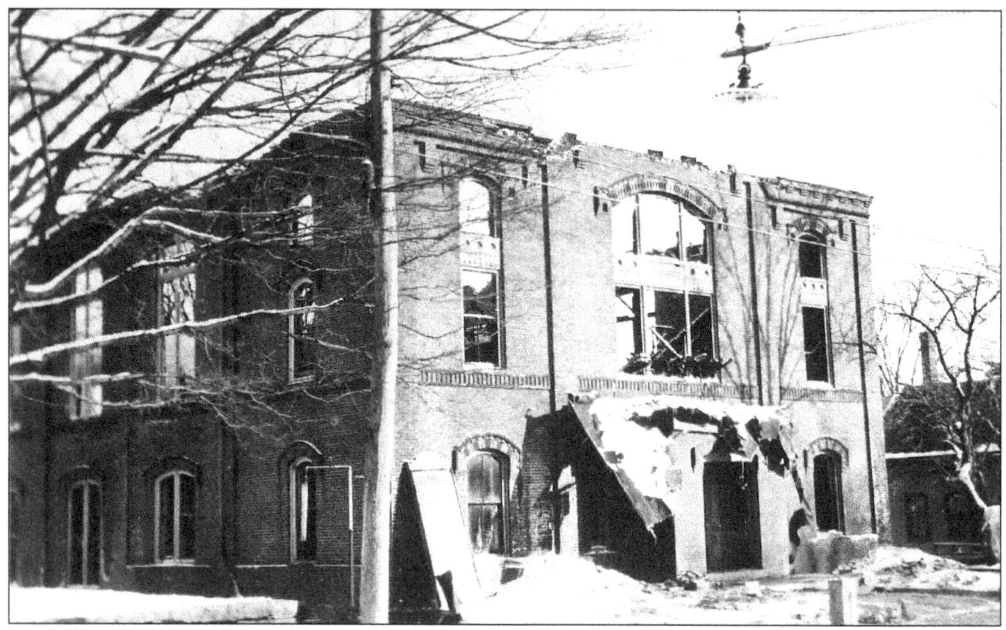

The fire which ravaged the Opera House on February 10, 1928, completely gutted the interior, destroying many town records as well as all the books in the town library.

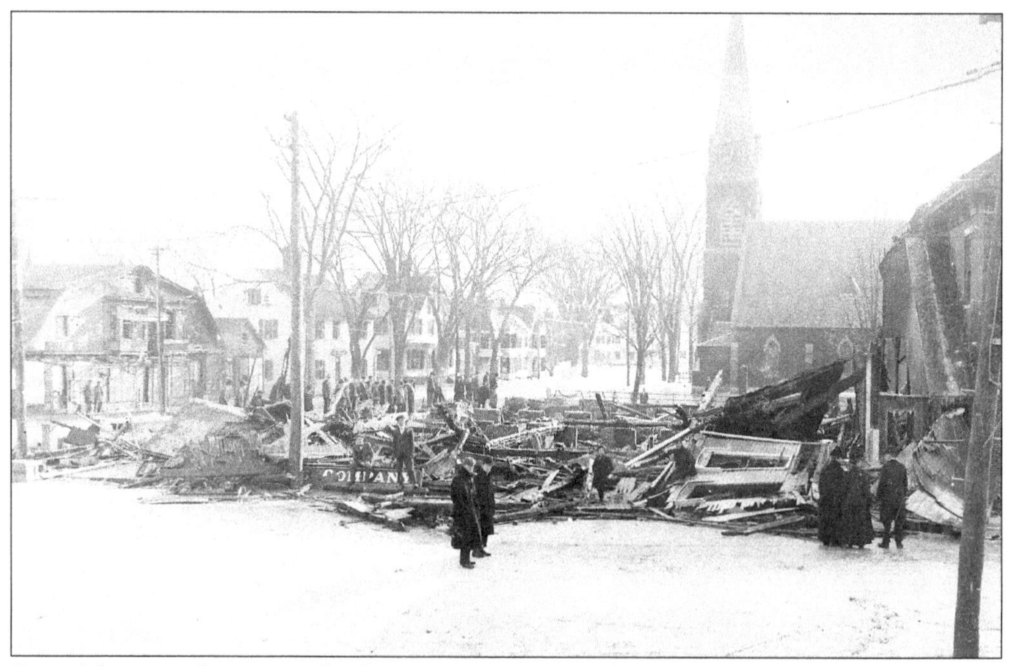

One of the worst disasters to the downtown area occurred on January 9, 1910, when a fire and resultant explosion destroyed the E.T. Willson Store and adjacent Barker Block. The bank and buildings across Main Street suffered damage but were saved.

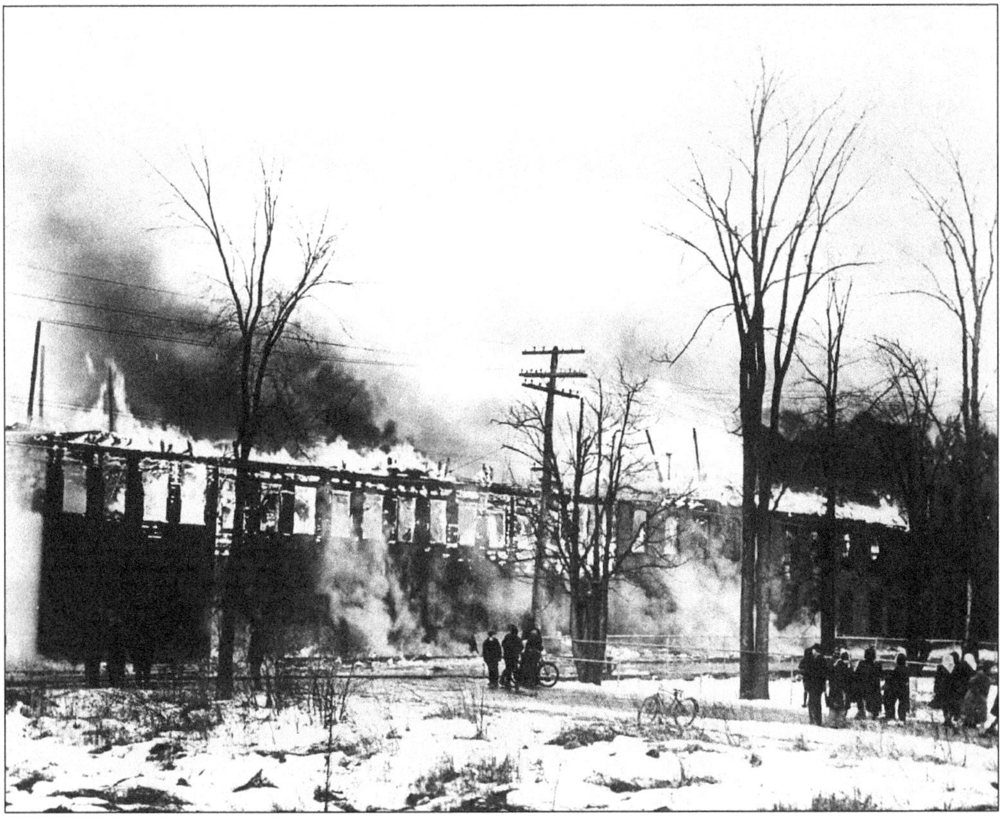

The rebuilt former Nute factory on the corner of East Grove Street, now owned by Dole and Waldron, burned again in 1944. Boarded up for years, it was eventually renovated into a food store.

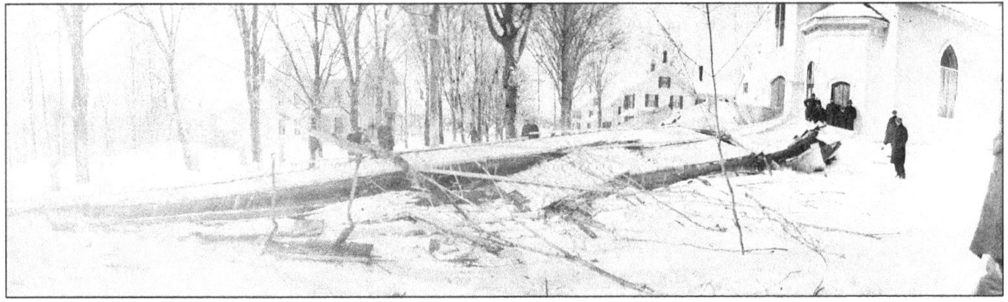

A dreadful winter snowstorm in March 1920 blew down the 139-foot steeple of the Baptist church. The town was isolated for four days.

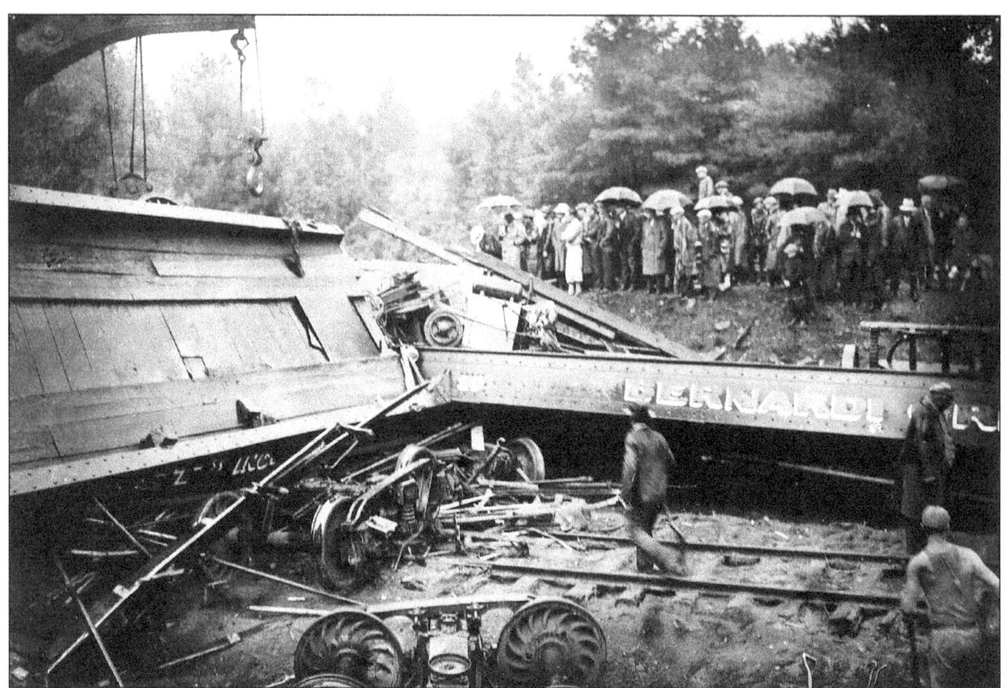

It was in July of 1928 that this circus train carrying "Bernardi's Greater Show" derailed near where the southbound tracks crossed Meeting House Hill Road. On its way from Lakeport to Gloucester, Massachusetts, the twenty-car train carried 368 people but, miraculously, only four were killed and eight injured. Thousands came to view the "great train wreck."

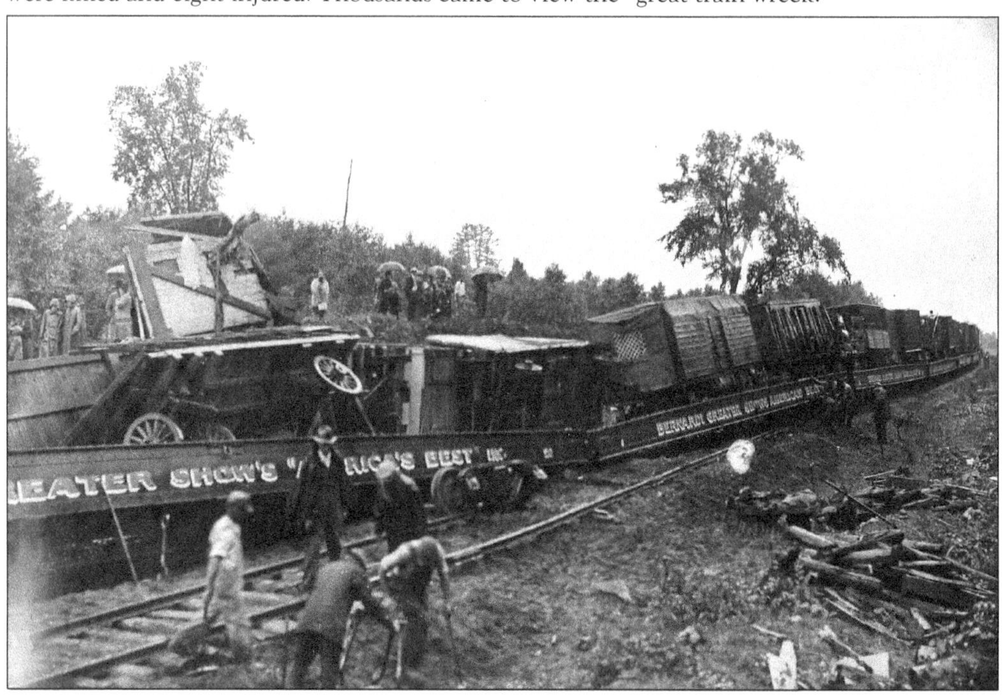

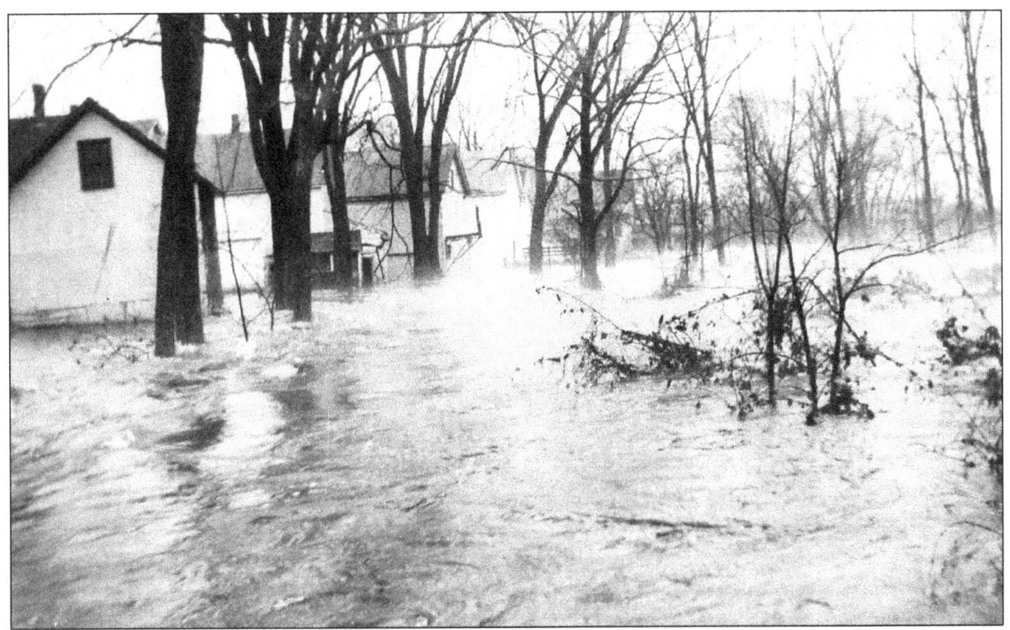

As viewed from the Tappan Street Bridge, flooding was a problem for Farmington residents before the Army Corps of Engineers dredged the rivers and reinforced the riverbanks.

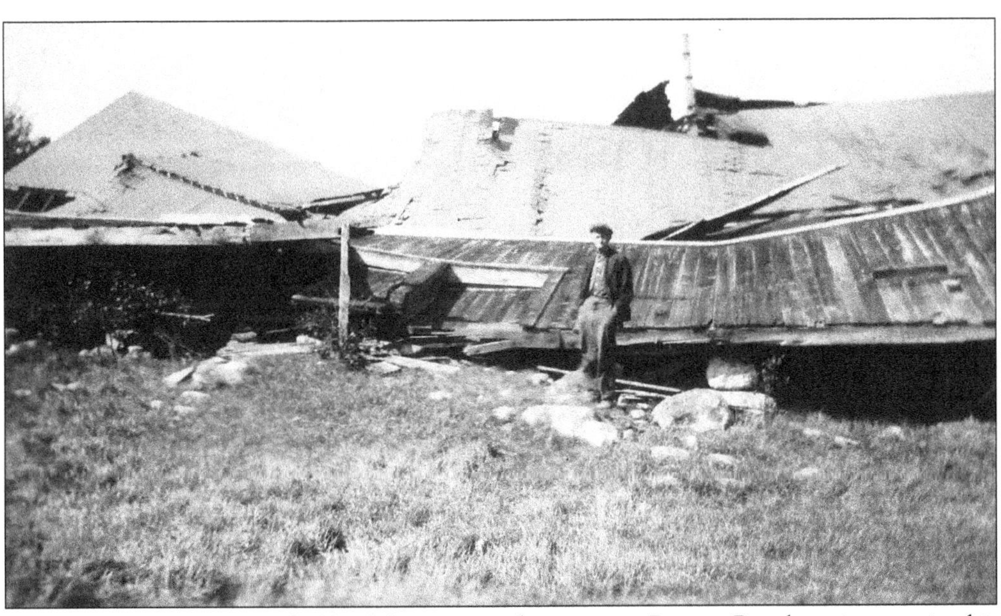

The infamous Hurricane of 1938 did not spare the town, as Roscoe Bowden witnesses in this photograph of Ware's barn on the Governor's Road.

NGTON, (N. H.) NEWS FRIDAY, OCTOBER 31, 1947

Farmington Escapes Being Wiped Out By The Greatest Fire in Local History!

In Path of Forest Fire, With Adverse Odds, Heroic Work by Hundreds of Persons Saved the Town From Total Destruction.

The above headline from The Farmington News says it all! Sparks from a train traveling between the Paulson and Meeting House Hill Roads started a catastrophic fire on October 23, 1947, which lasted three days. Due to heroic efforts by the citizens, no lives were lost and only a few buildings destroyed in Farmington, although Rochester was not so fortunate. The map below, (redrawn from State Fire Marshall Richard Curtis' map in *The Rochester Currier*), shows the Farmington portion of the 10,500 acres covered by the fire.

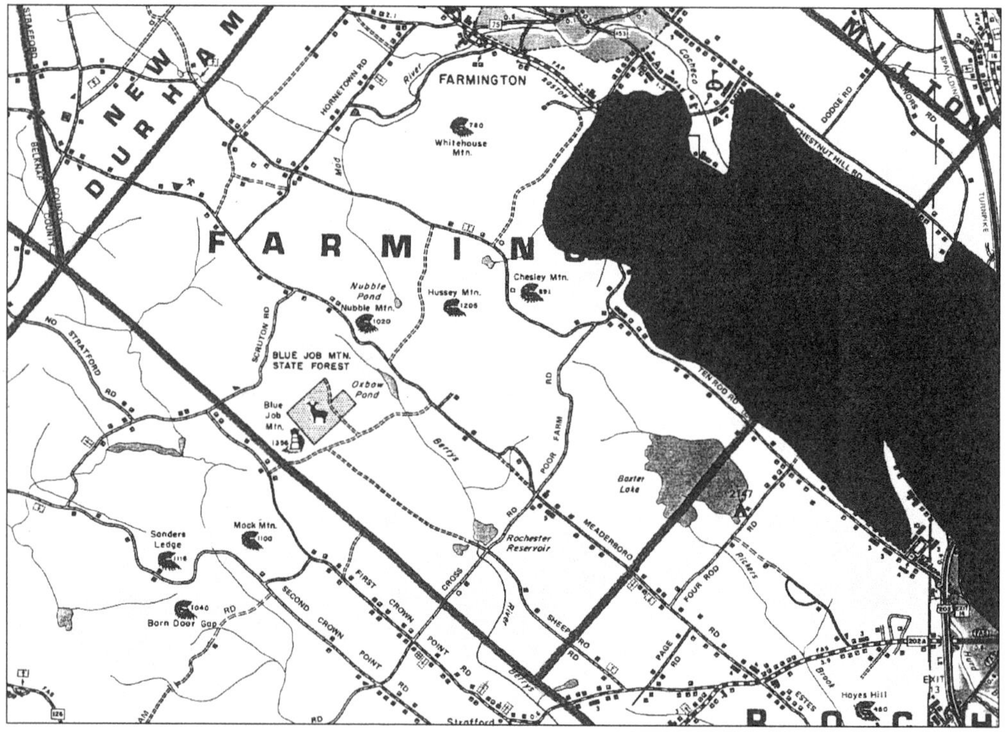

Six

Education: Schools and Sports

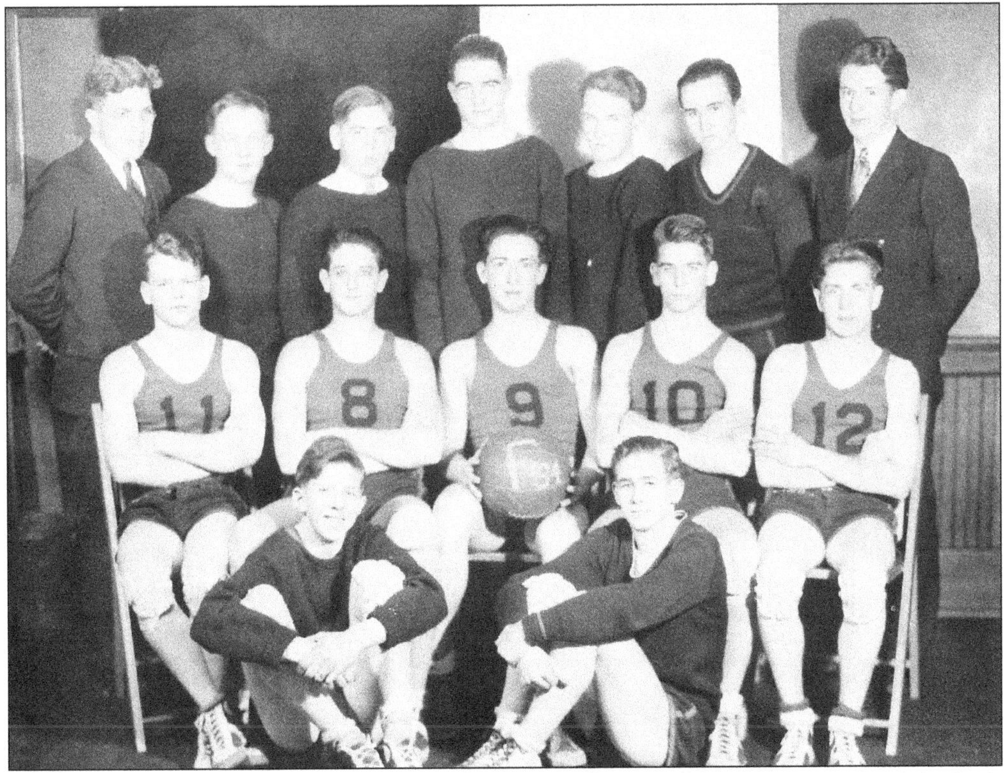

Farmington has always been known as a "basketball town." In this 1934 picture of the high school team are: (on floor) Tom Davenhall and Francis Mooney; (seated) Raymond Martineau, James Liberty, Floyd Richards, Valmore Martineau, and Lindon Burnham; (standing) principal Jesse Pellerin, Leo Nute, Maurine Hayes, Ralph Gullison, Charles Spear, Normal Fall, and coach Stanley Towle.

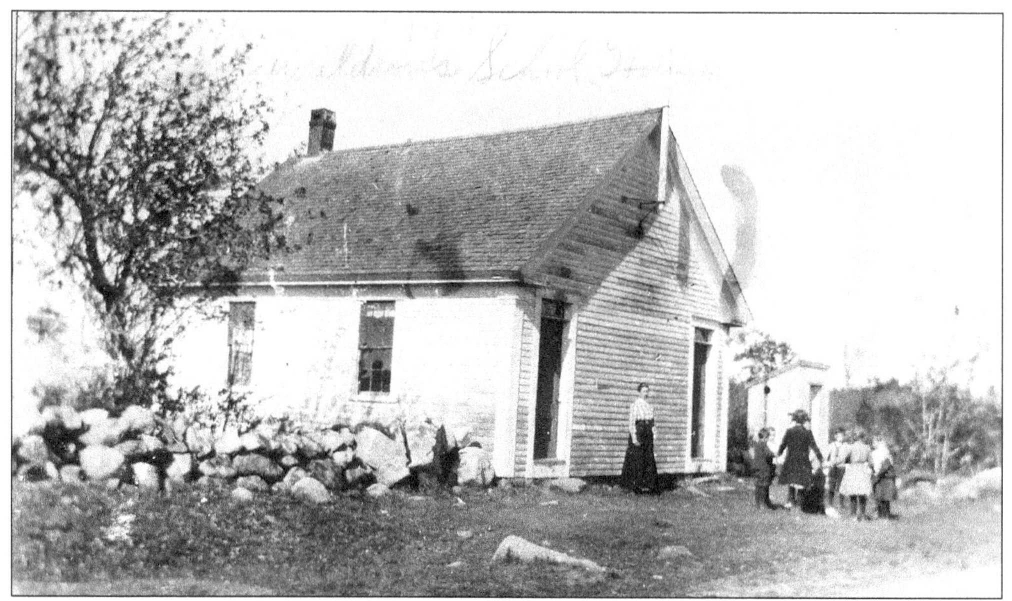

The Waldron Schoolhouse on the Bay Road was typical of the one-room buildings in outlying areas after the township was divided into sixteen school districts in 1805. Note the conveniently located privy!

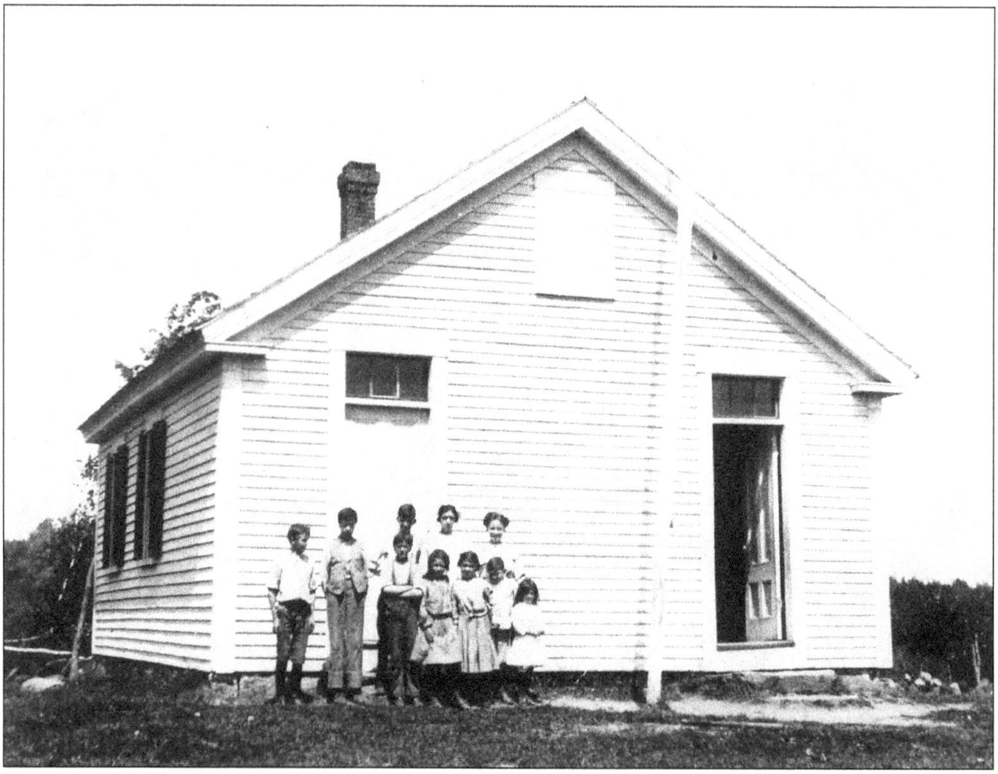

Teacher Floss Locke stands before the Ten Rod Road School in 1911 with her nine pupils. A rural school for over a hundred years, this building was transported three miles into town for use as a classroom behind the Main Street School.

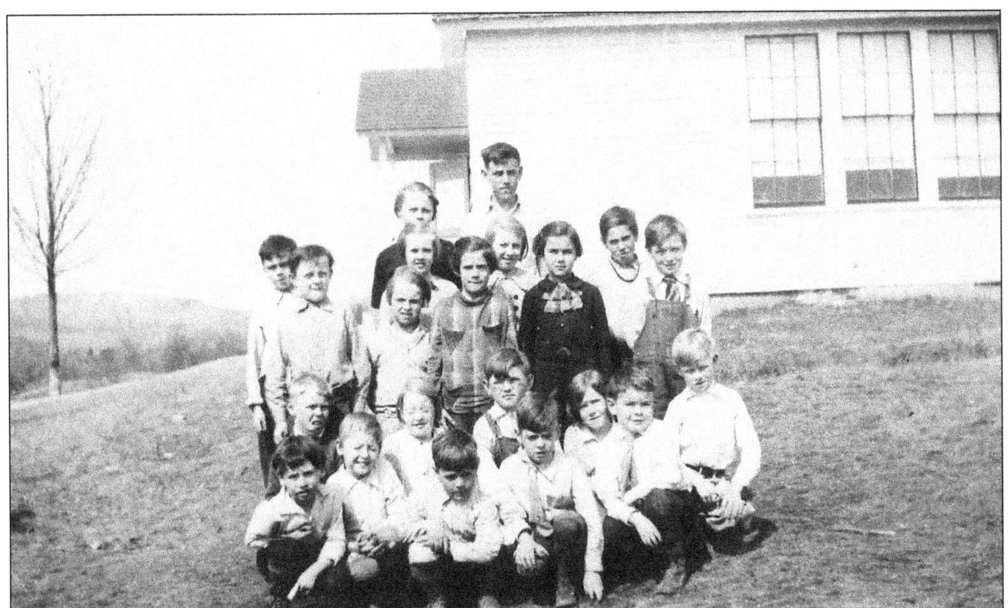

With all eight grades taught in one room, these are the pupils of the Merrill's Corner School on Meaderboro Road in 1935. The building is now a home.

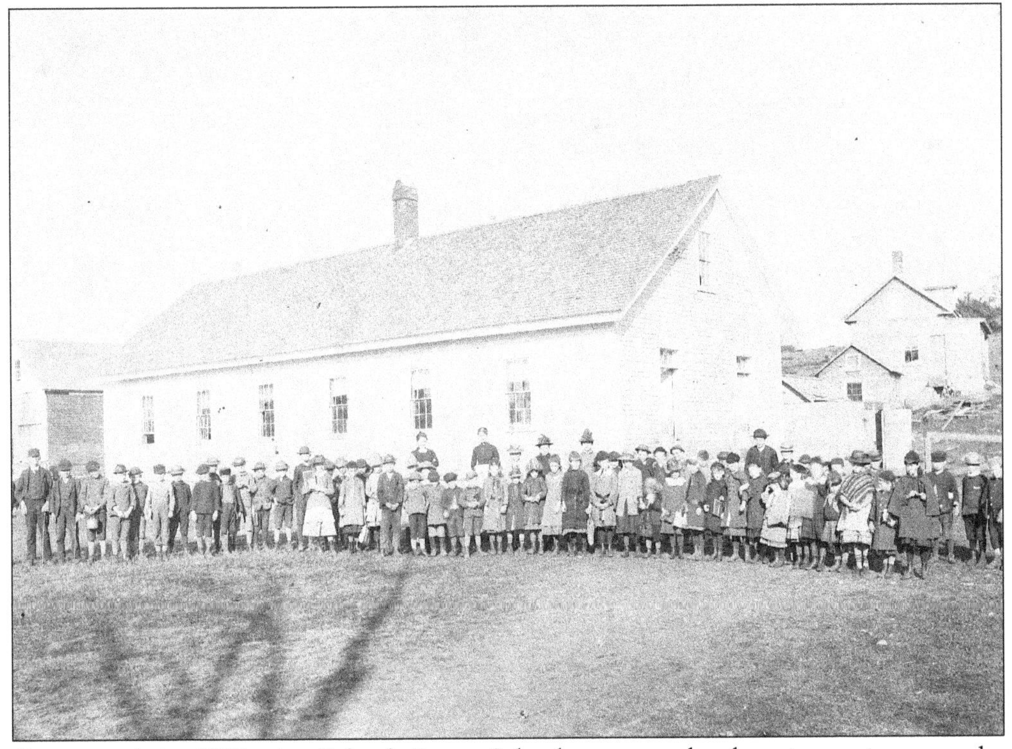

Constructed in 1859, the School Street School accommodated various primary grades until 1952.

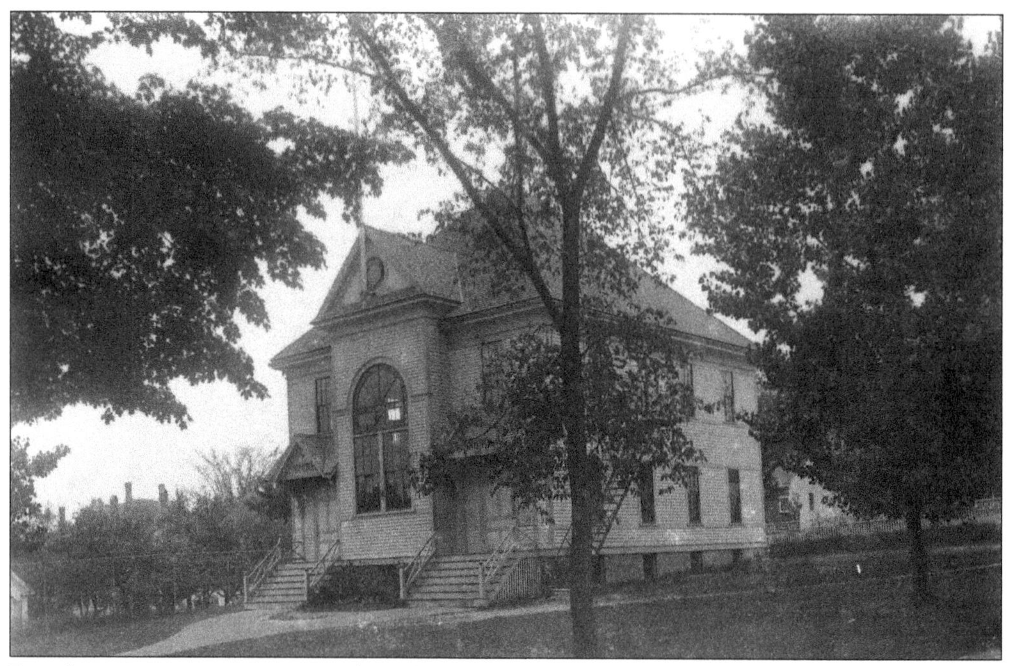

Four large rooms were contained in this two-story school on Glen Street where pupils were educated from 1890 to 1952.

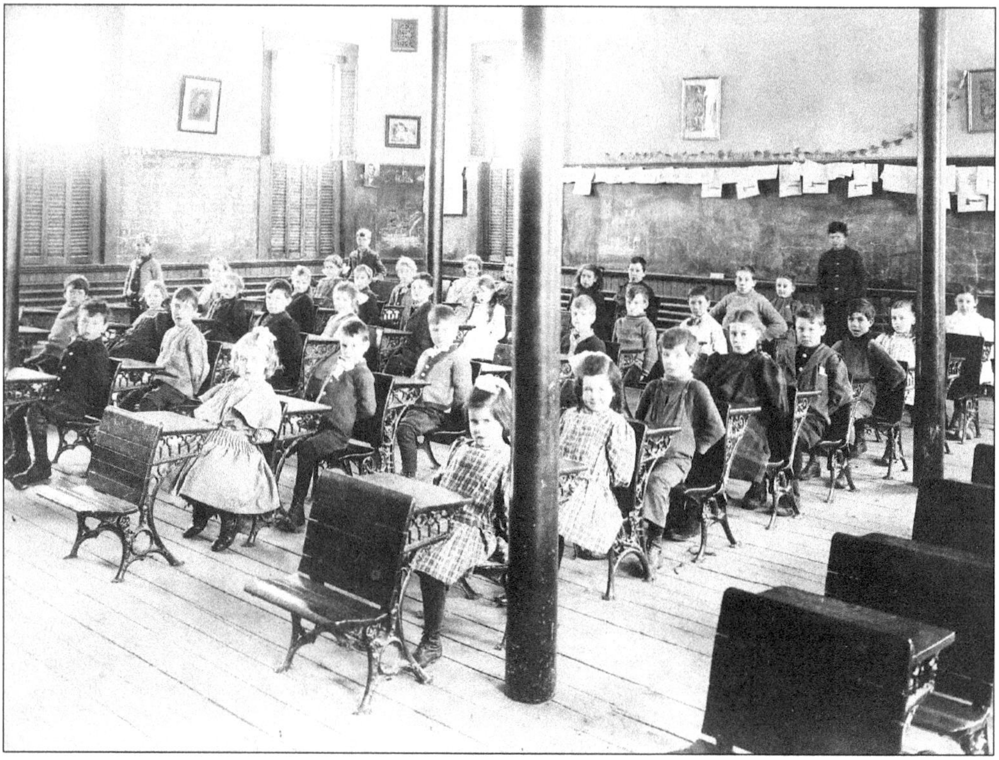

Discipline was obviously very strict at the Glen Street School!

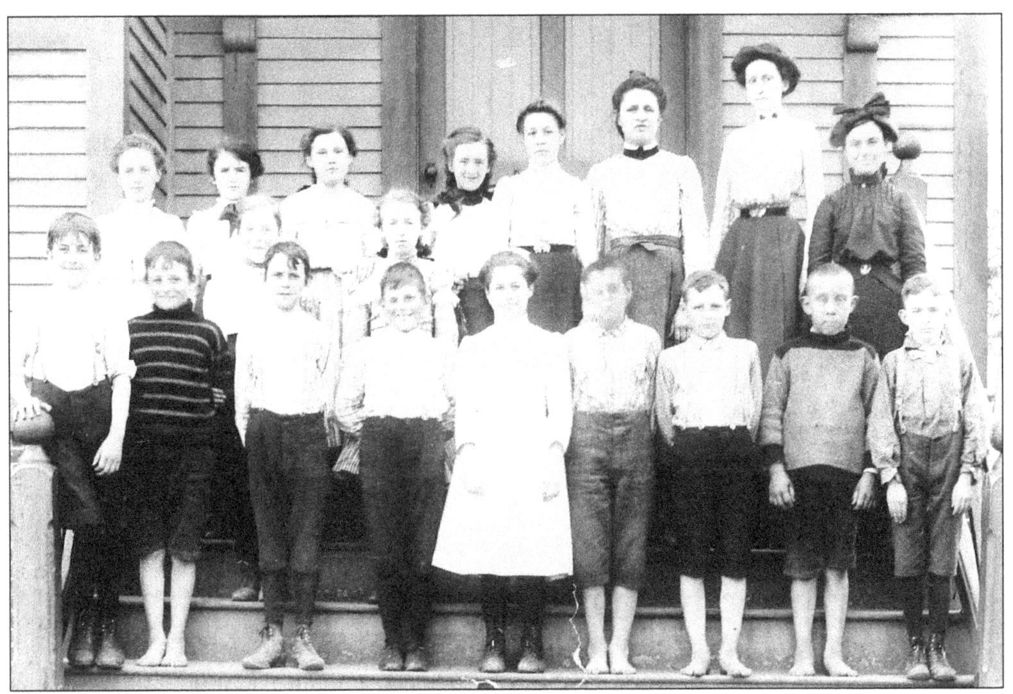

Shoes must have been a luxury for some of these Glen Street pupils.

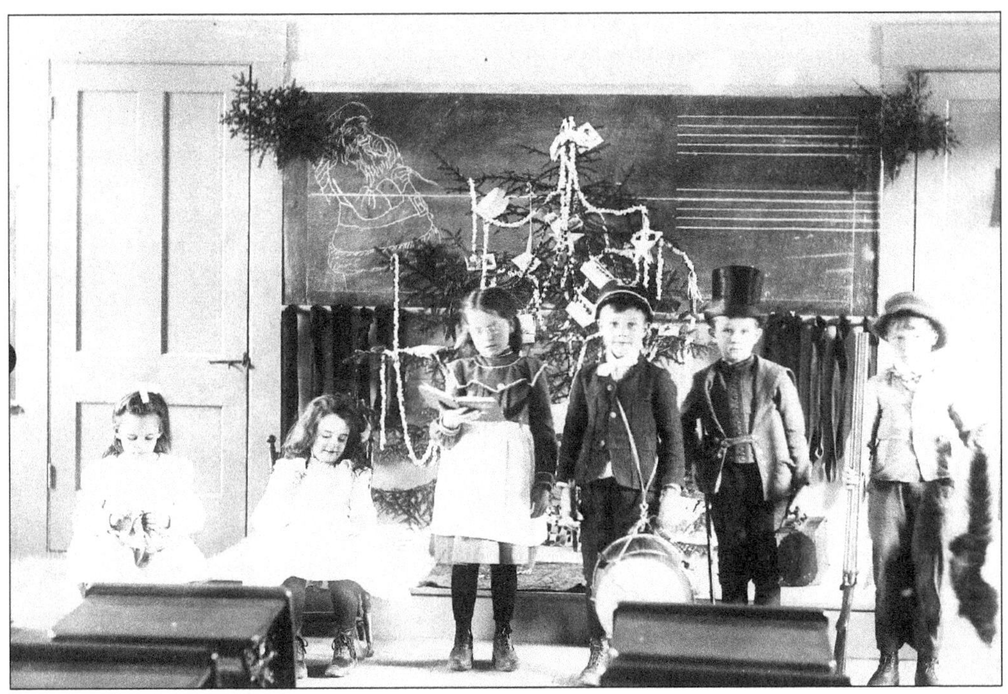

With such costumes as these, one wonders at the theme of this play! Participants are Helen Brown, Lillian Drum, Helen and Ralph Card, Harold Towle, and ? Gilman.

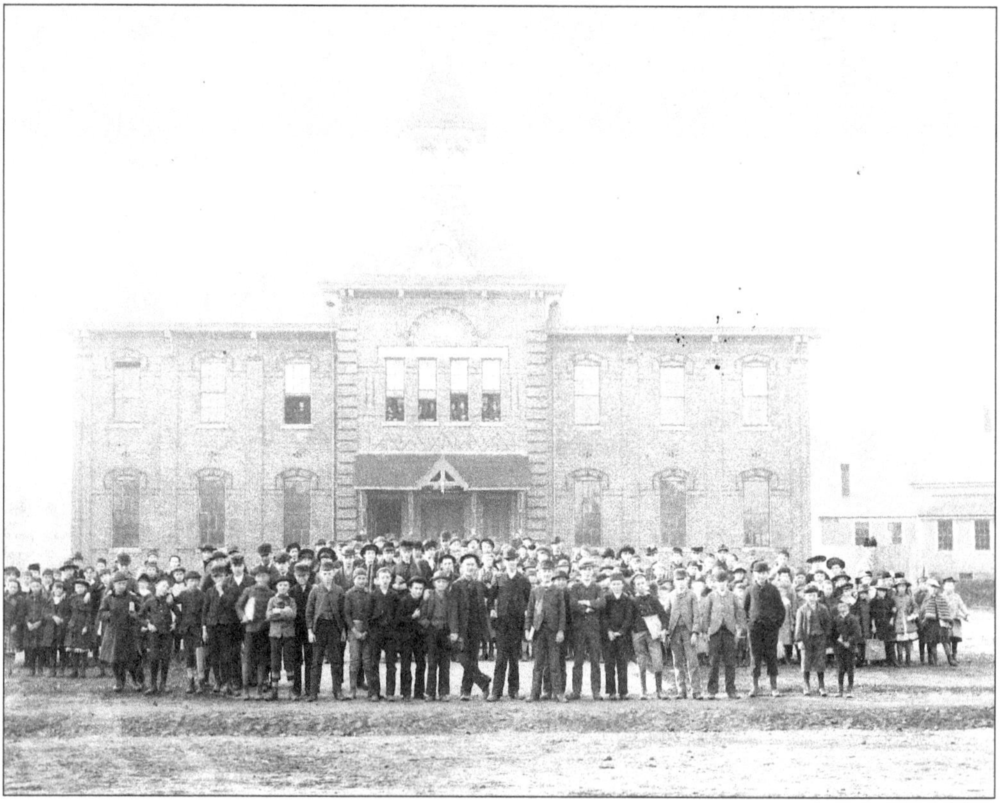

Reputed to be the oldest school in continuous use in New Hampshire, the Main Street School was built as a junior and senior high school in 1876 and used as a junior high until 1996.

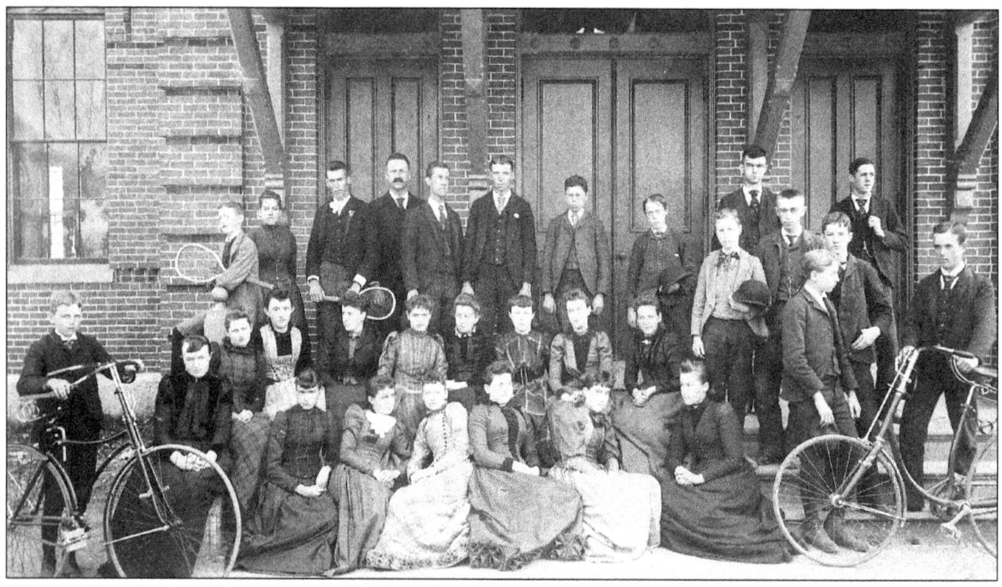

The student body of Farmington High School poses for a picture in 1891.

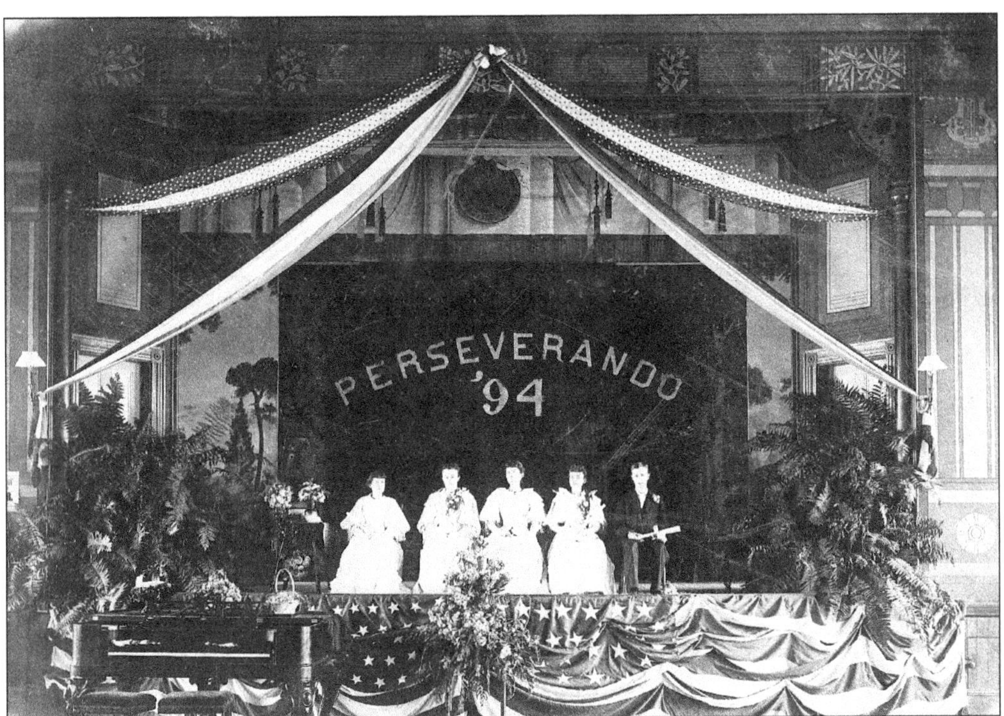

The high school graduating class of 1894 is shown here on the Opera House stage: Helen Barker, Susie Dow, Myra Davis, Ethel Card, and Herbert Browne.

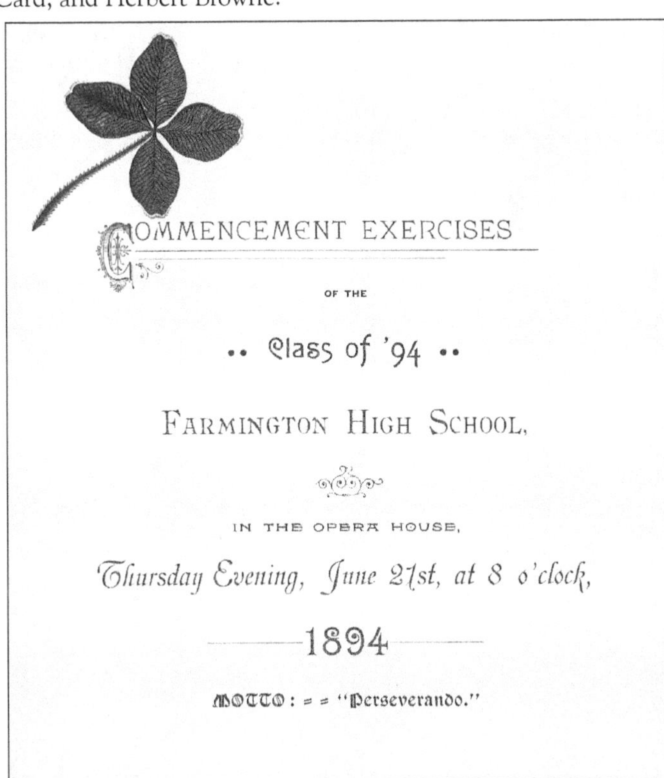

COMMENCEMENT EXERCISES

OF THE

•• Class of '94 ••

FARMINGTON HIGH SCHOOL,

IN THE OPERA HOUSE,

Thursday Evening, June 21st, at 8 o'clock,

1894

MOTTO: = = "Perseverando."

An 1894 Farmington High School commencement program.

Farmington High School.

RANK BILL.

For the Term ending November 22, 1872.

Senior Class.	Punctuality.	Deportment.	Scholarship.	Rank.
COLBATH, FLORENCE	100	100	95.4	98.4
FLANDERS, ARTHUR	93.1	100	89	94
HORNE, ELLA	100	100	94.7	98.2
HUSSEY, CHARLES	100	99.5	93.1	97.5
McLANE, JOHN	97.1	100	89	95.3
NUTE, ALICE	100	100	94	98
PARMENTER, NELLIE	99.8	99.7	87.2	95.5
WALDRON, ARTHUR	100	99.7	94.1	97.9
WALDRON, HARRY	100	100	95.7	98.5
Middle Class.				
HALL, HANNAH	100	97.5	89.6	95.7
HORNE, NELLIE	100	99.8	85.9	95.2
HODGDON, LIZZIE	100	100	67.5	89.1
HAYES, FRANK	99.1	99.7	88.5	95.4
LEIGHTON, FRANK,	94.7	100	65	86.5
LEIGHTON, CHAS.	81	100	68.9	83.3
McDUFFEE, IDA	96.4	99.7	73.2	89.7
NUTTER, FRANK	76.8	99.1	73	82.9
PARKER, SAMUEL	100	100	90	96.6
TUTTLE, ALLISON	100	99.8	90.1	96.6
WIGGIN, CORA	99.7	100	60	86.5

Junior Class.	Punctuality.	Deportment.	Scholarship.	Rank.
BLAISDELL, ELTELLE	97	100	75.3	90.8
BLAISDELL, JOSIE	97.1	98.8	78.4	91.
BEARD, GEORGE	88.1	98.7	82.7	89.8
CHAMBERLAIN, FANNIE	90.5	99.5	90.3	93.4
COFFIN, EMMA	100	99.8	85.6	95.1
CHESLEY, ETTA	94.8	99.5	70.6	88.3
CHILD, ELMER	98.4	99.5	70	89.3
EDGERLY, ELLA	85	99.8	85.3	90
FLANDERS, ELOISE	100	99.8	93.2	97.6
GOODALL, DORA	95.7	99.8	70	88.5
HAMLIN, ANNIE	99.8	100	90.4	96.7
HERRING, SADIE	99.2	99.7	71.7	90.2
MELLOWS, GEORGE	100	99.7	70.1	89.9
PARKER, NELLIE	96	99.8	92	95.9
PEAVEY, SARAH	87.1	100	90.1	92.4
PIKE, IZEL	91.4	99.7	91.5	94.2
PINKHAM, FRANK	92.7	99.8	65.3	85.9
SMITH, SADIE	100	100	90.6	96.8
SMITH, FRANK	92.1	99.4	76	89.1

E. J. GOODWIN, Teacher.

In the Scale of Rank, 100 is considered Perfect.

In 1872 a student's punctuality and deportment were as important as his scholarship!

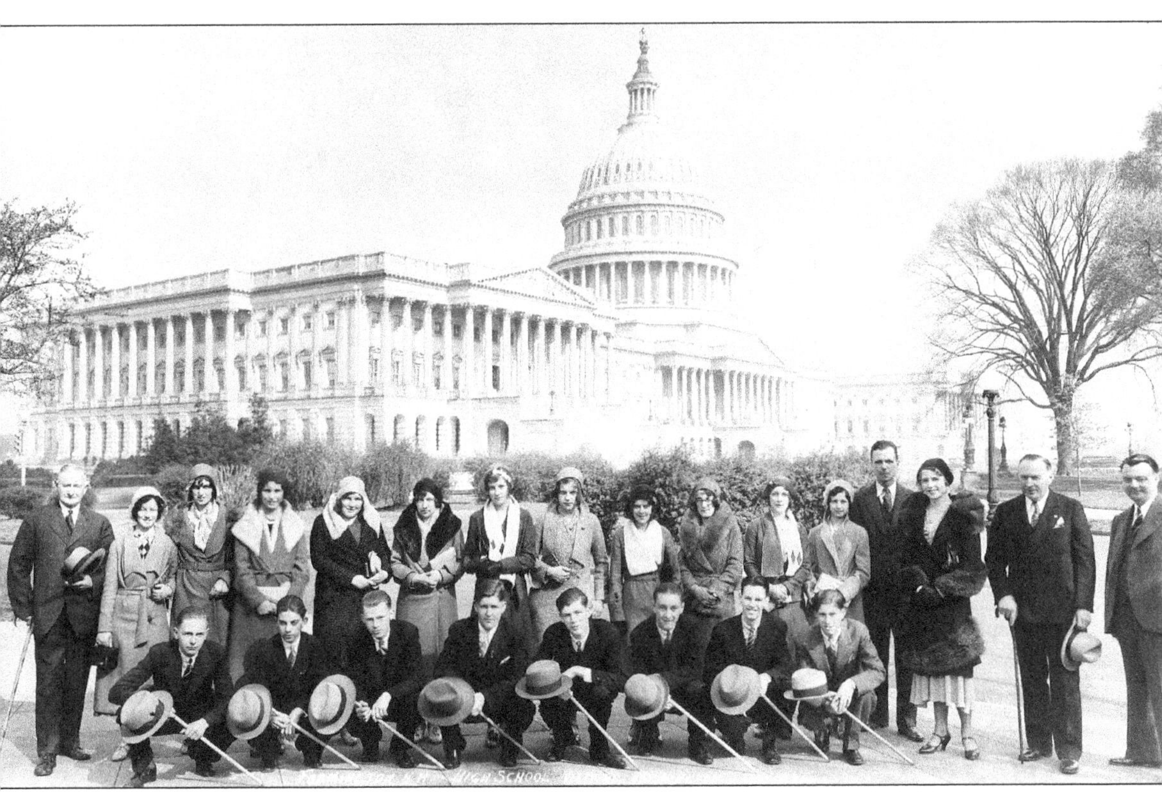

This Farmington High School class trip to Washington, D.C., took place in 1931. My, haven't fashions changed!

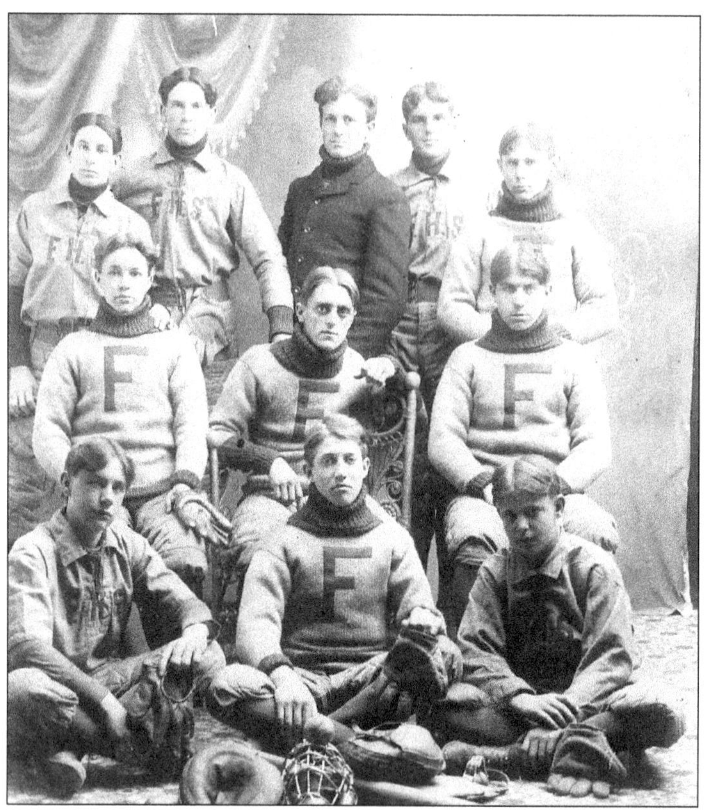

The Farmington High School baseball team, c. 1903.

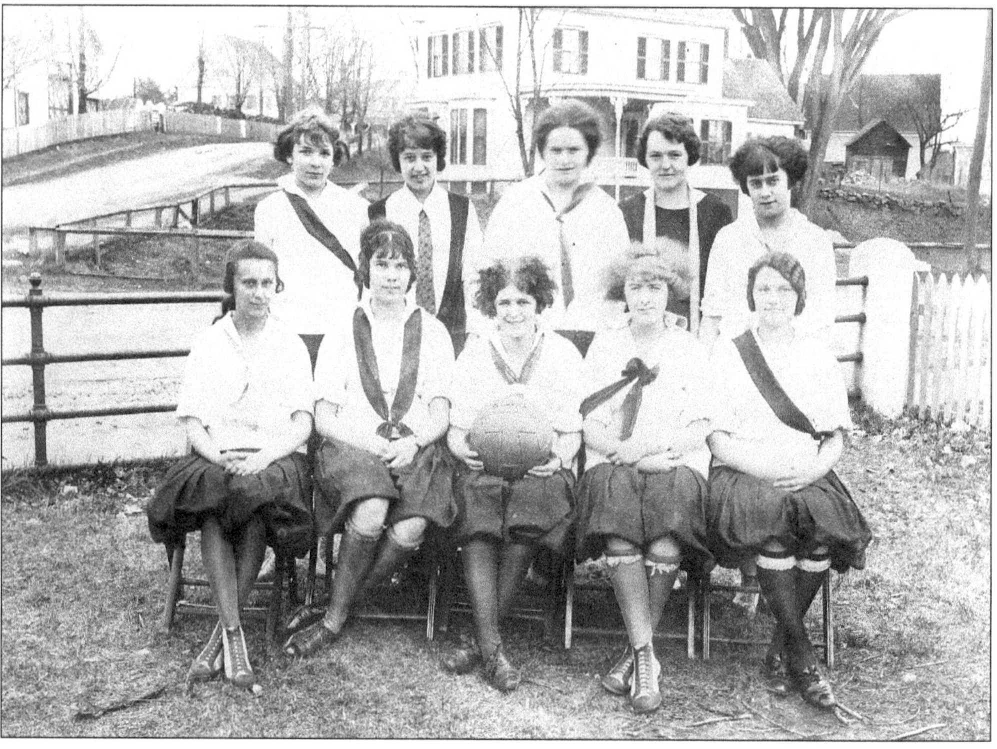

The 1925 high school girls basketball team consisted of: (front row) Evelyn Otis, Rhuma Hayes, Molly Stanley, Beatrice Perkins, and Pauline Hayes; (back row) Beatrice Hartfield, Norma Brown, Dorothy Burbank, Evelyn Parker, and Ruth Webster.

Seven

Organizations and Churches

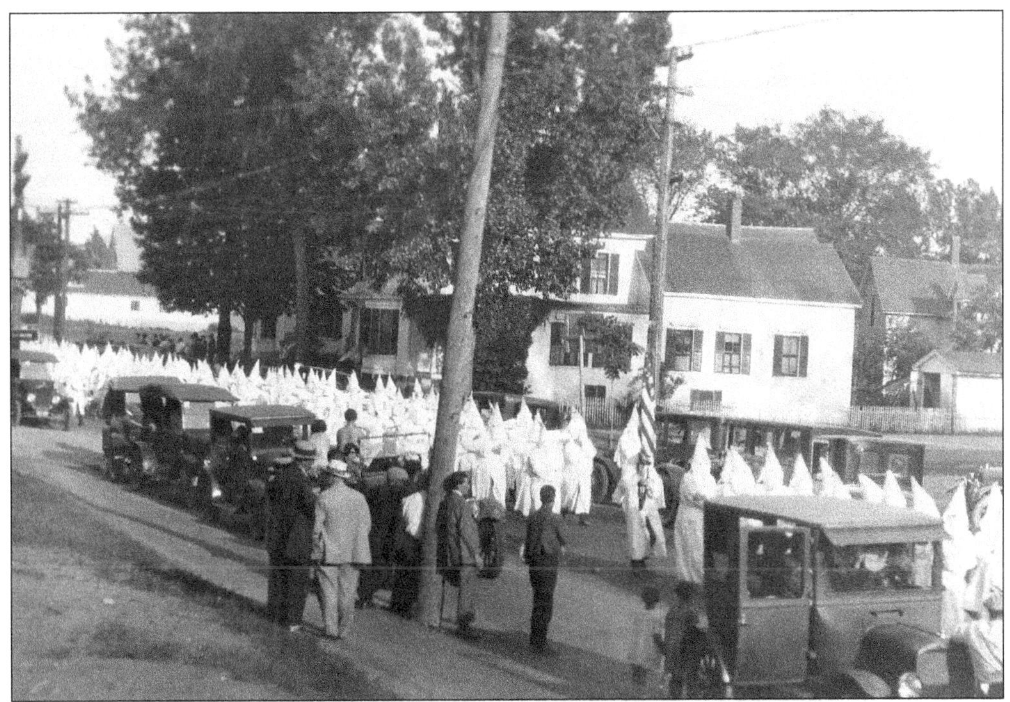

Years ago the Ku Klux Klan had chapters in forty states, including those of New England. A 1926 Klan conclave in Farmington is shown marching up South Main Street.

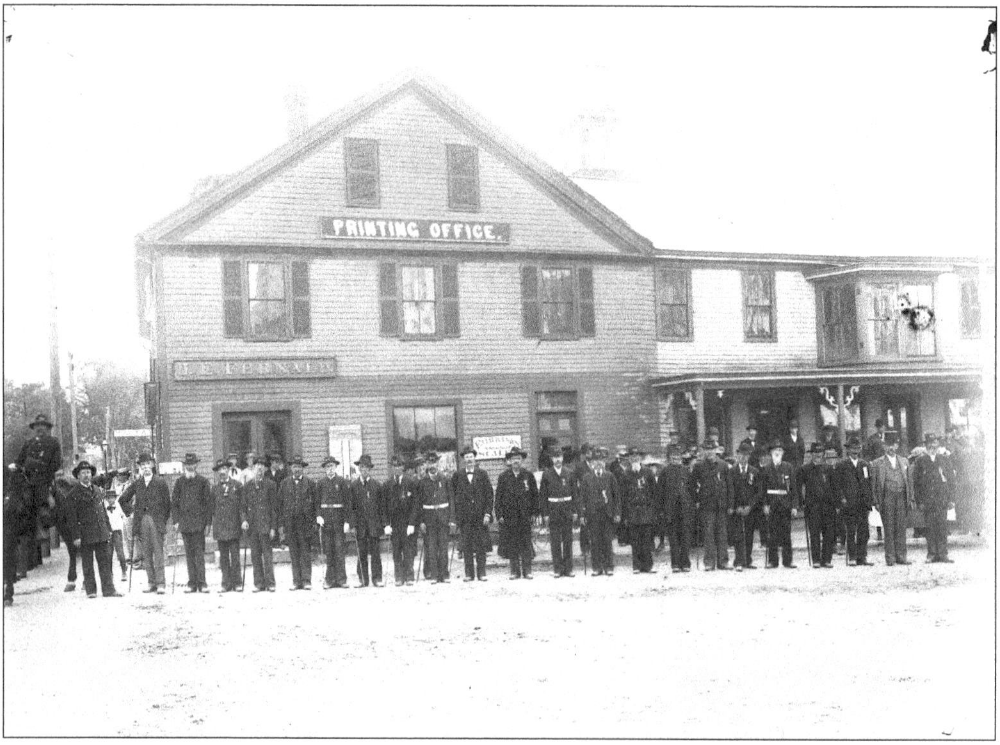

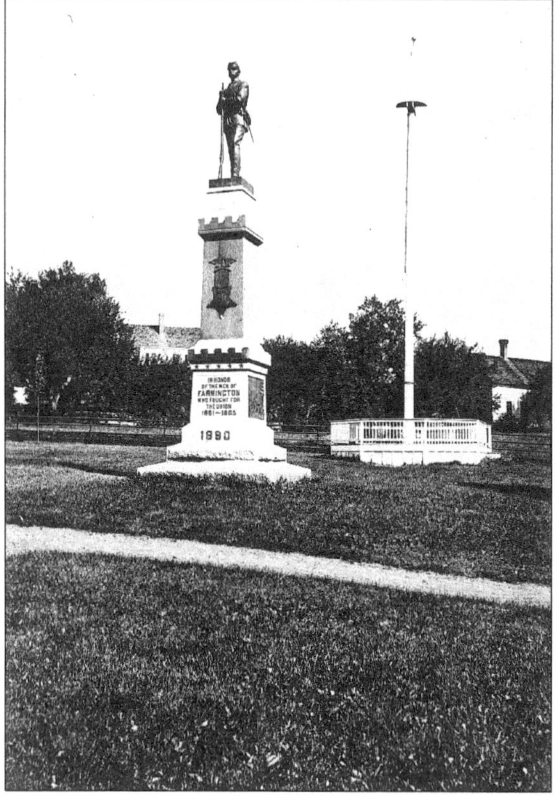

Farmington men have always eagerly responded to their country's call to war. Records show over two hundred defended the Union during the Civil War. Surviving Grand Army of the Republic men are shown in later years. When the Women's Relief Corps raised funds for a commemorative monument, James B. Edgerly presented land to the town for its location, henceforth known as Edgerly Park.

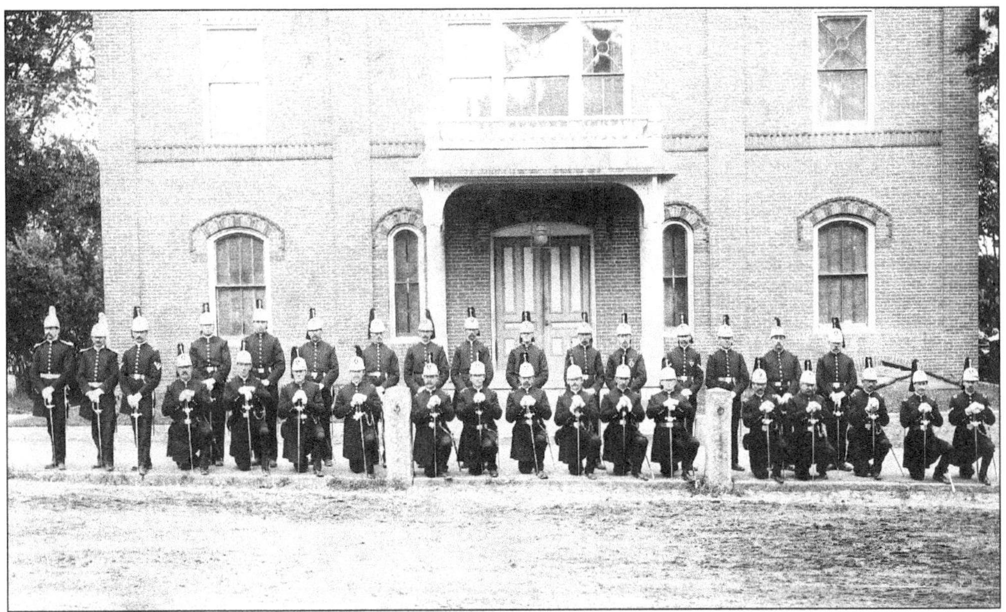

The Knights of Pythias was a fraternal benevolent organization. Its Uniform Rank, a prize-winning drill squad, is shown above in full regalia. The seated gentleman in the 1910 photograph below is Harry S. Parker, for whom the rank was named.

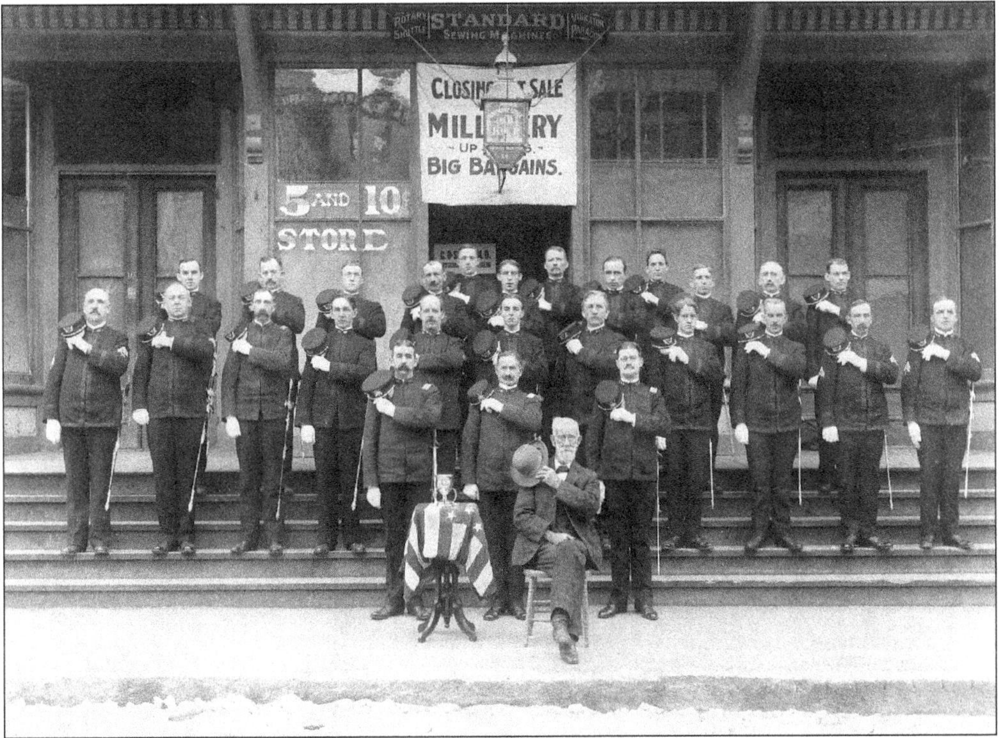

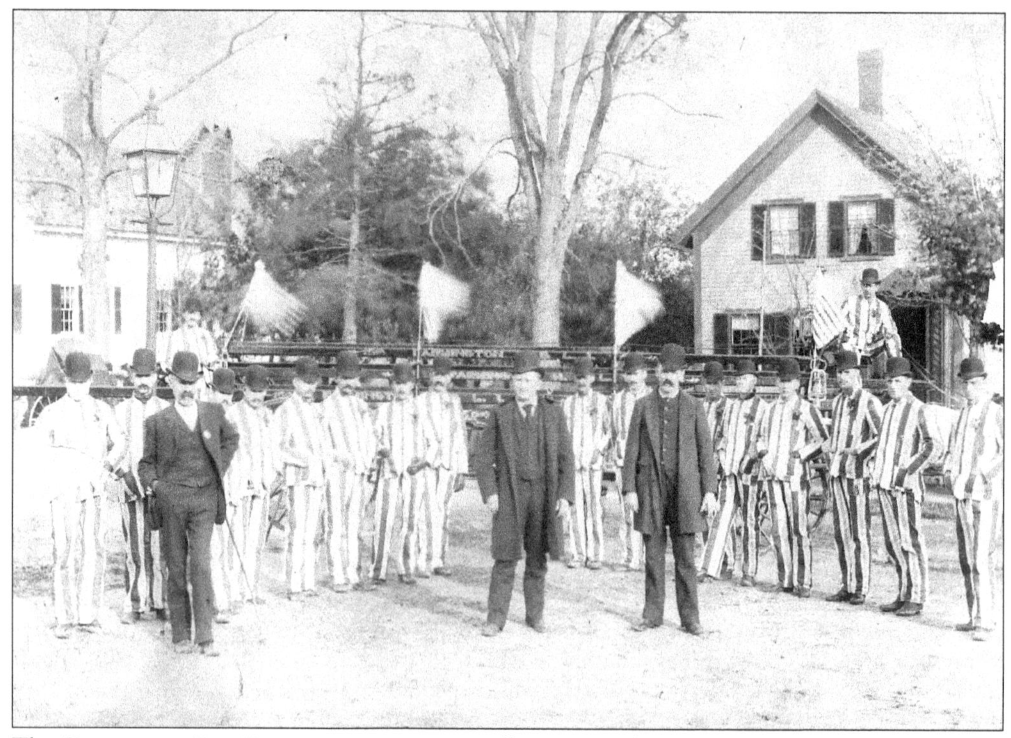

The Farmington Fire Department was originally composed of two companies: the Hook and Ladder Company and the Engine Company. The Hook and Ladder men in this 1860 picture were a colorful group with their gray uniforms trimmed with red, white, and blue stripes.

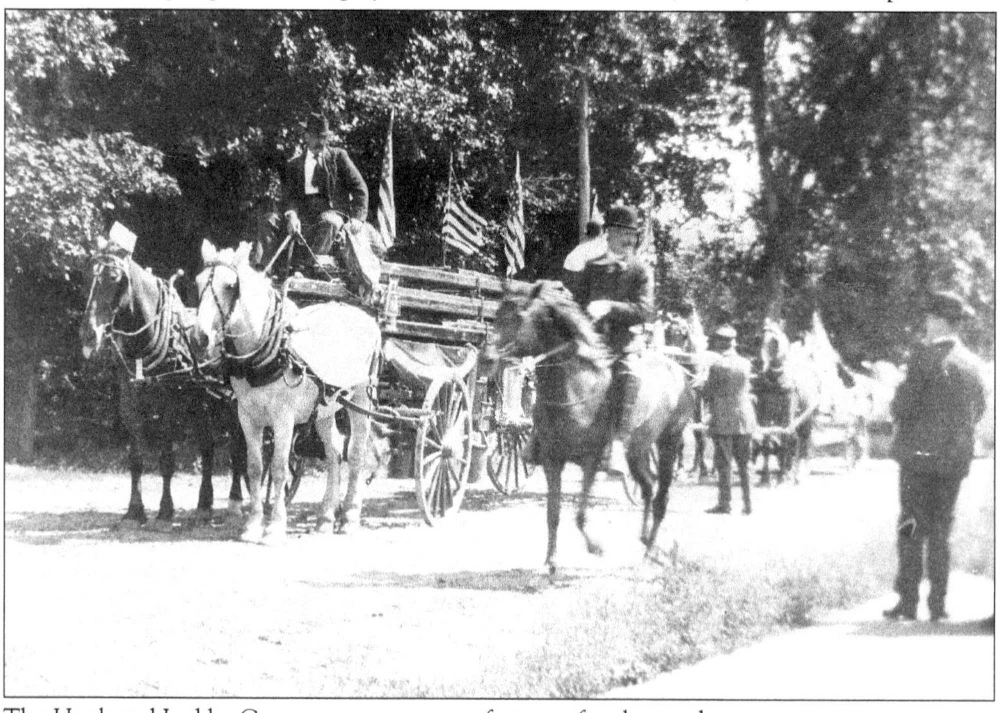

The Hook and Ladder Company wagon was a feature of early parades.

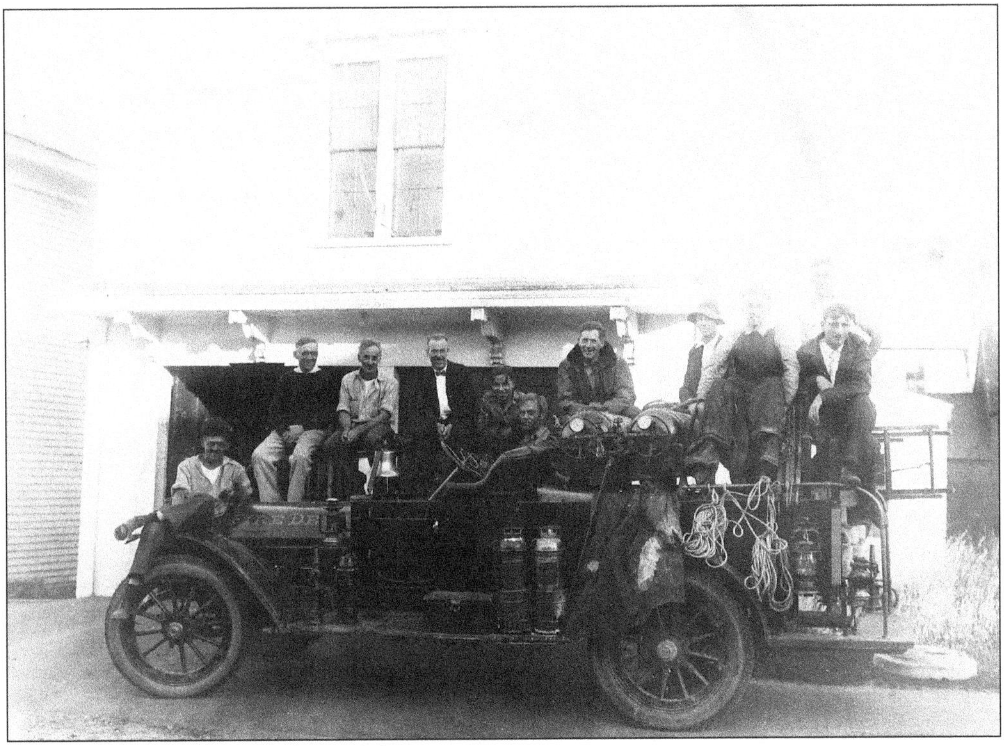

The men shown here, members of the Farmington Fire Department in 1929, are Ralph Burham, Ernest Kelley, Earle Edgerly, Don Waldron, Charles Child Jr., C. Child Sr., Lester Leonard, Sam Gray, John Lepene, and Everett Gray.

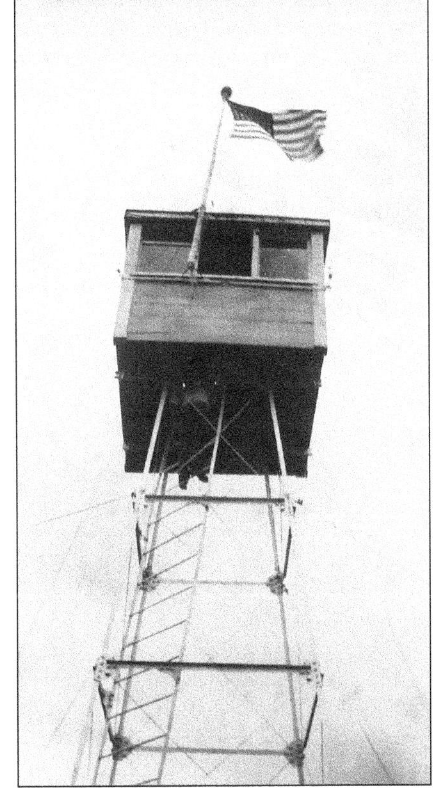

The fire tower atop 1,350-foot Blue Job Mountain began operation in 1912. Manned by a watchman living in a nearby cabin, it was closed in 1983 with the advent of aerial surveillance.

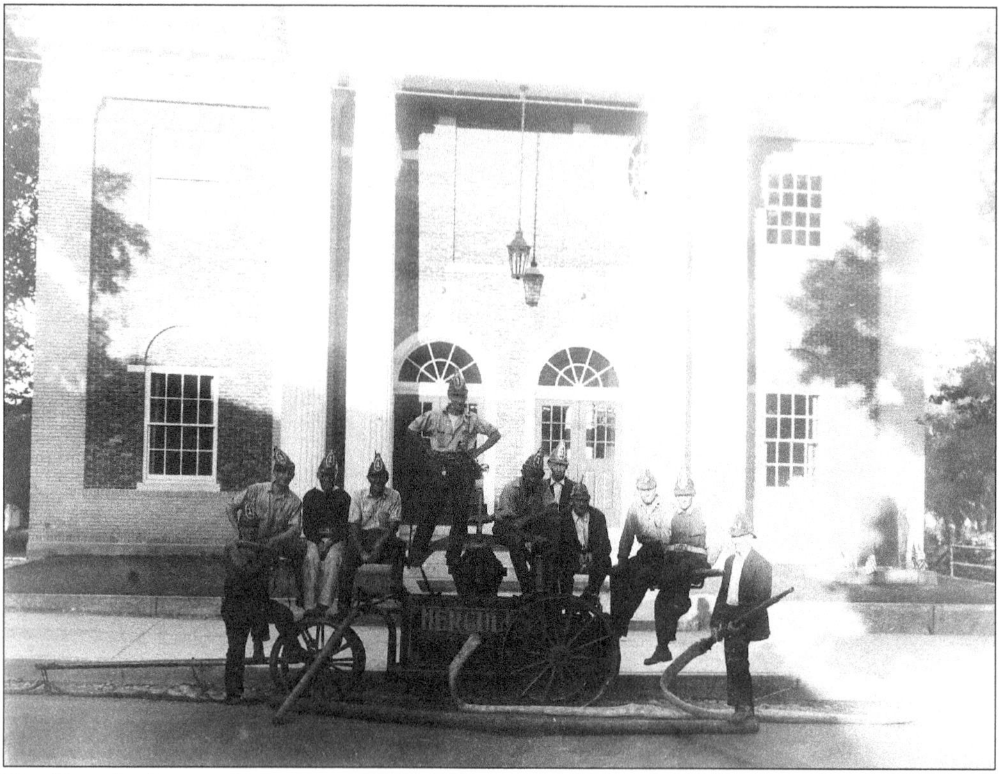

The Hercules Engine Company was named for its pumper, shown here in front of the new Town Hall. This venerable apparatus is now owned by a descendant of the manufacturer, having been rescued from the storefront window of a Boston insurance company.

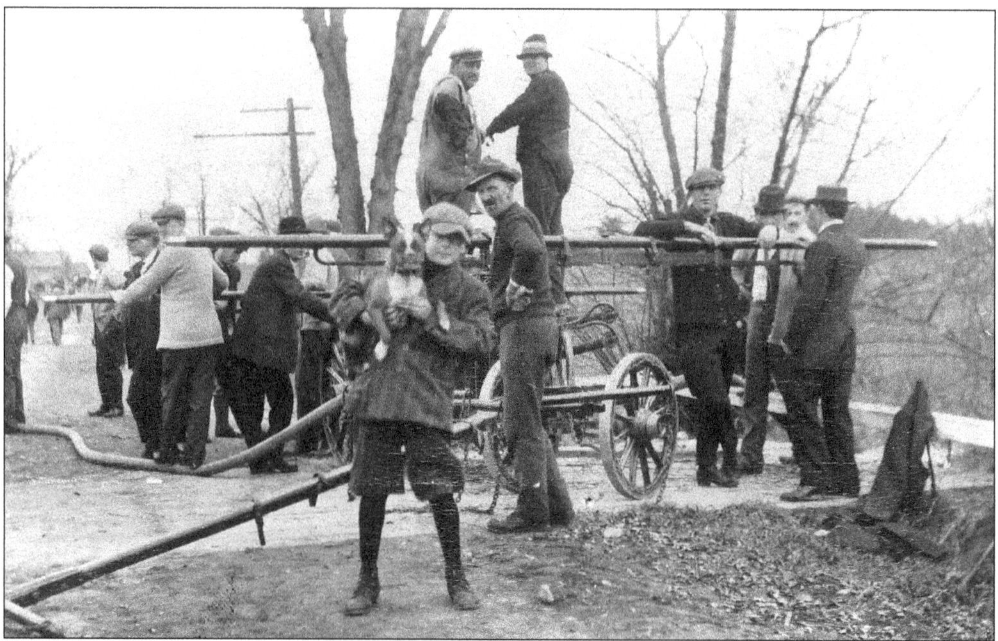

The old Hercules is drawing water to fight the Breen fire on November 11, 1911.

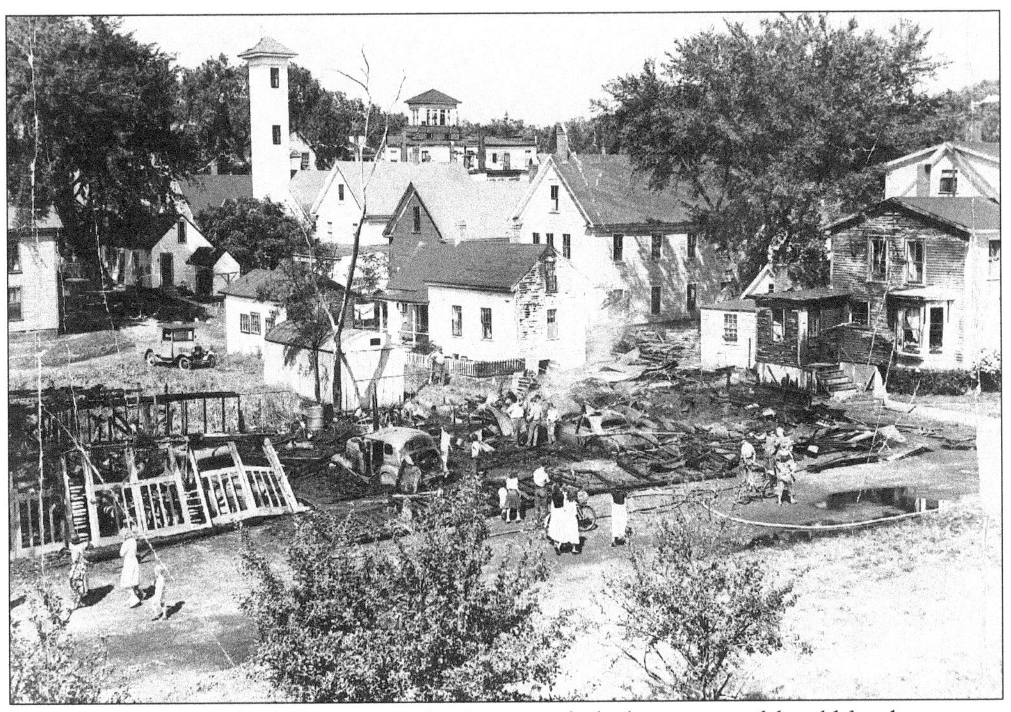

Shown is the aftermath of a fire on Crowley Street, with the hose tower of the old fire department building on Mechanic Street visible in the background.

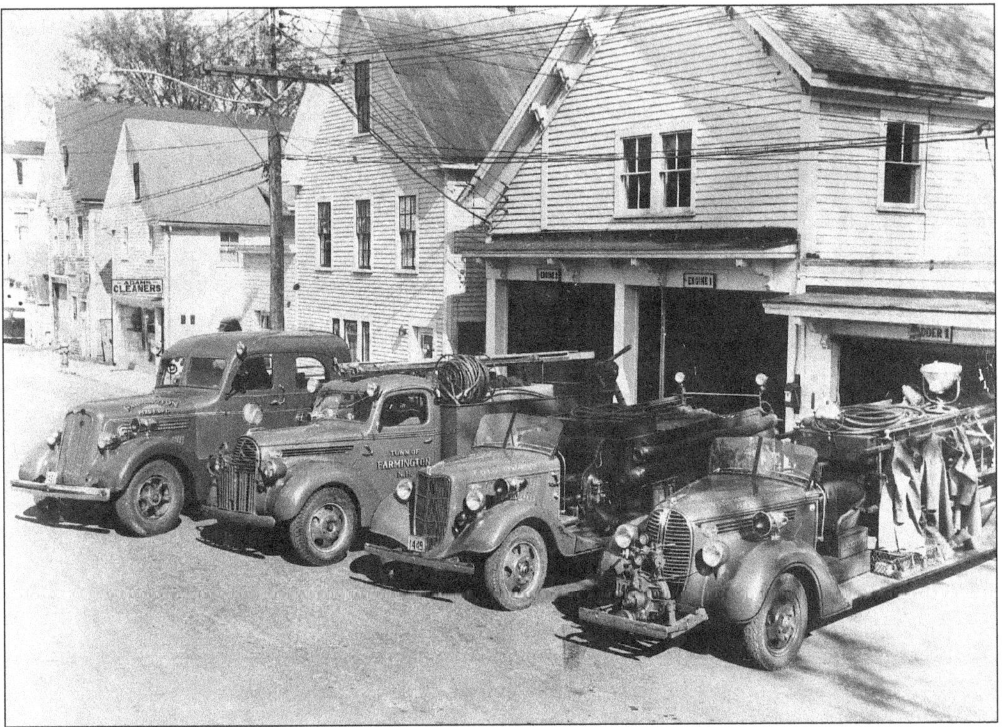

This picture taken in front of the Mechanic Street firehouse includes, on the left, the 1942 Seagrave truck which was given to the town by Mr. H.O. Rondeau.

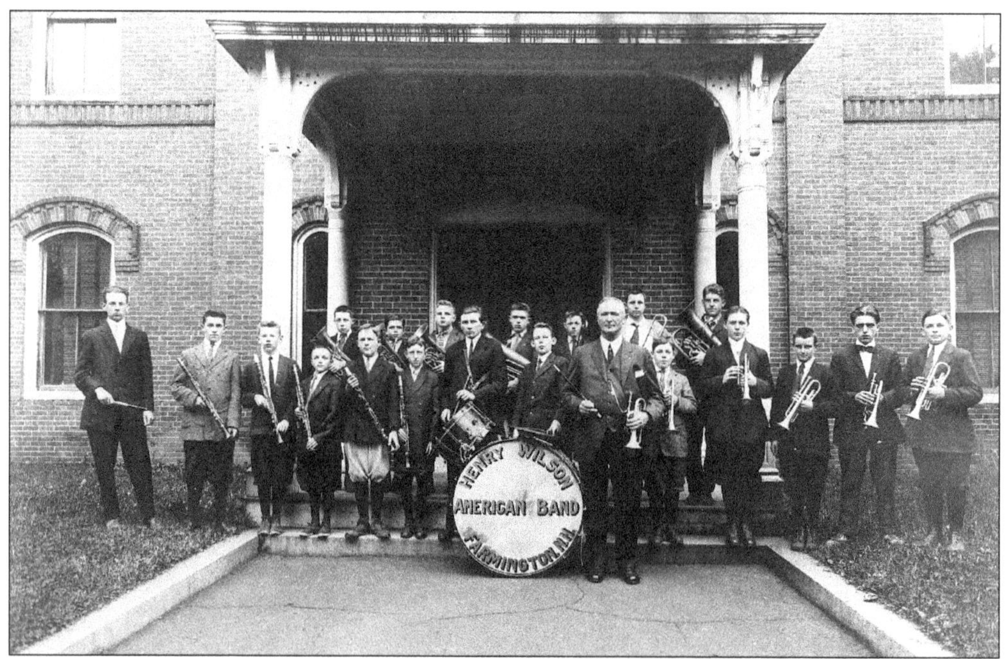

J. Frank Butler (left), made sightless at the age of four by scarlet fever, devoted his life to the youth of Farmington. The founder of the Henry Wilson Boy's Band, he gave lessons on all instruments besides conducting the town band. A plaque honoring his memory may be seen in the Town Hall.

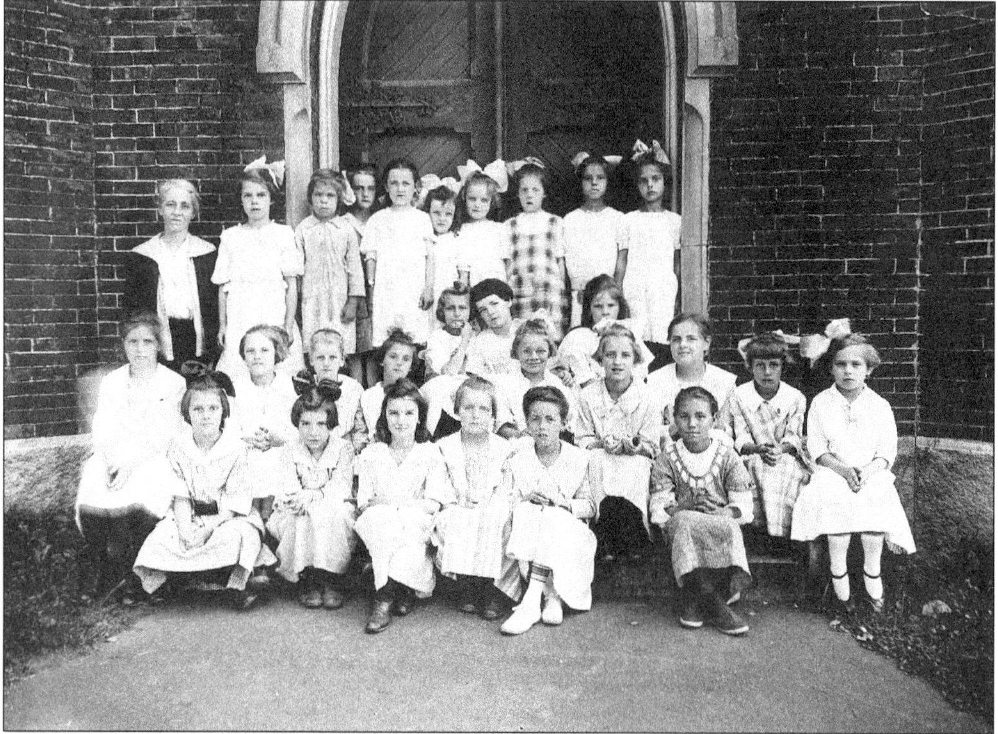

The Pollyanna Club in front of the Congregational church in June 1919.

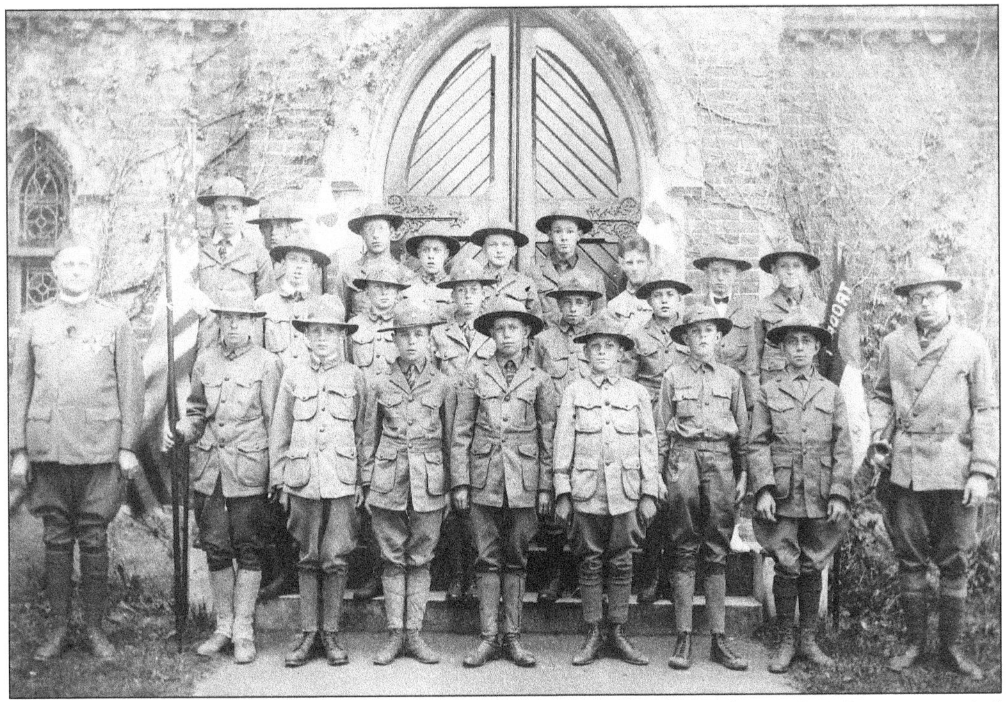

Farmington has a long history of Boy Scouting going back to 1912. These 1922 Scouts were led by Scoutmasters Leslie Ham and Norman Davis.

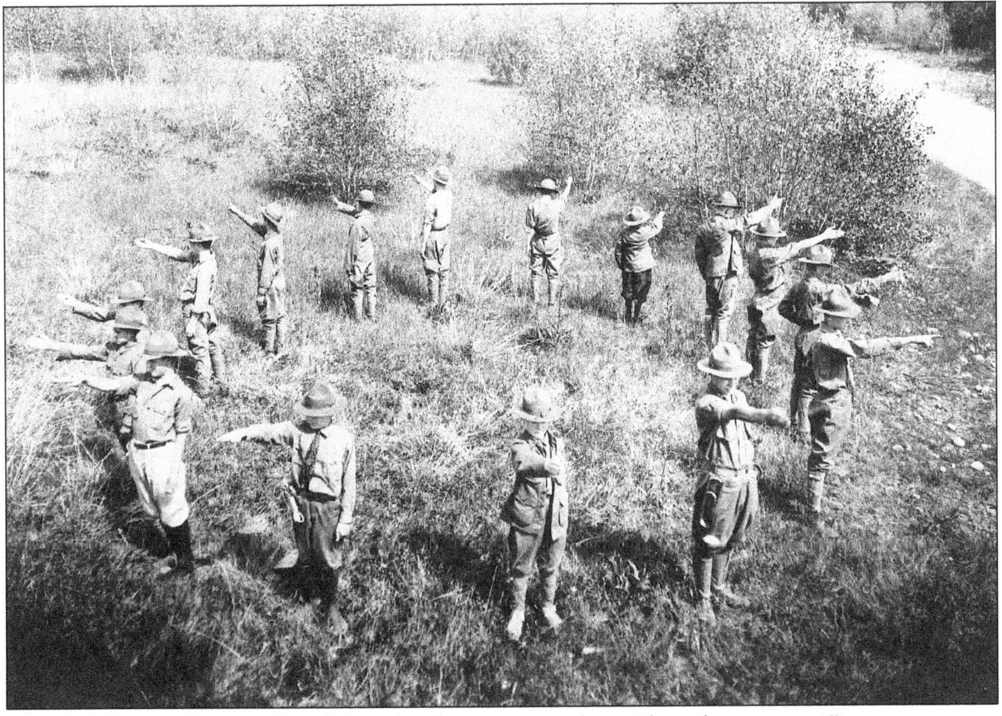

Scouts didn't get lost on their hikes, for they were taught to "box the compass!"

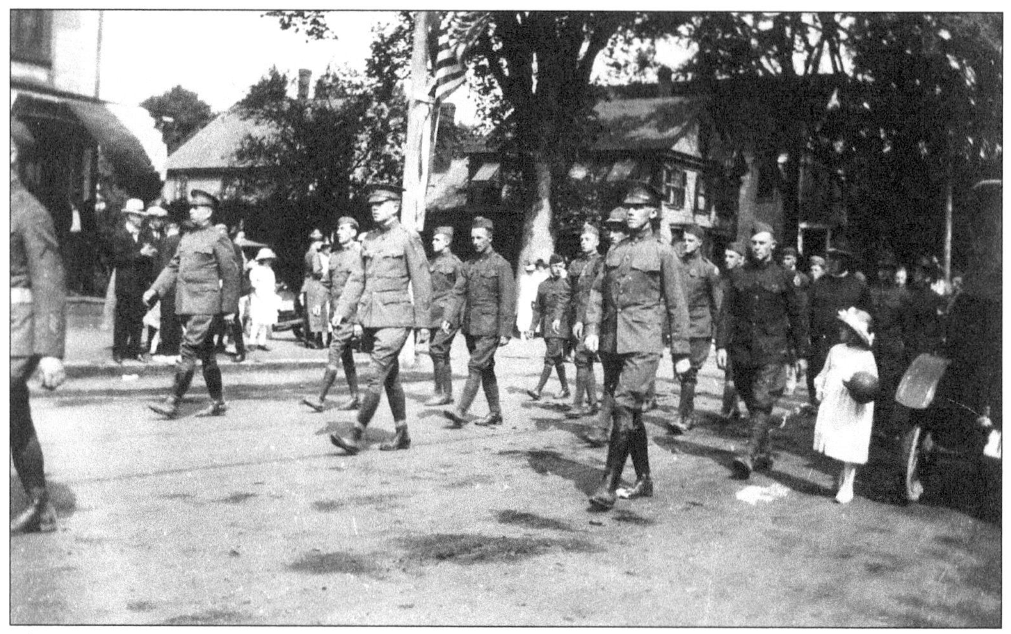

This Armistice parade took place on August 23, 1919.

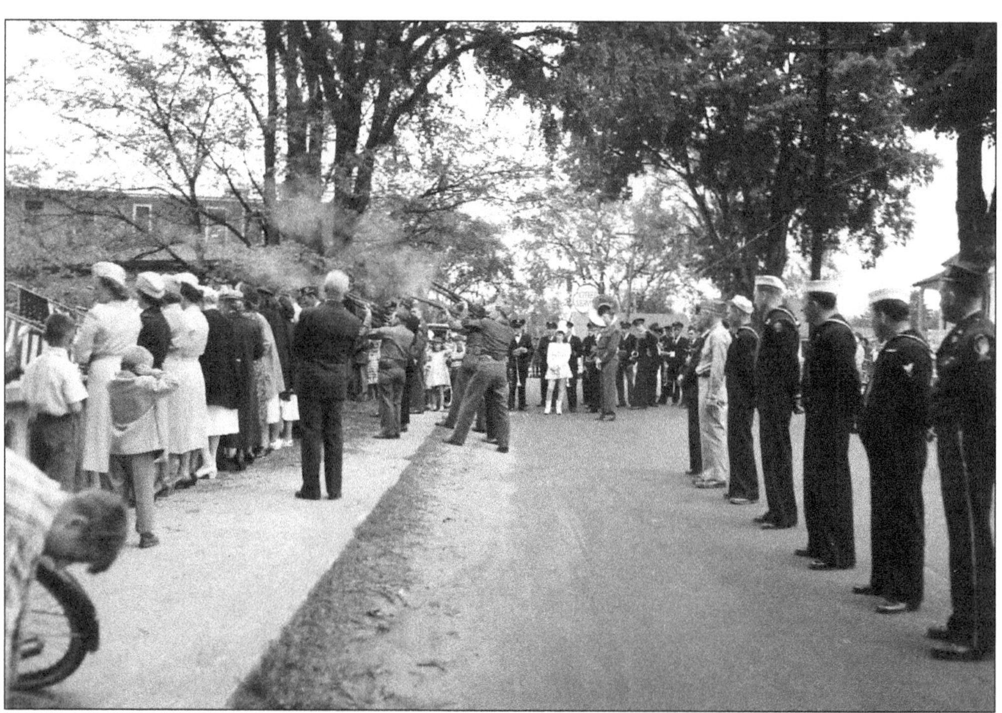

Patriotism was strongly in evidence at the annual Memorial Day parade, when a commemorative wreath was cast from the bridge into the Cocheco River.

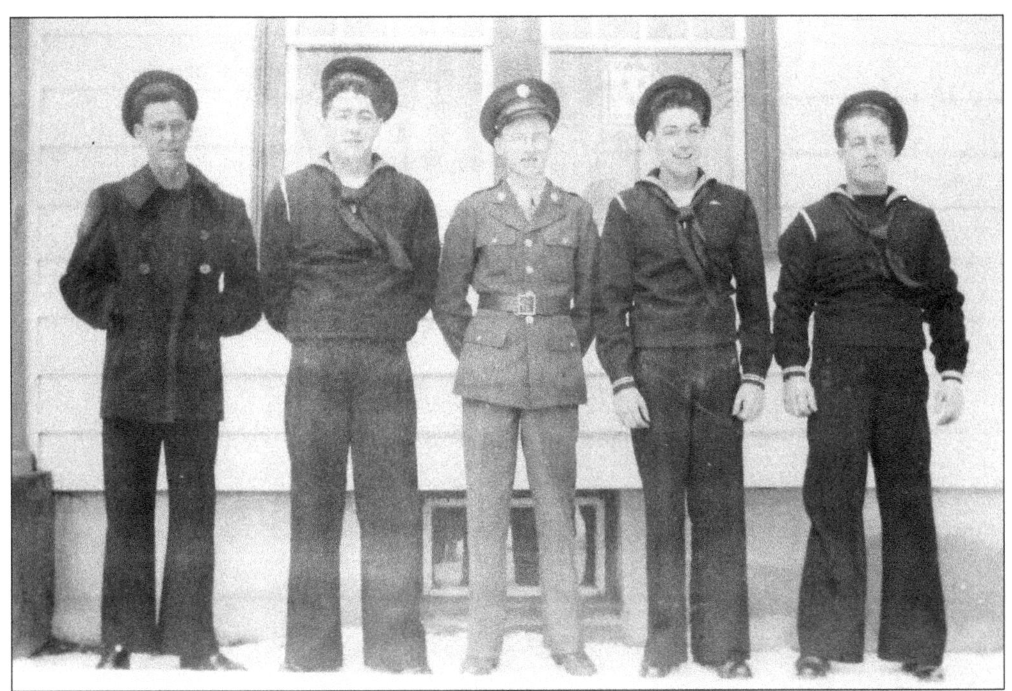

Many families in town sent men to battle during World War II. Shown here are "Meat" Merrill, Carl Worster, Eddy Gray, and George and Bob Worster.

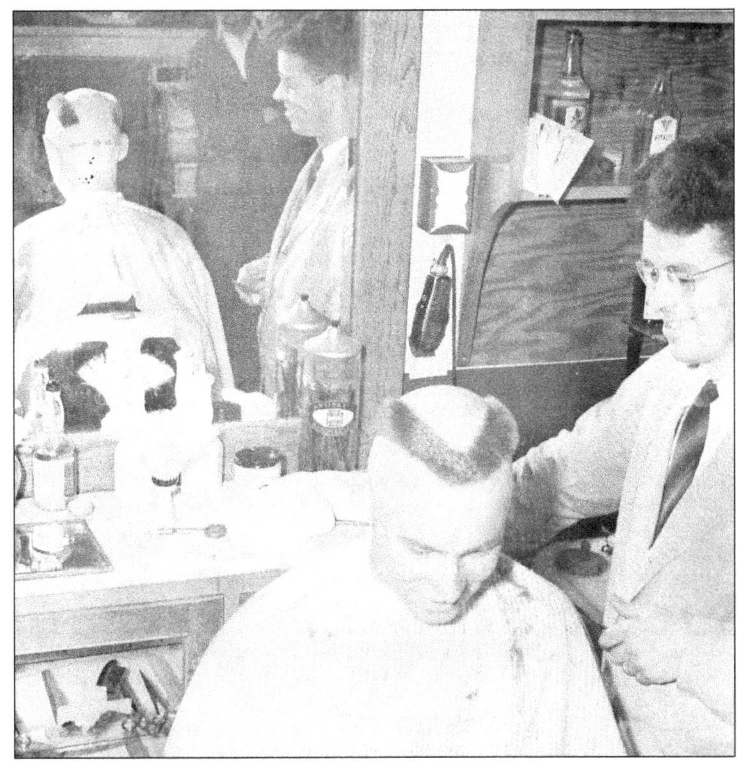

Lee Russell celebrated the end of World War II with a "V for Victory" haircut by barber Rufus Rundlett.

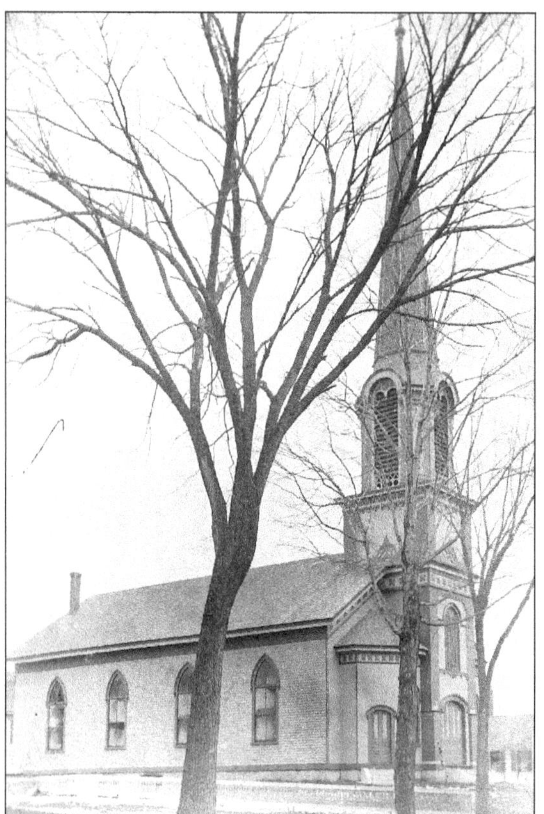

The oldest church building in town is the First Baptist, dedicated in 1857. This 1904 picture shows it with its original steeple, which was destroyed in 1920 and replaced with an octagonal dome.

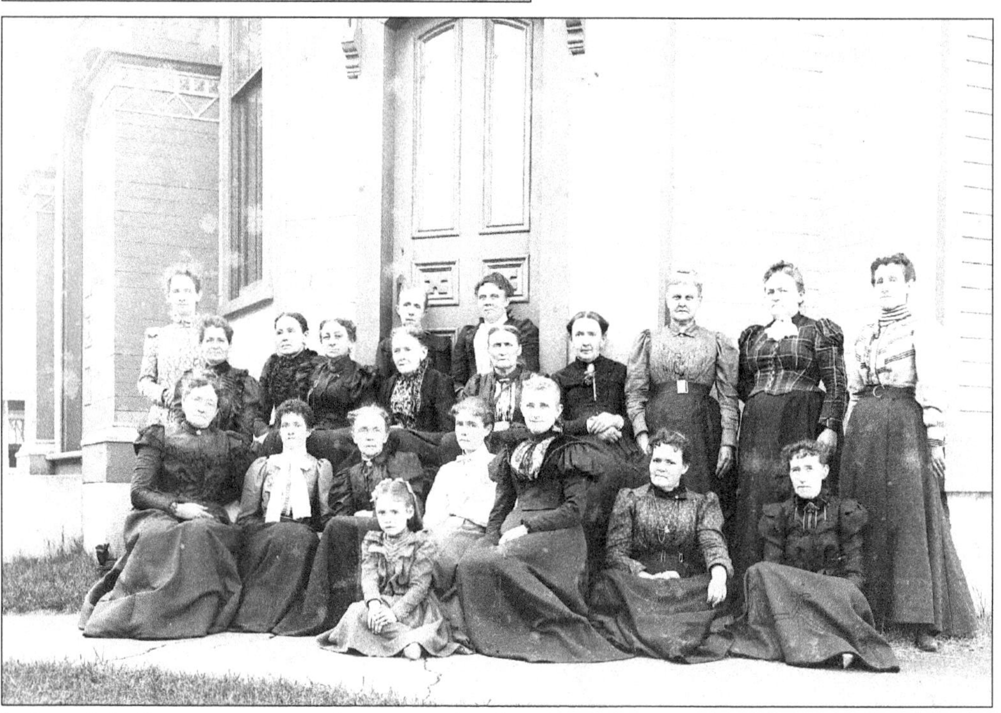

Ladies of the Baptist sewing circle pose on the church steps.

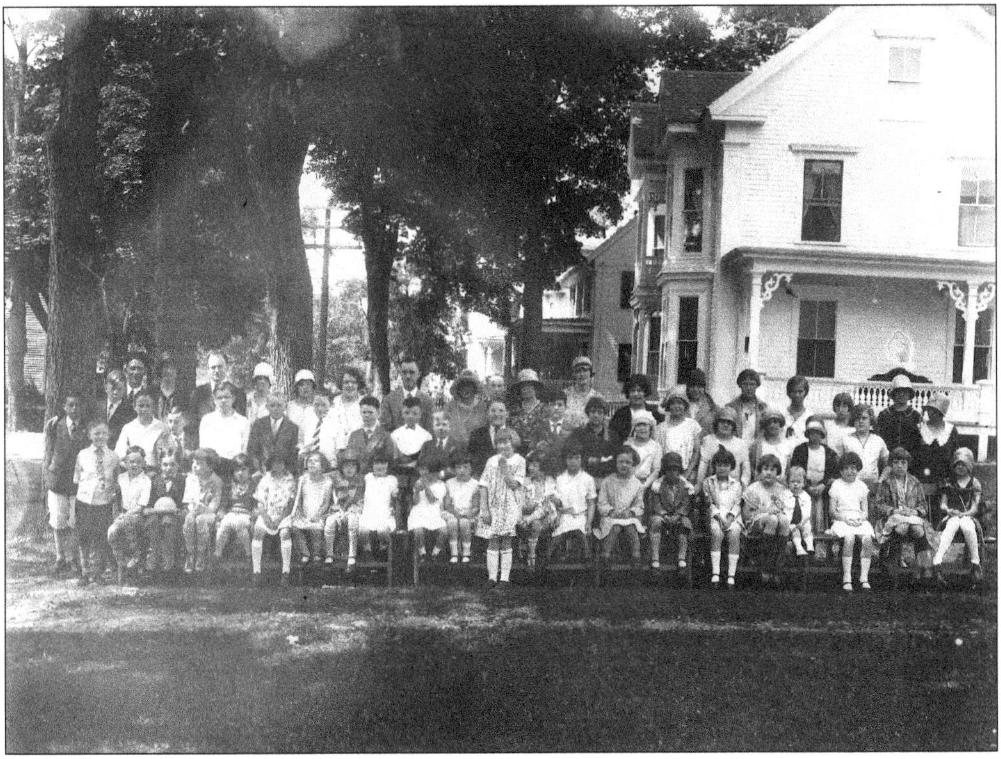

Baptist Bible School students in their Sunday best sit still for a portrait.

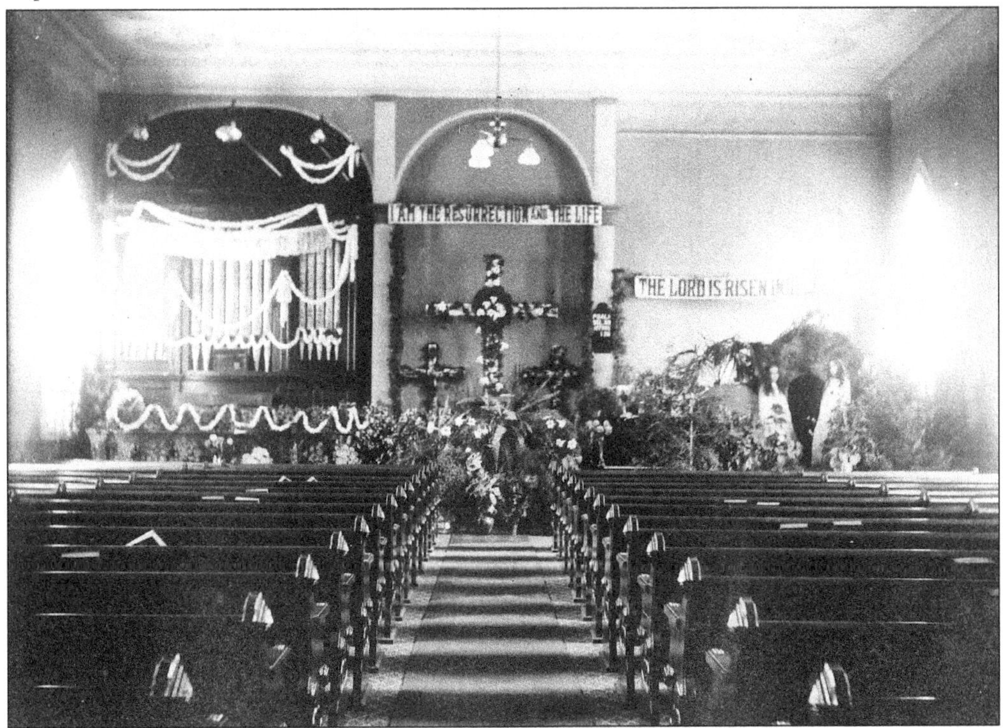

The interior of the Baptist church is shown at Easter time.

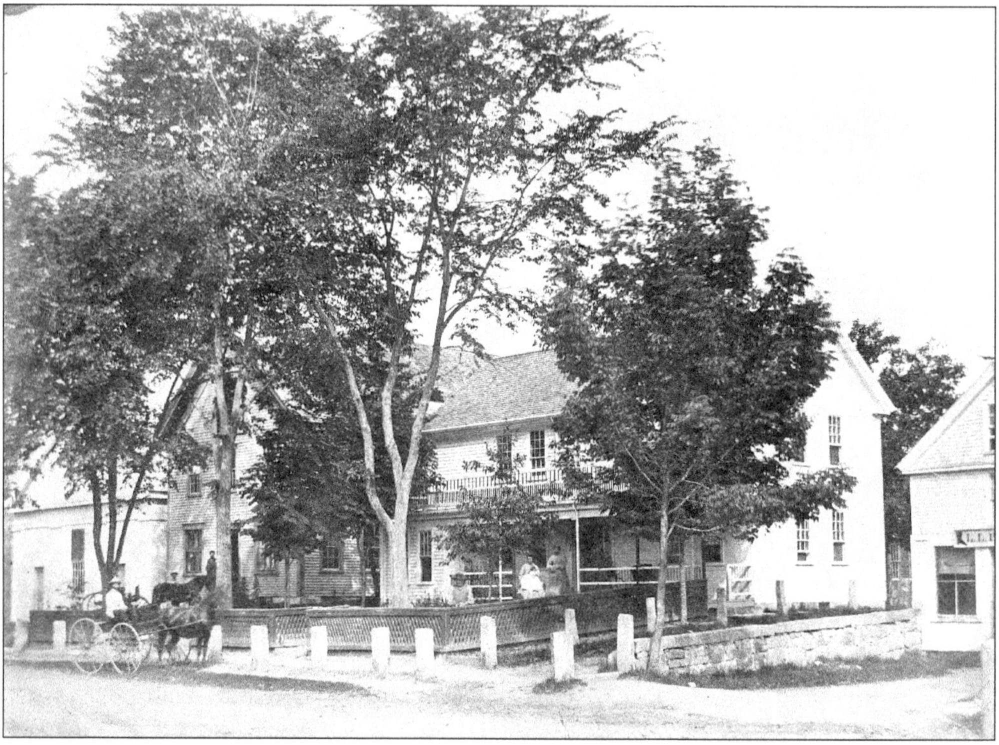

The First Congregational Church and parsonage occupied these buildings, constructed in 1844 on Central Street land donated by Judge George Whitehouse.

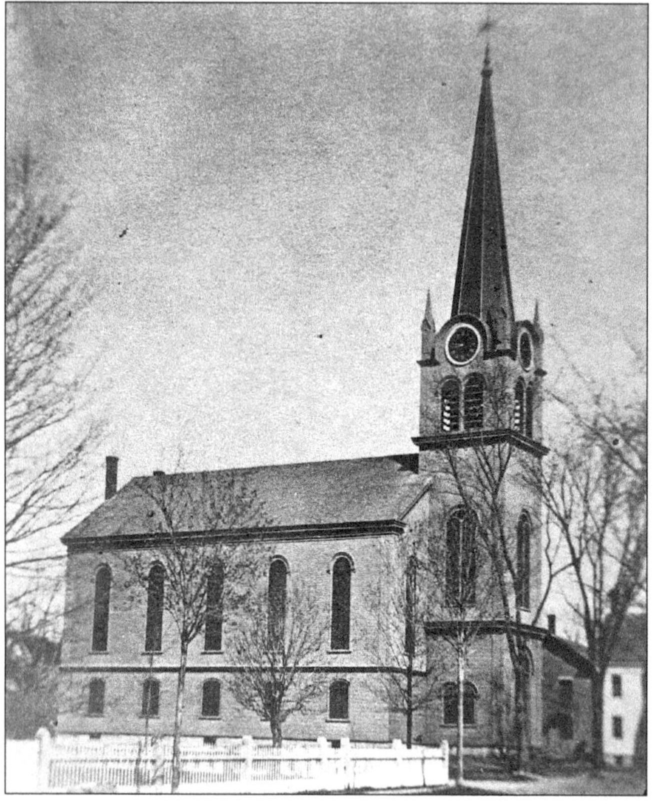

In 1870, this two-story wooden Congregational church was erected on Main Street. It was in use only five years before being reduced to ashes in the terrible fire of February 10, 1875.

One year later, in 1876, the brick church in use today was dedicated. Its steeple holds the Town Clock and a large bell engraved with the words, "Ring to the Memory of Henry Wilson, Farmington's Honored Son."

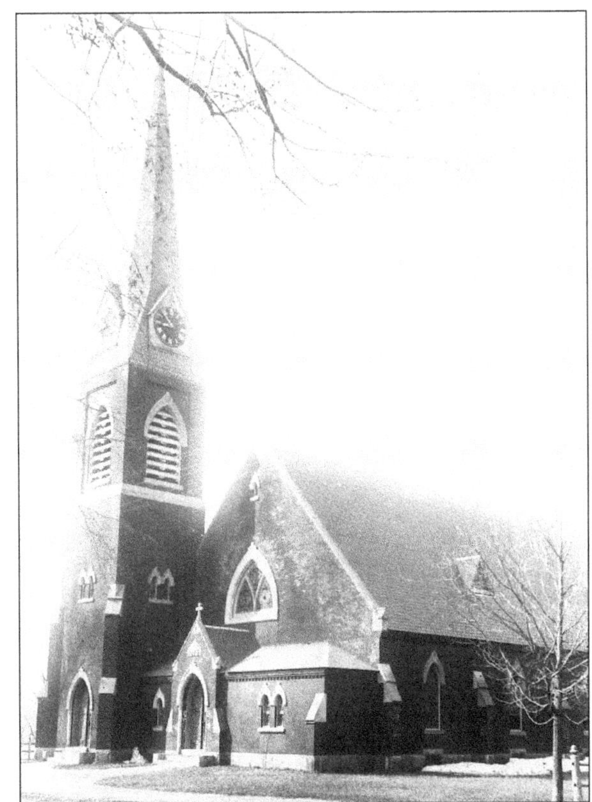

These beautiful chandeliers and massive organ pipes have been replaced since this picture was taken of the present Congregational church interior.

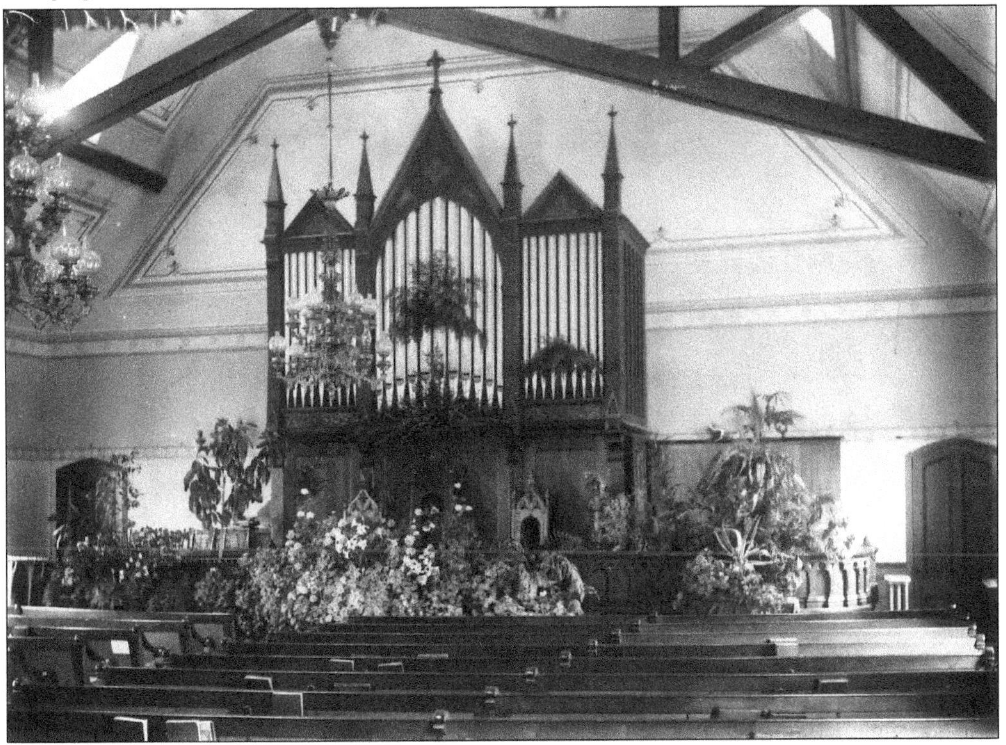

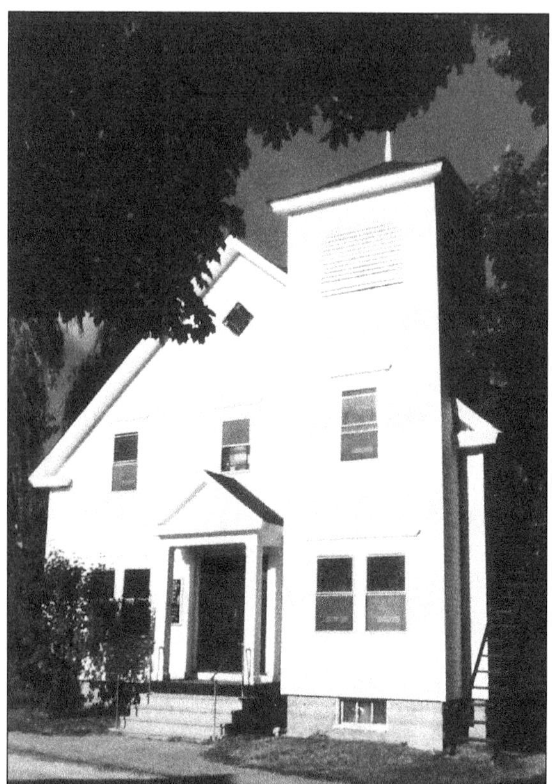

The Advent Christian Church on Orange Street had its beginnings in Farmington in 1869. Its parsonage and parish hall are located nearby.

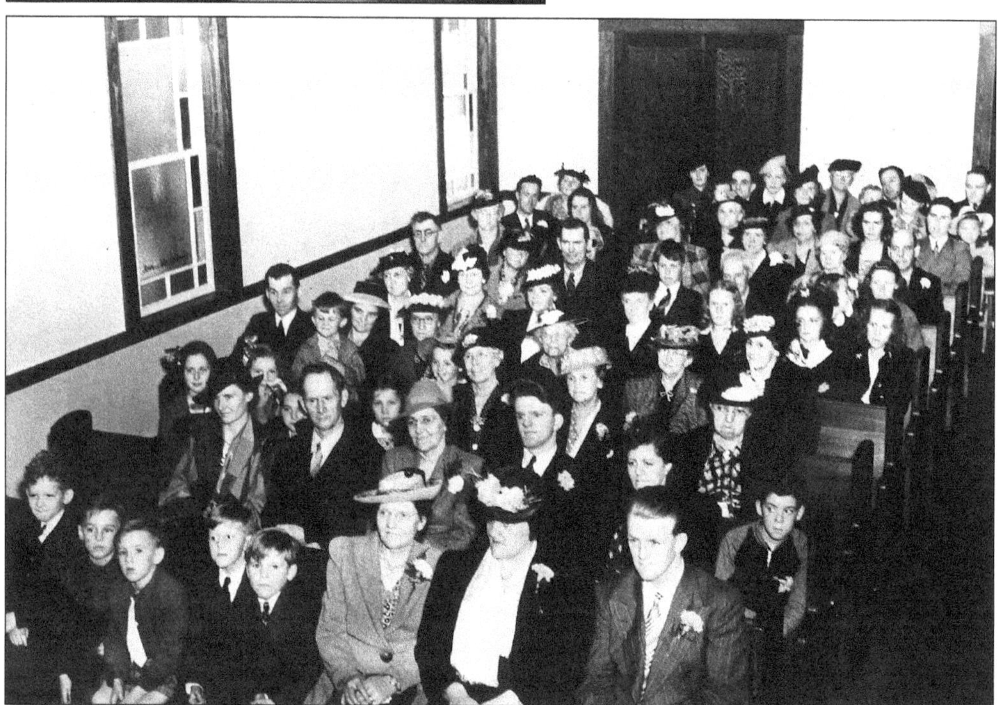

This 1941 photograph shows many families worshiping together during a Mother's Day service at the Advent Church.

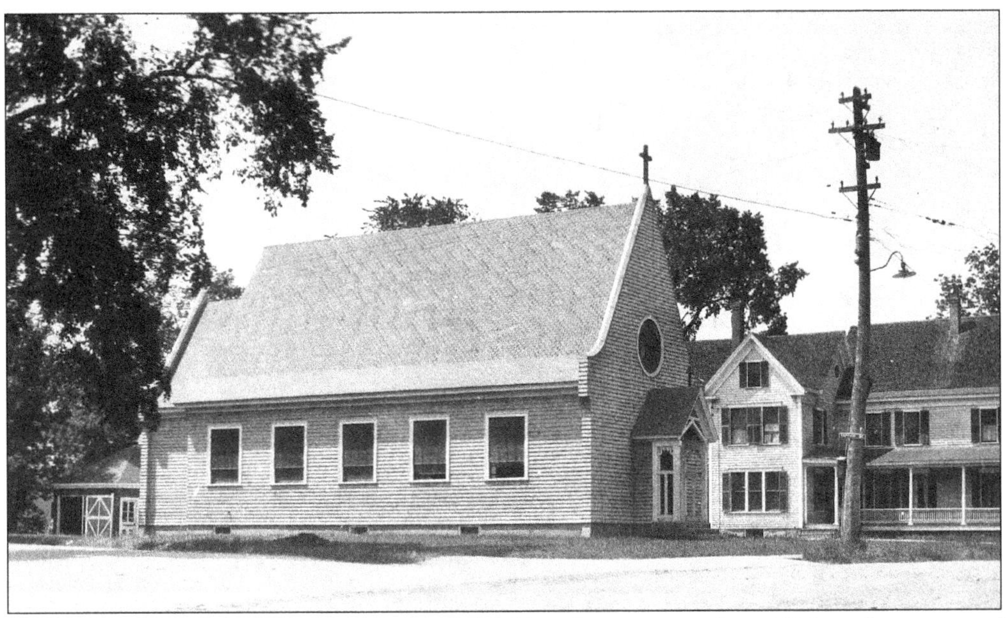

This original building of St. Peter's Catholic Church was erected in 1923 at the corner of Central and Tappan Streets. The expanding parish made necessary a larger building, which was constructed in 1955.

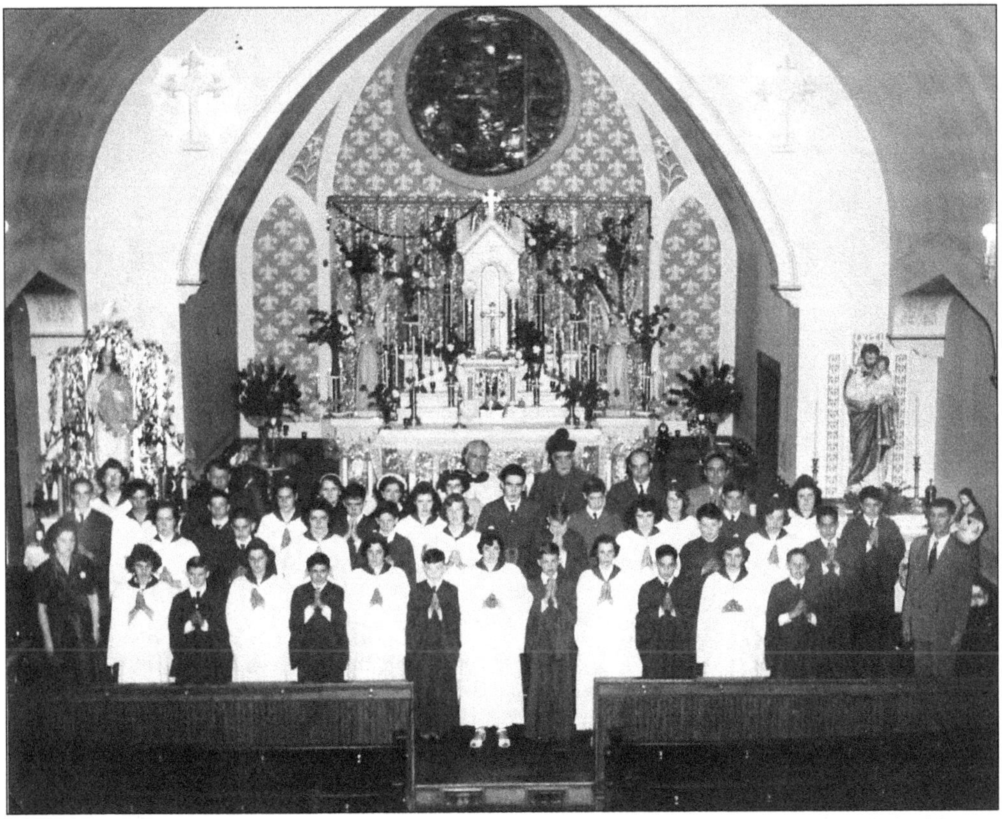

The 1953 Confirmation class of St. Peter's stands before the altar in the first church building.

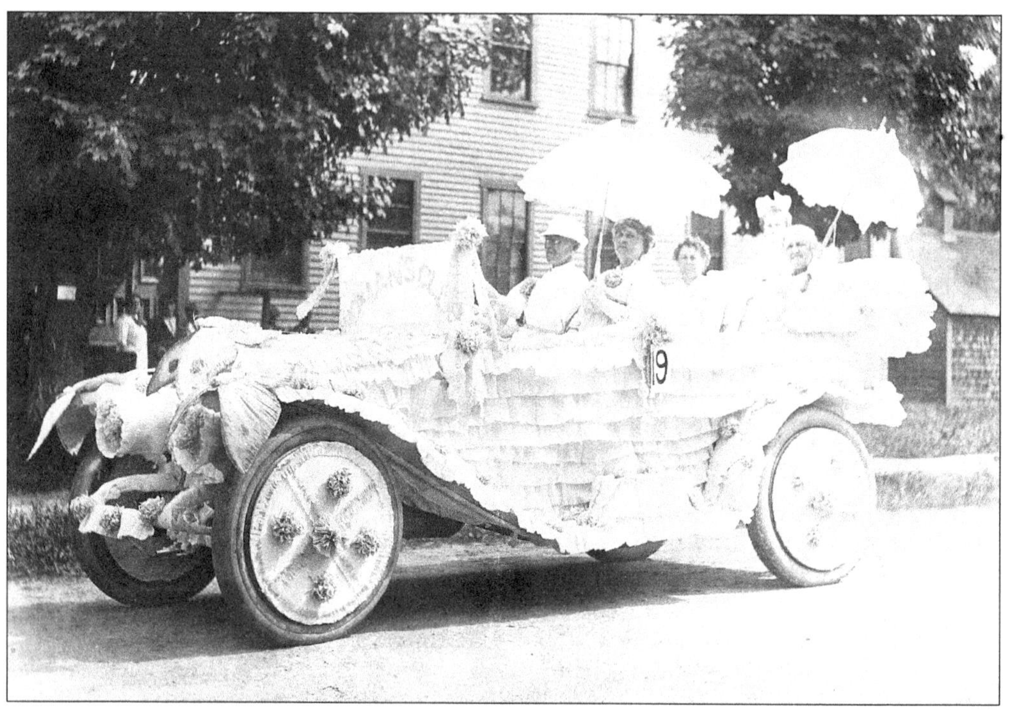

The Farmington Woman's Club was represented by this prize-winning float in the 1934 Old Home Day Parade.

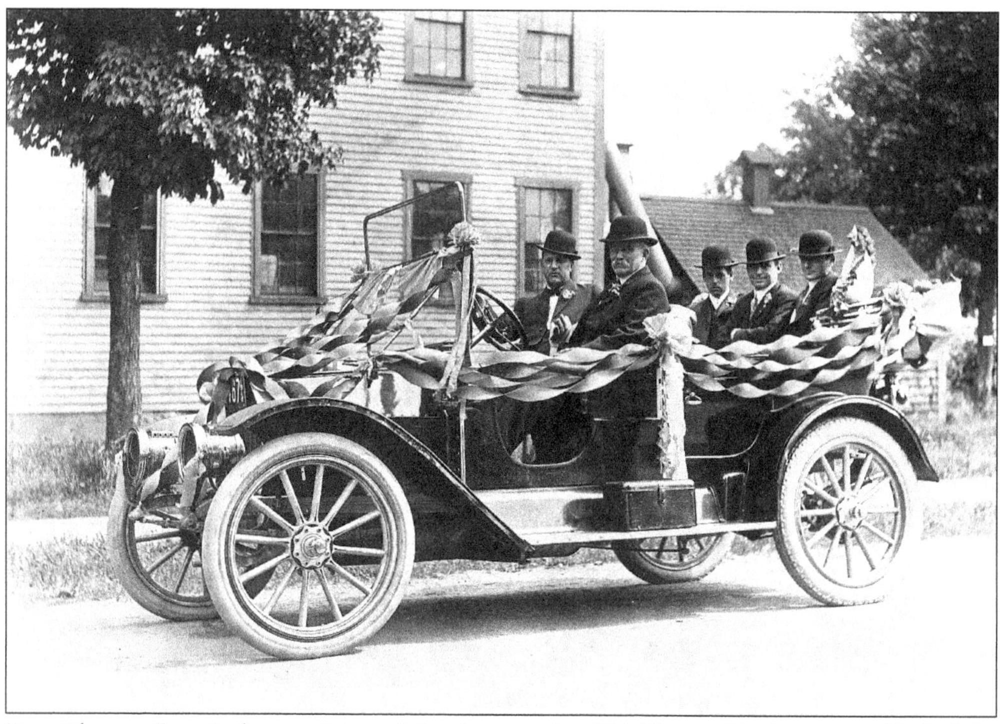

Five "dapper Dans" also participated in the parade. Old Home Week was established by gubernatorial proclamation in 1898 to encourage hometown reunions.

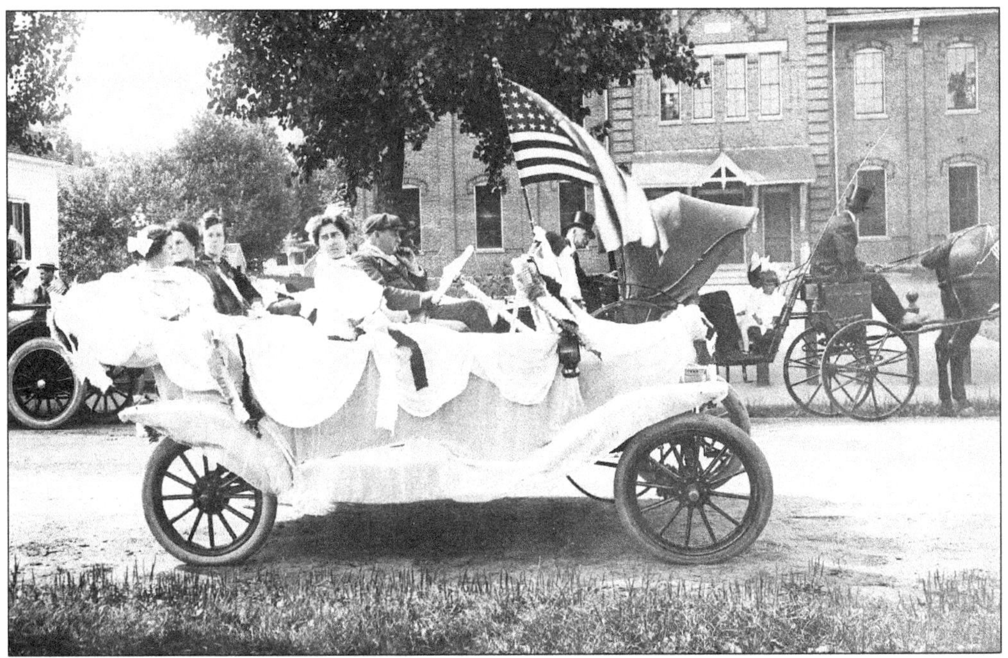

Will Nute drove members of the Pythian Sisterhood in this parade car. Mrs. Ella Chandler sits beside him.

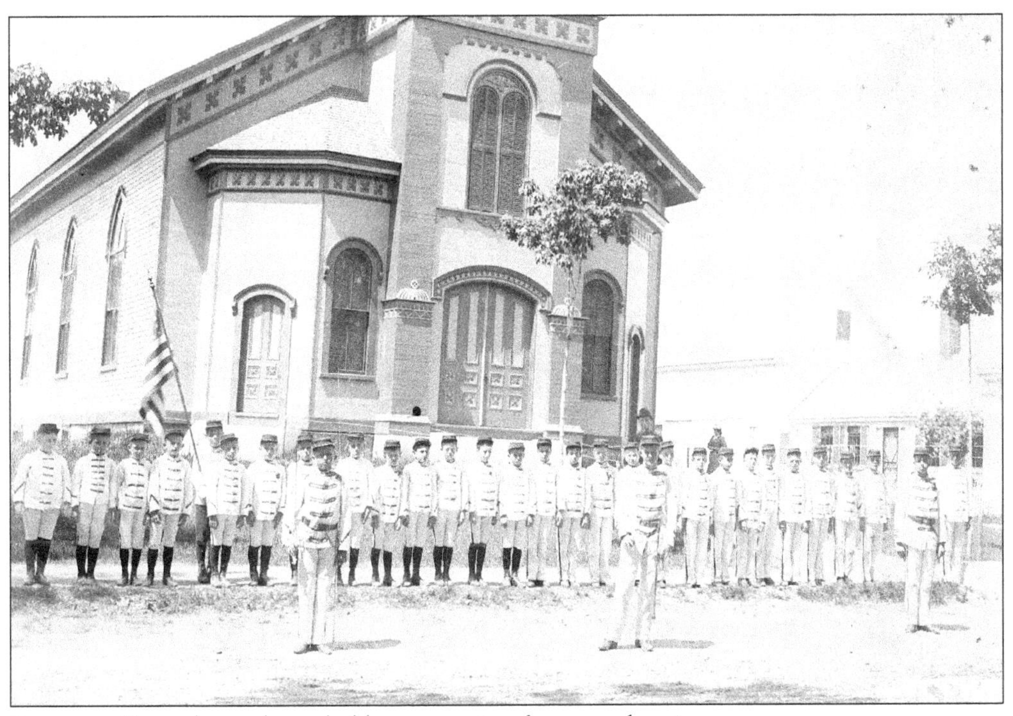

Snappy uniforms have always held an attraction for young boys!

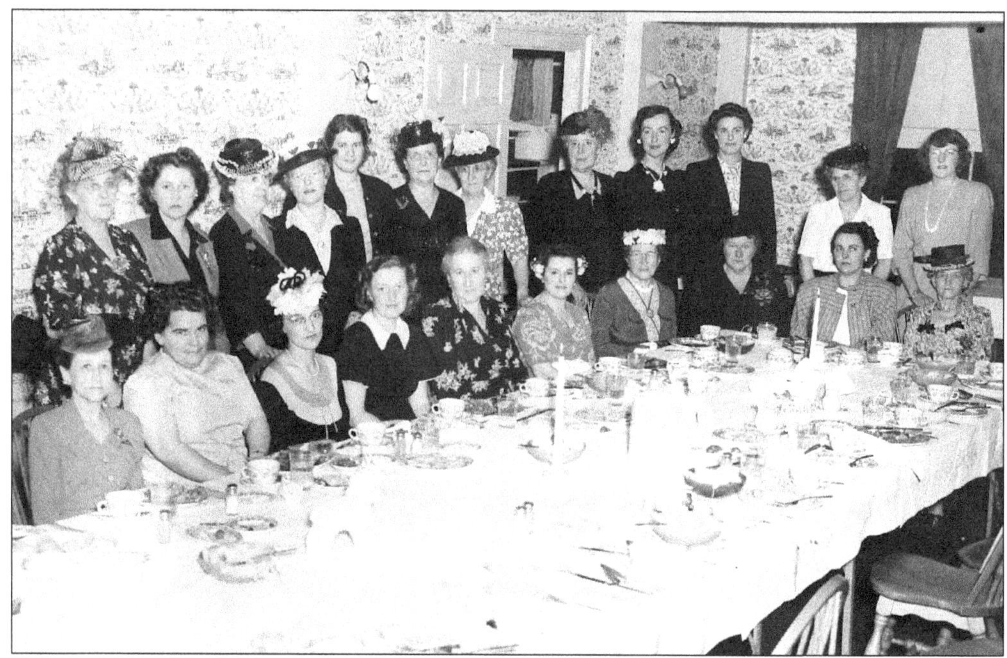

Ladies of the Farmington Woman's Club gather for luncheon. The club was organized in 1910 as a community service and social group. Its clubroom is on the second floor of the Goodwin Library.

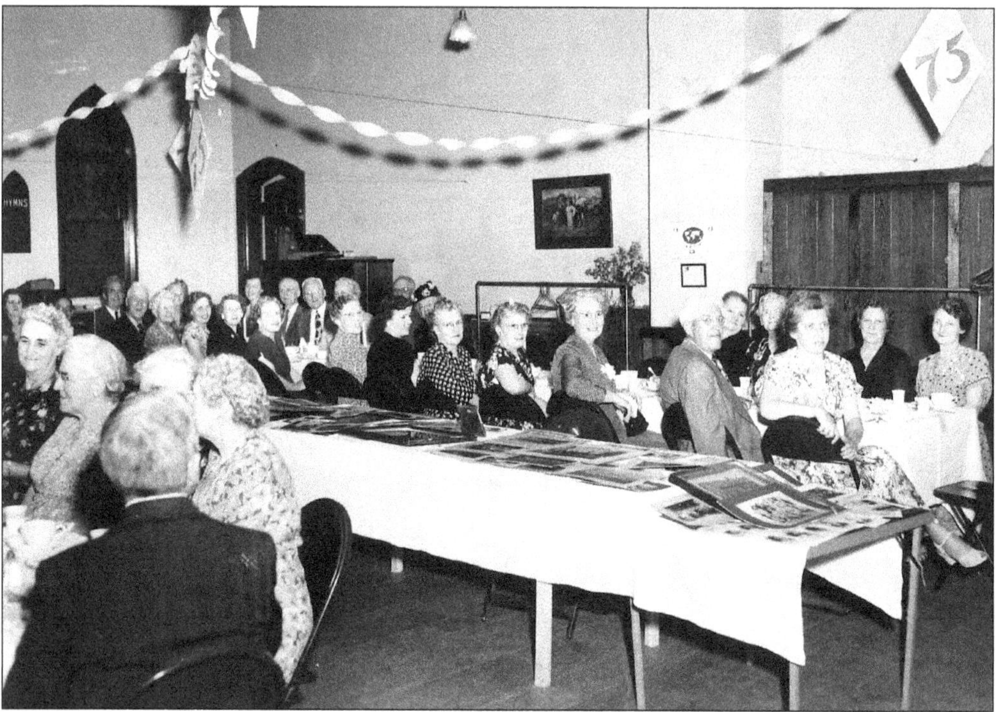

A dinner meeting in 1951 of the original Farmington-New Durham Historical Society. The Farmington Historical Society became independent in 1993; it meets monthly in the Goodwin Library's Henry Wilson Room.

Eight

Fun and Games

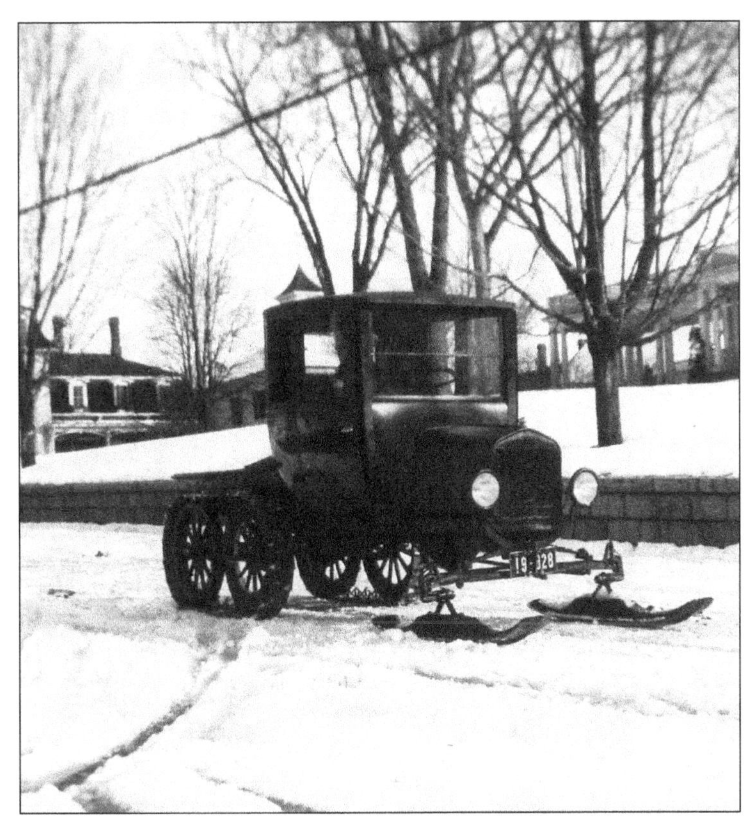

Walter Young bought this early snowmobile from its inventor, Virgil White of West Ossipee, who made his patented machine from a converted Model T Ford.

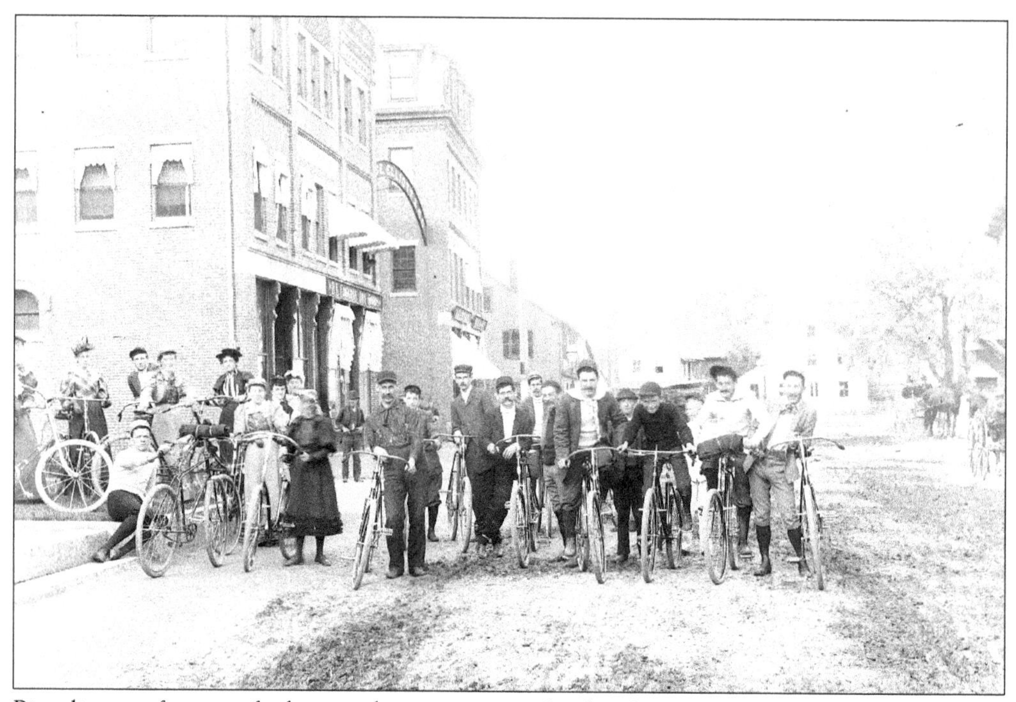

Bicyclists out for some fresh air and exercise pause for the photographer on Central Street.

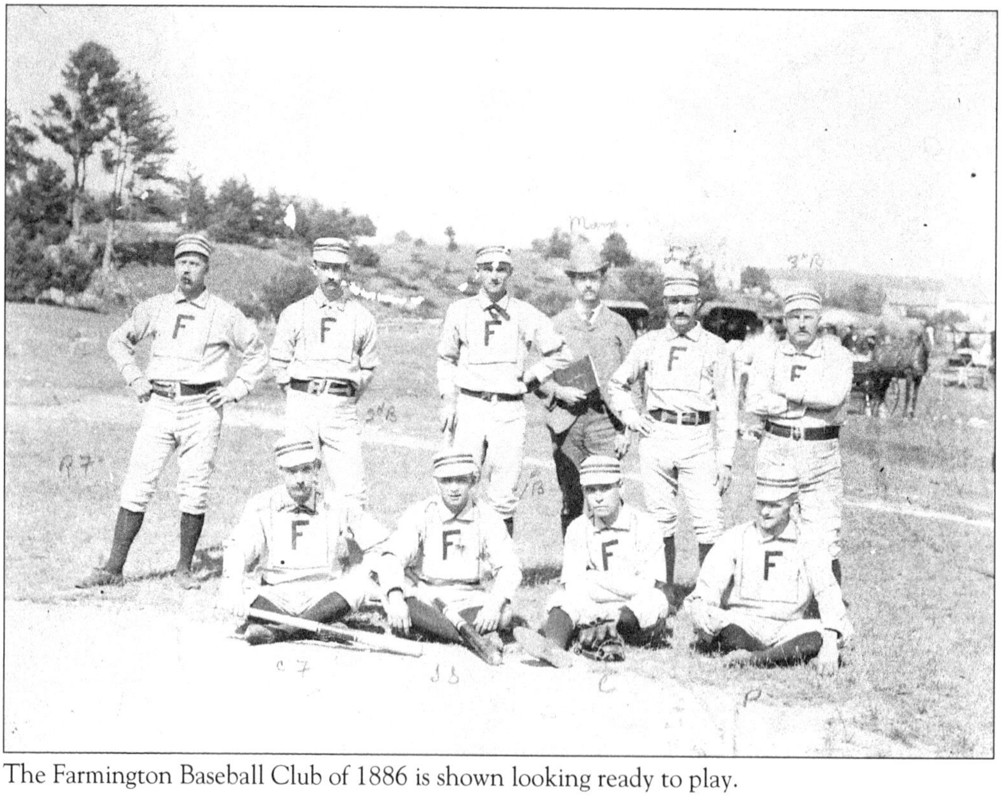

The Farmington Baseball Club of 1886 is shown looking ready to play.

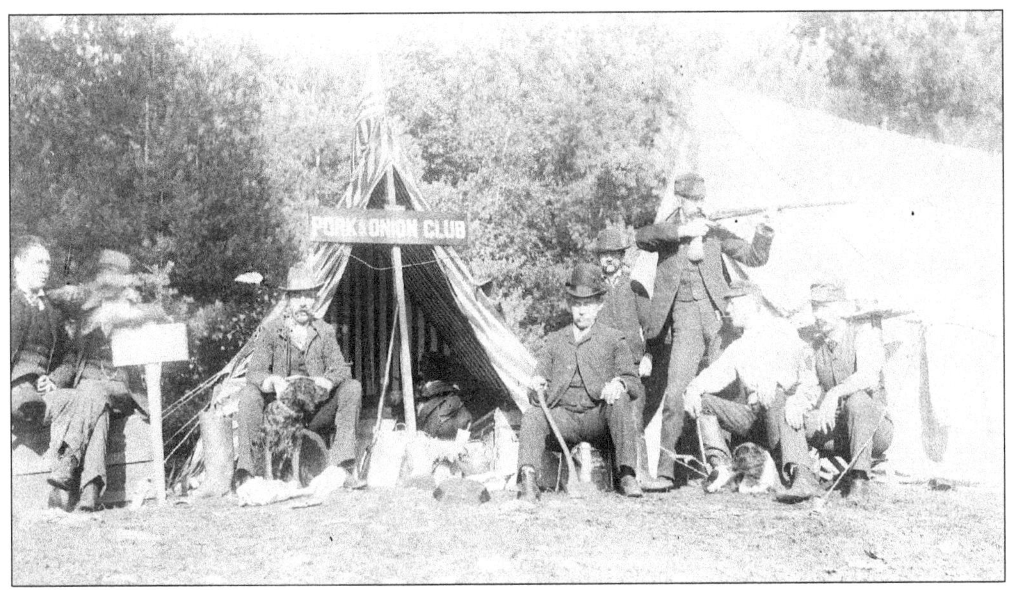

Was this jolly group an outdoor dining club or just well-dressed sportsmen-campers?

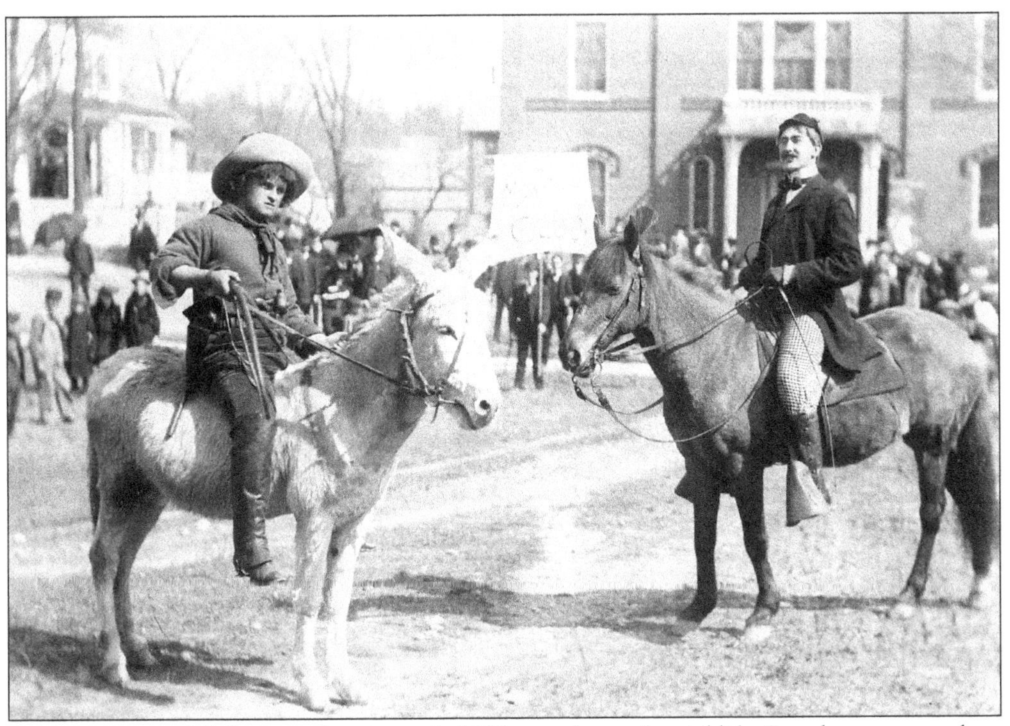
A great variety of clubs existed in the early 1900s as a focus of social life. Seen here are members of the Montauk Club in front of the Opera House.

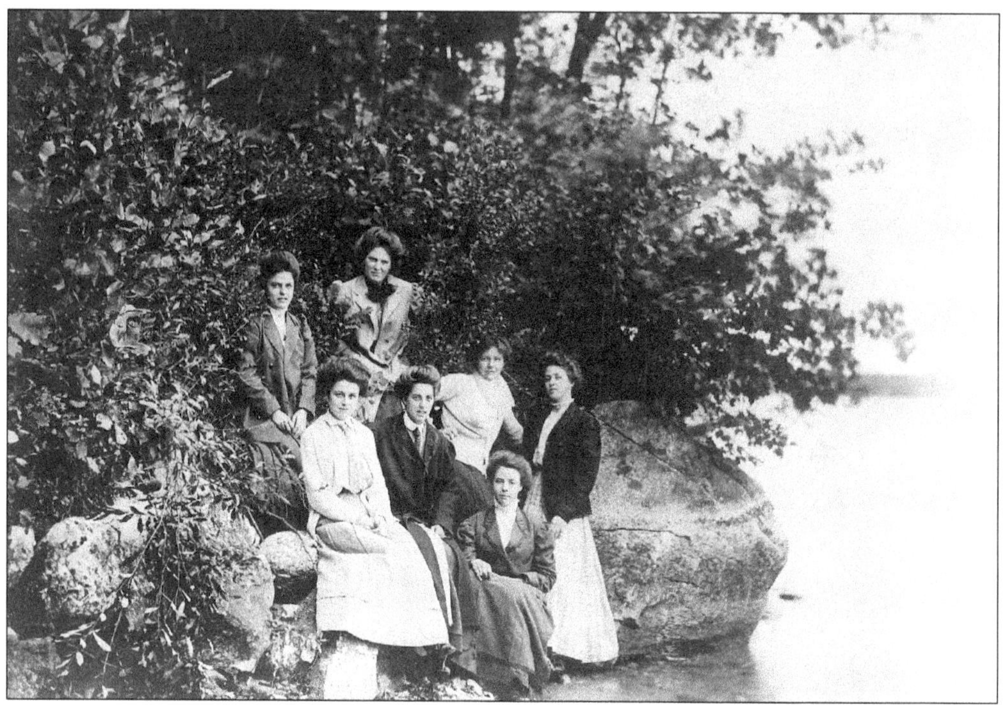

Among these ladies enjoying a lakeside outing are Hattie T. Lefavour, Edna H. Jewell, Maude McLean, Altire Corson, and Violet Jones.

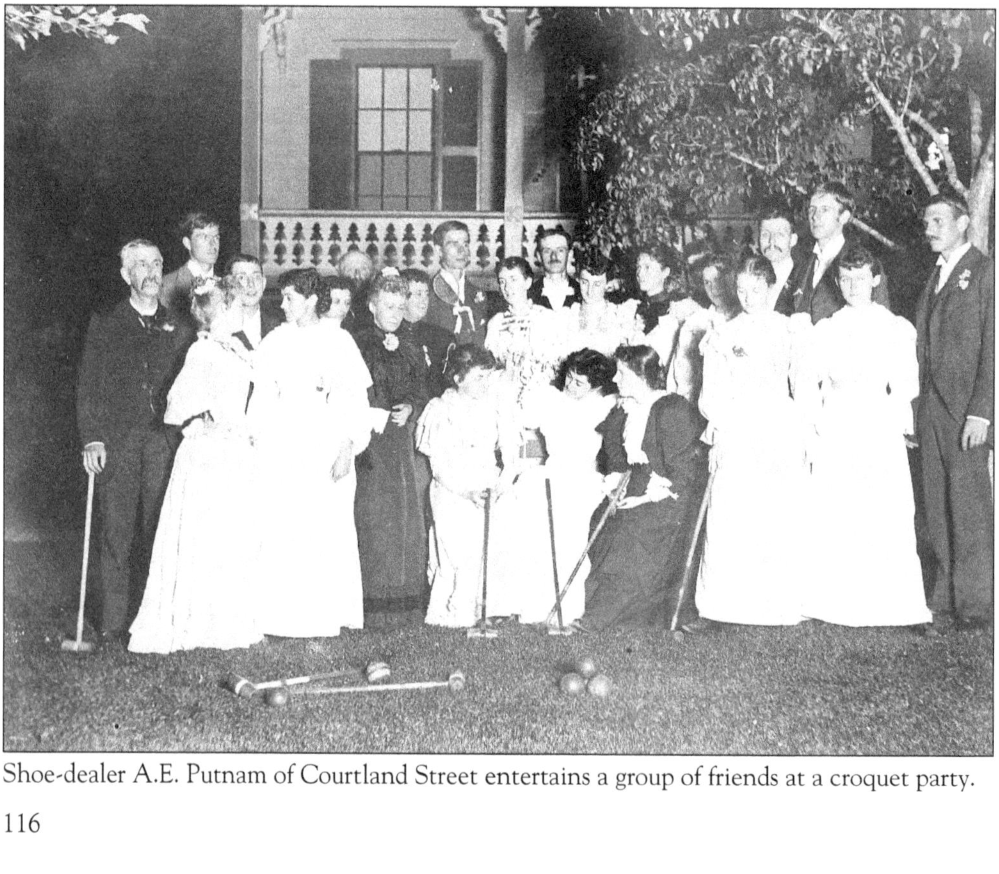

Shoe-dealer A.E. Putnam of Courtland Street entertains a group of friends at a croquet party.

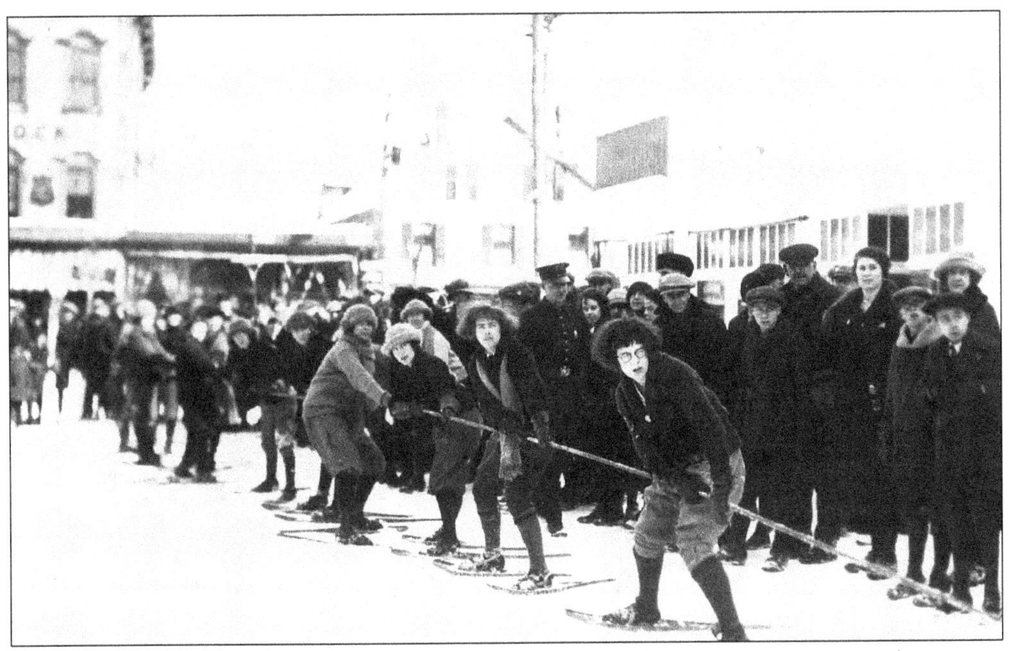

A tug-of-war on snowshoes! Winter fun took many forms before skiing became popular.

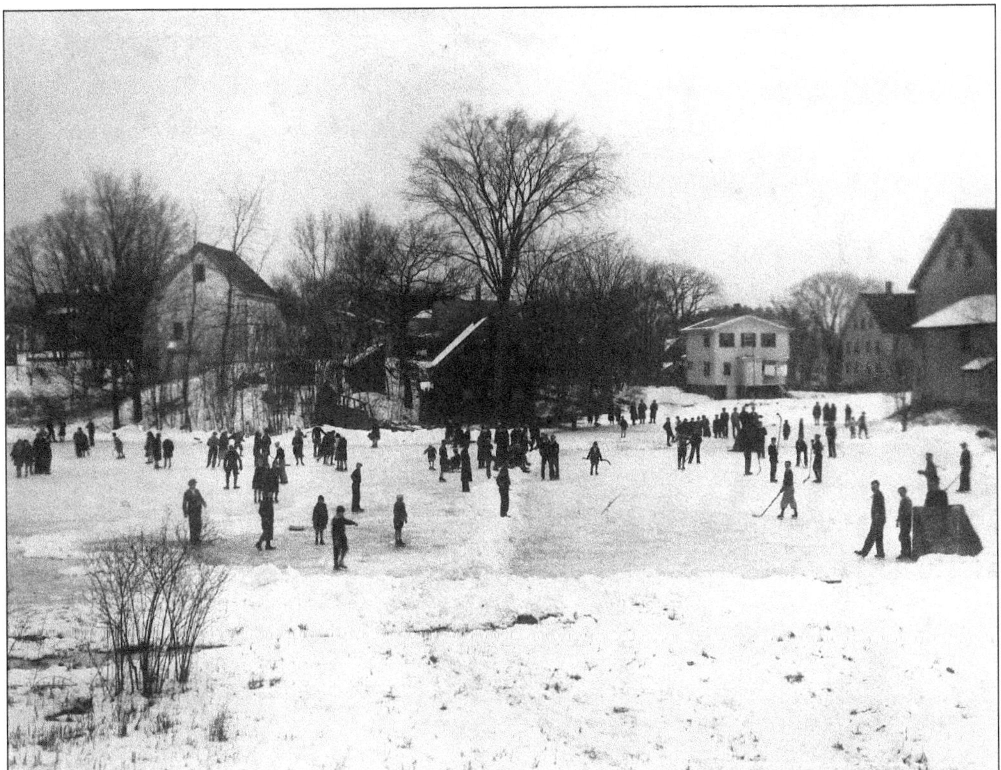

Another winter activity was skating on the Union Street pond, in use until 1963.

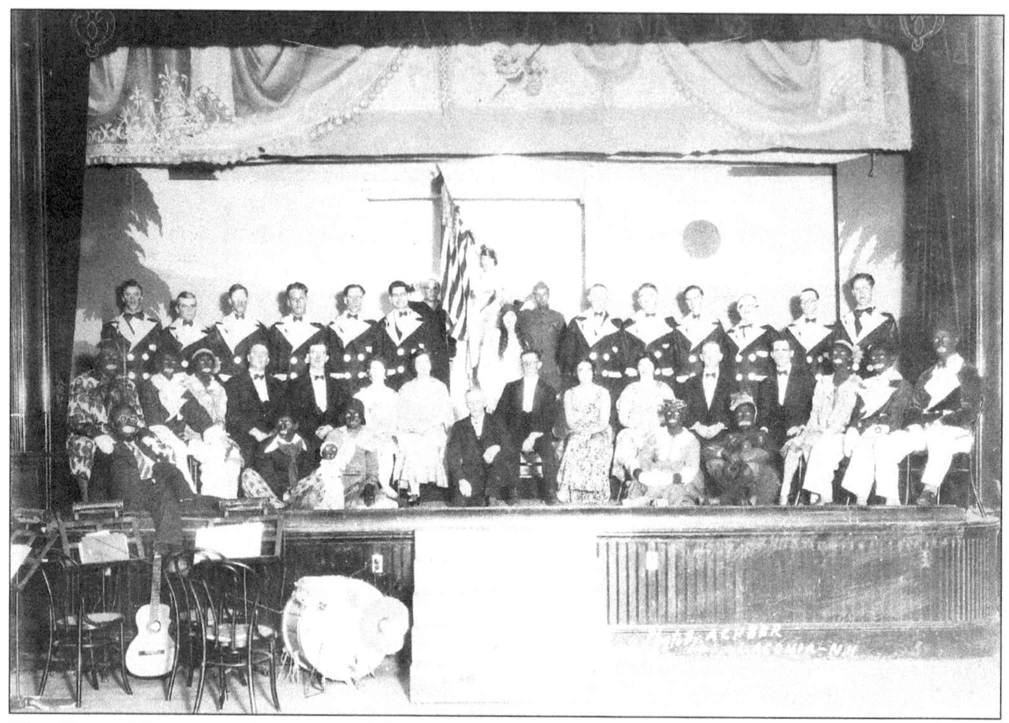

The Opera House was the scene of this early minstrel show.

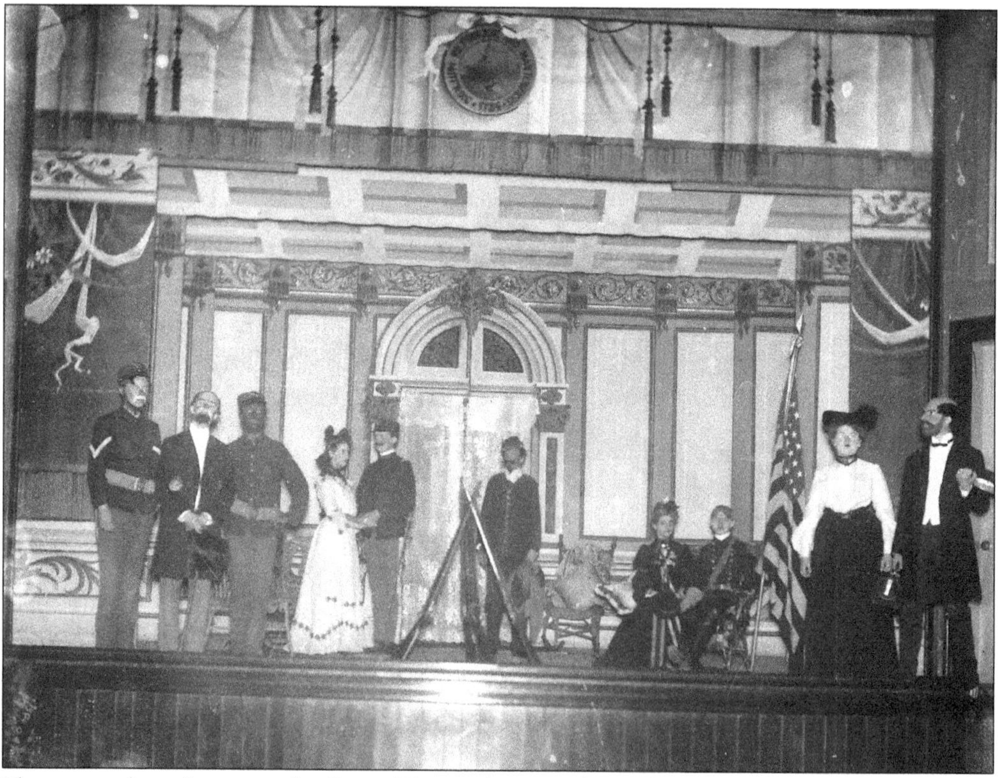

Plays were also a feature at the Opera House; this one obviously had a Civil War theme.

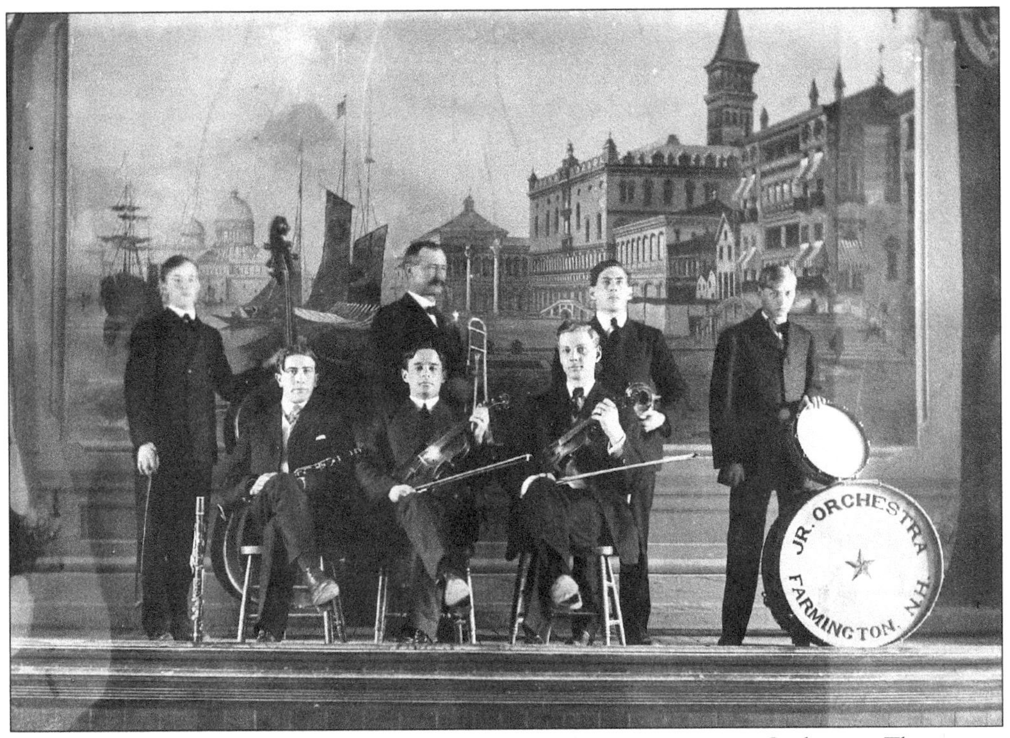

An elegant backdrop provides a classical tone for the town's Junior Orchestra. The cornet player is John Place.

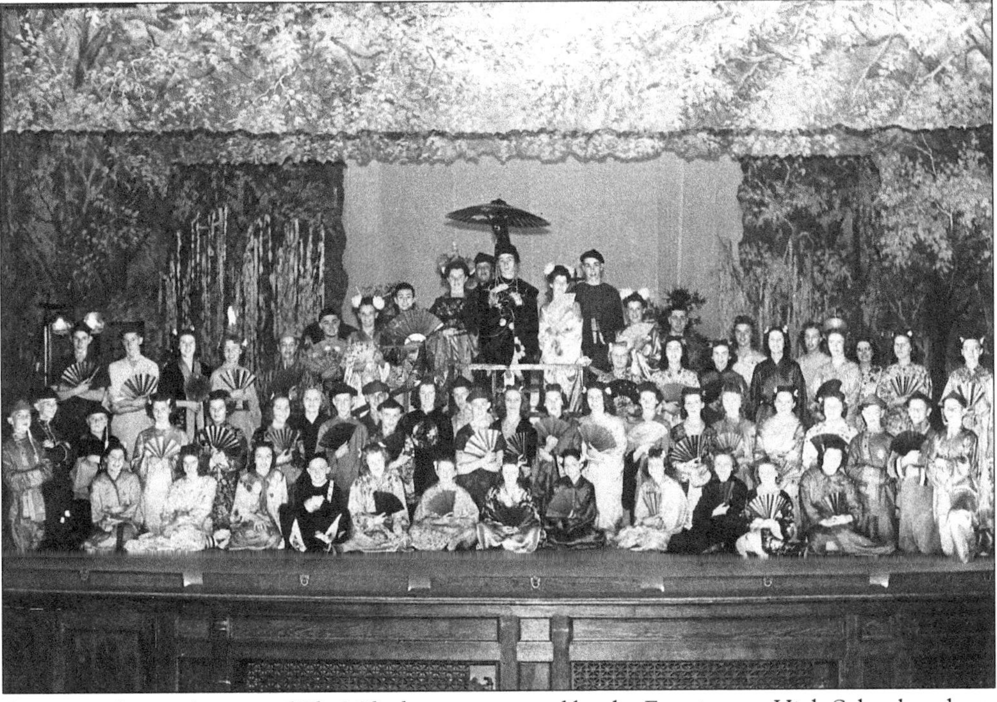
A spectacular production of *The Mikado* was presented by the Farmington High School students on April 15, 1941, at the Town Hall.

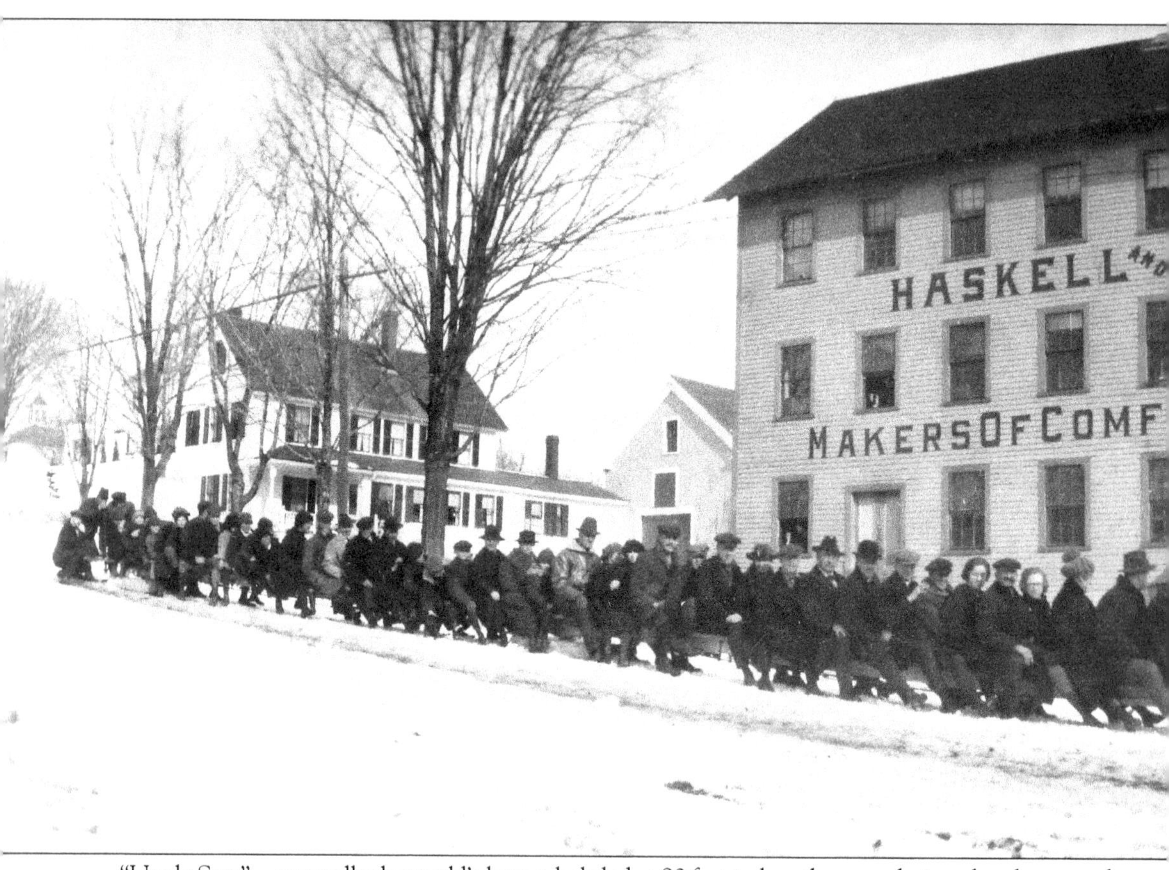

"Uncle Sam"—reputedly the world's largest bobsled at 90 feet in length—was designed and operated by Hervey Pearl. Built at the B.F. Perkins Carriage Shop in 1899, the sled weighed 6 tons loaded.

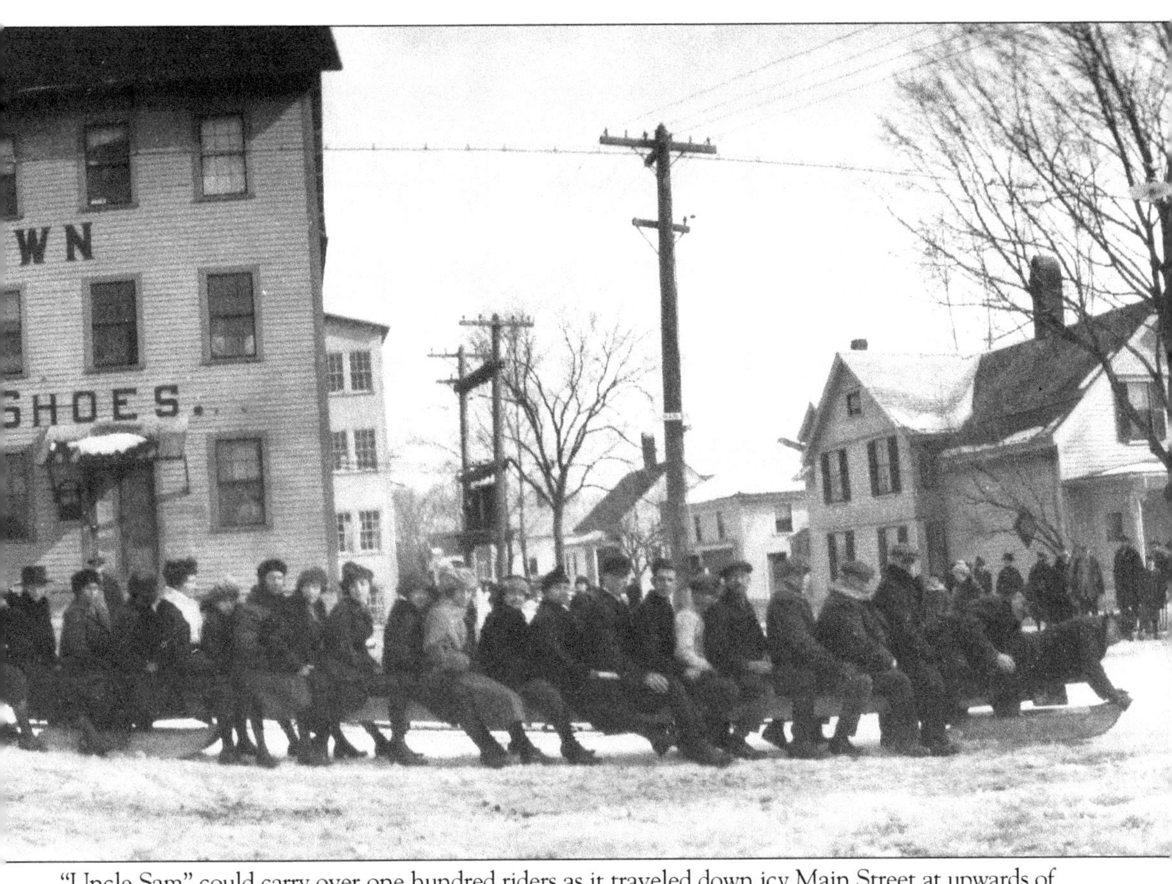

"Uncle Sam" could carry over one hundred riders as it traveled down icy Main Street at upwards of 60 miles per hour! Three of the four sections are preserved at Cameron's Garden Center.

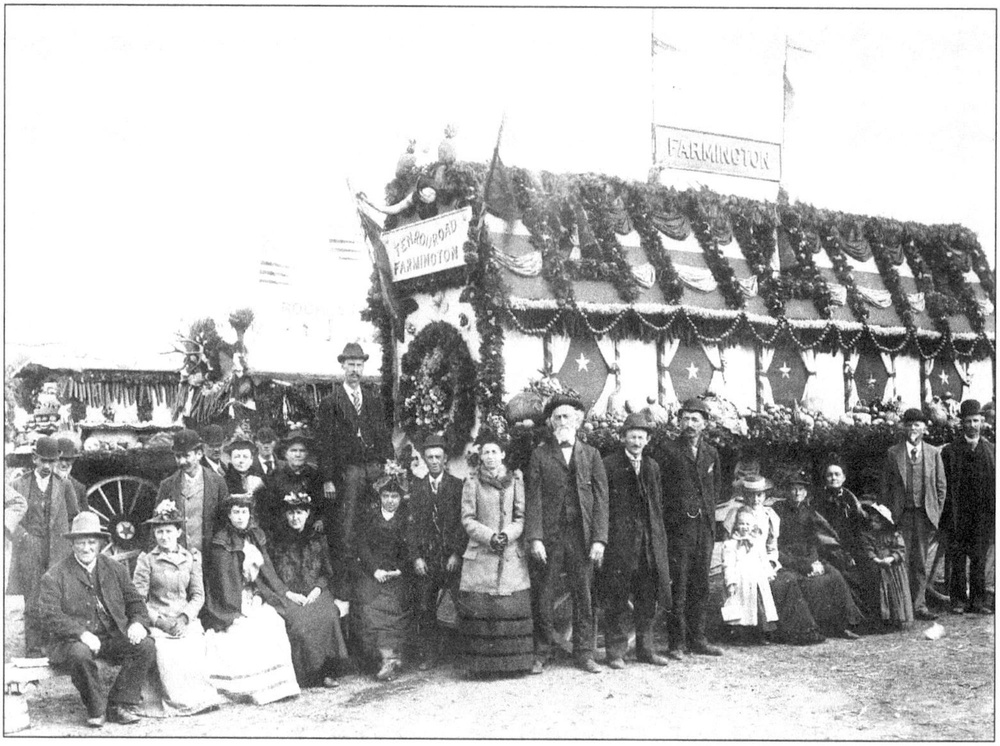

Lavishly decorated with home-grown produce by farmers of the Ten Rod Road section of Farmington, this float was awarded first place in the 1893 Rochester Fair Parade. Participation in the fair was the social highlight of the year—even the schools closed for the event.

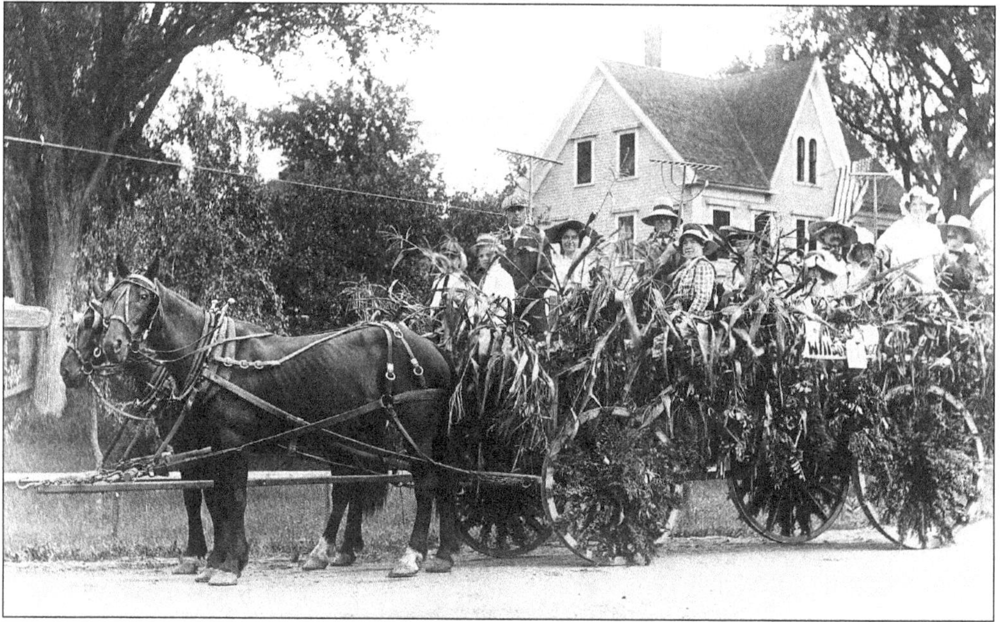

A horse-drawn parade float carries members of the Henry Wilson Grange. This order of the Patrons of Husbandry was organized in 1893, meeting first in the Odd Fellows Building and, since 1959, in its own building on Mechanic Street.

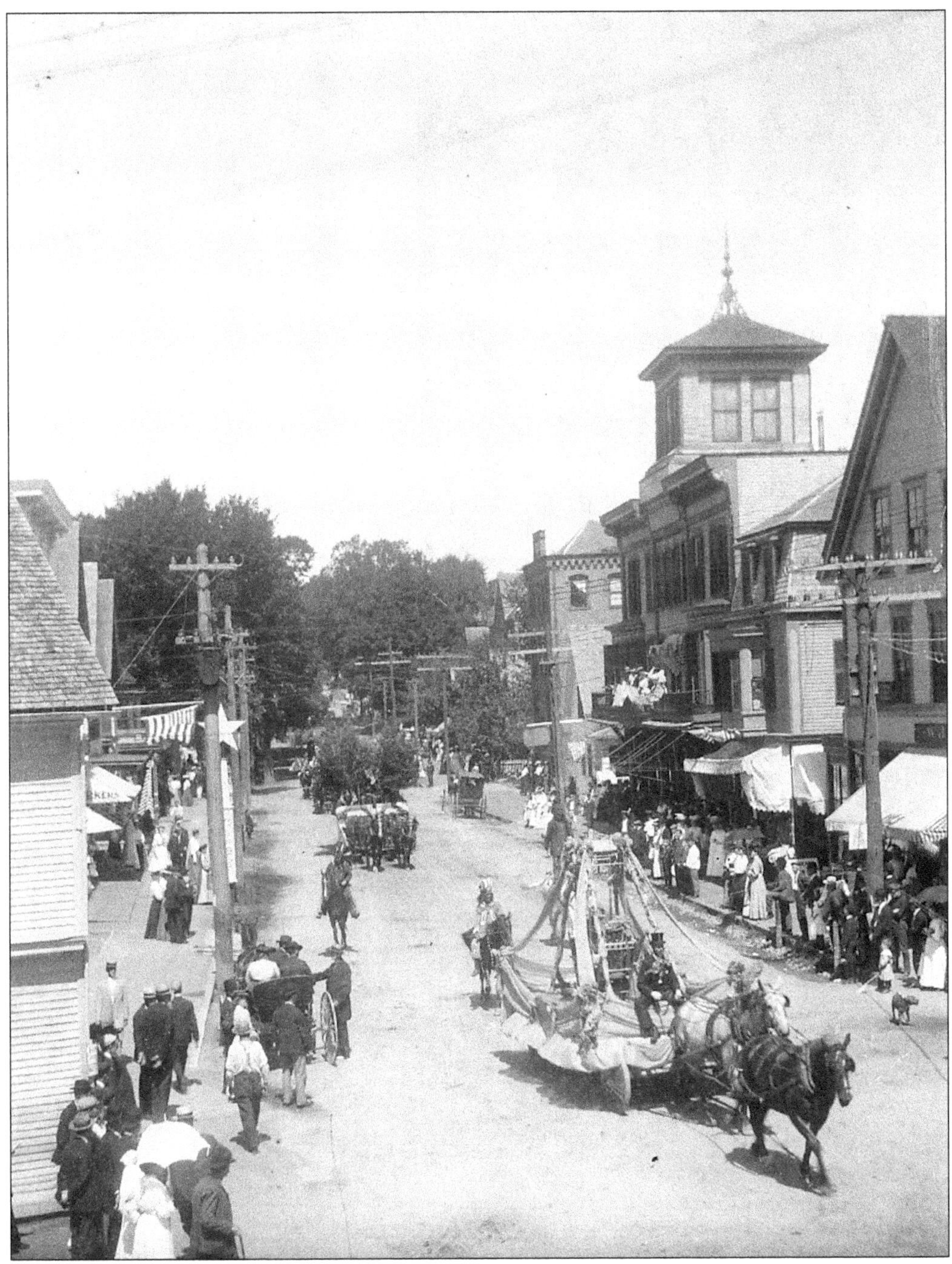

The Roberts Drug Store float in the foreground won first prize in this 1904 Old Home Day Parade on Main Street.

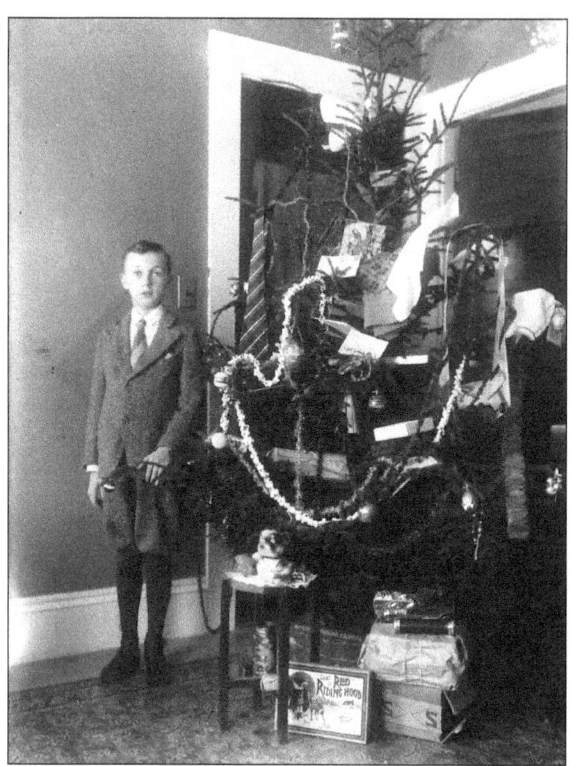

Sumner Evans is all dressed up to celebrate Christmas next to his gift-decorated tree.

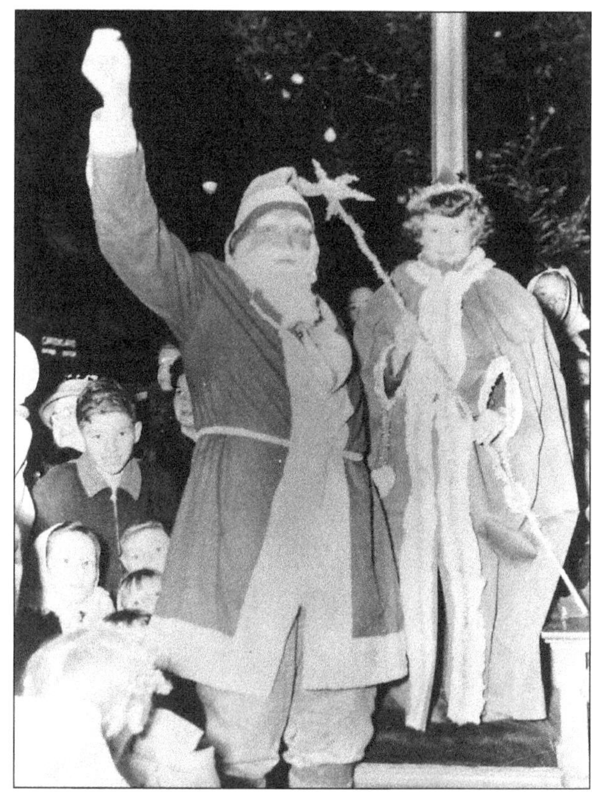

Santa and the "Spirit of Christmas" wish all the children a happy holiday.

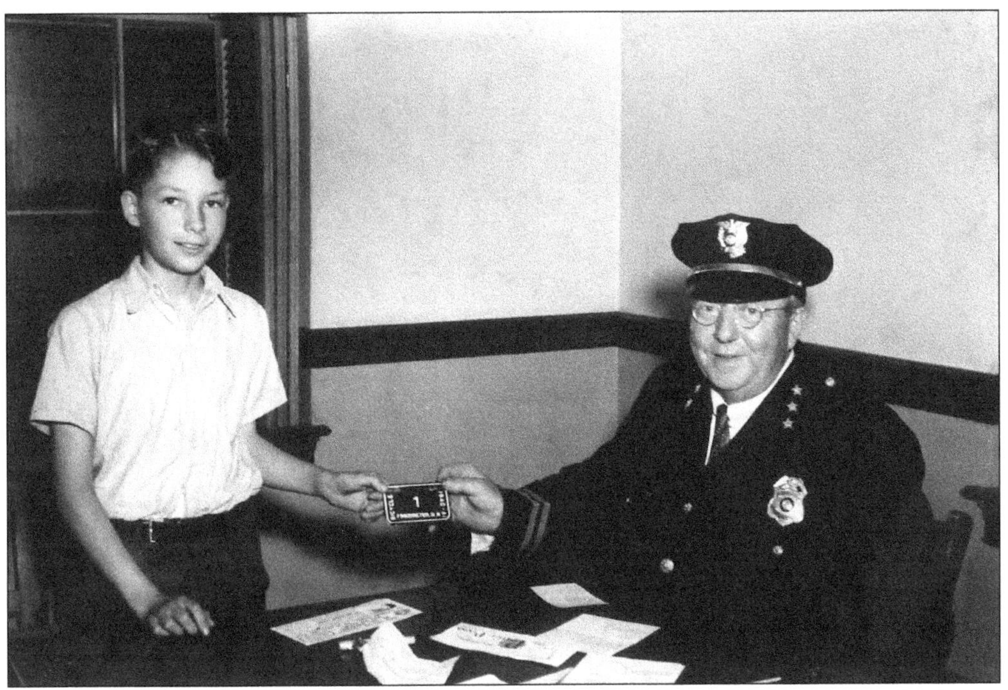

Chief Leon Furber presents the first bicycle license plate in 1940.

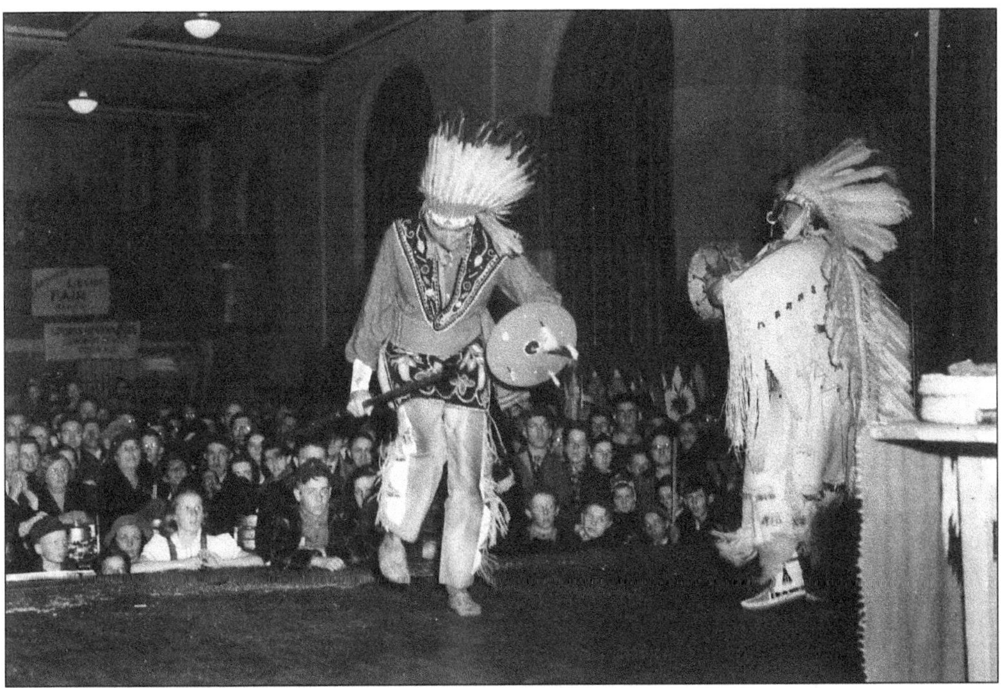

In the depths of winter the Farmington Fish and Game Club would hold its annual Sportsmen's Show in the Town Hall. There would be exhibits of sporting goods and, at this 1940 show, Indians doing a war dance!

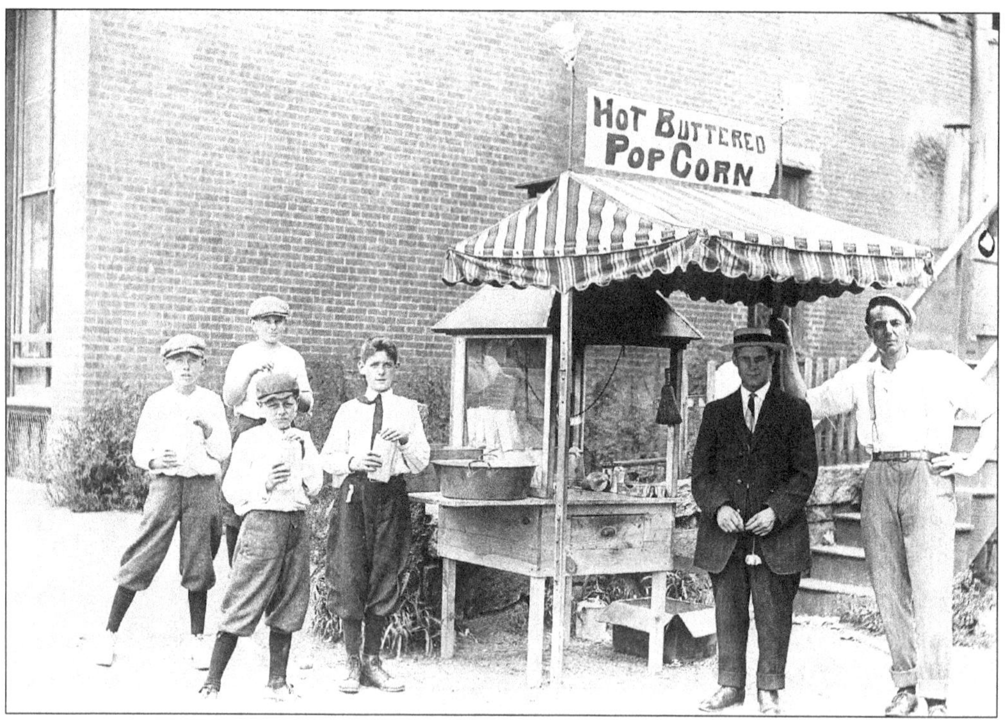

Some things never change!

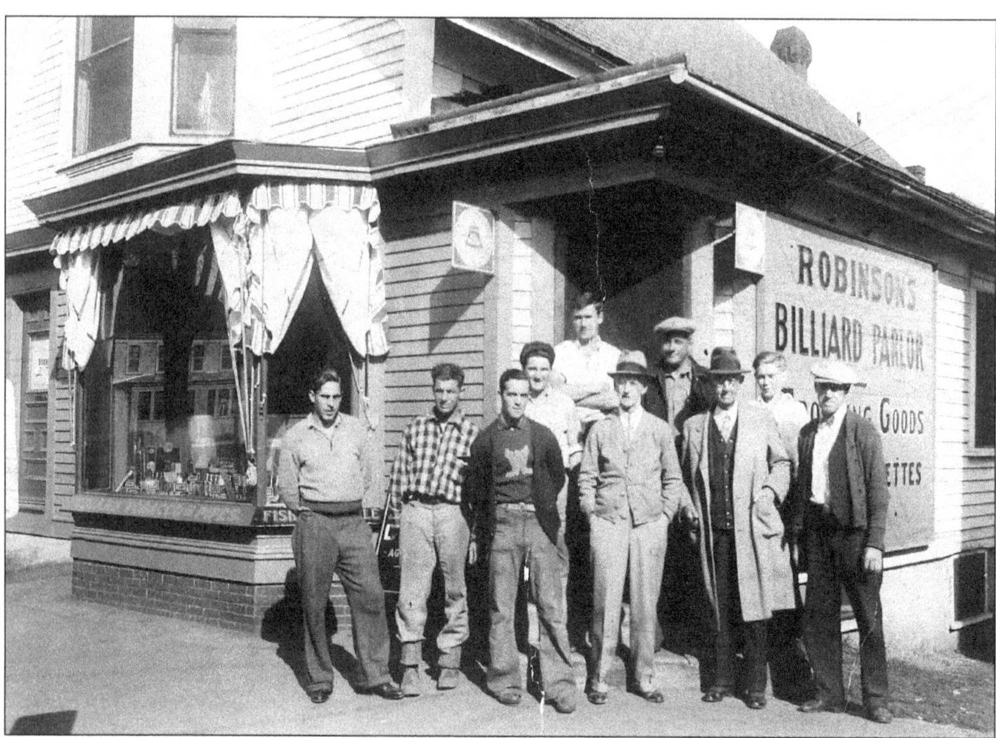

This Main Street establishment was where some of the boys spent their time before the days of video arcades.

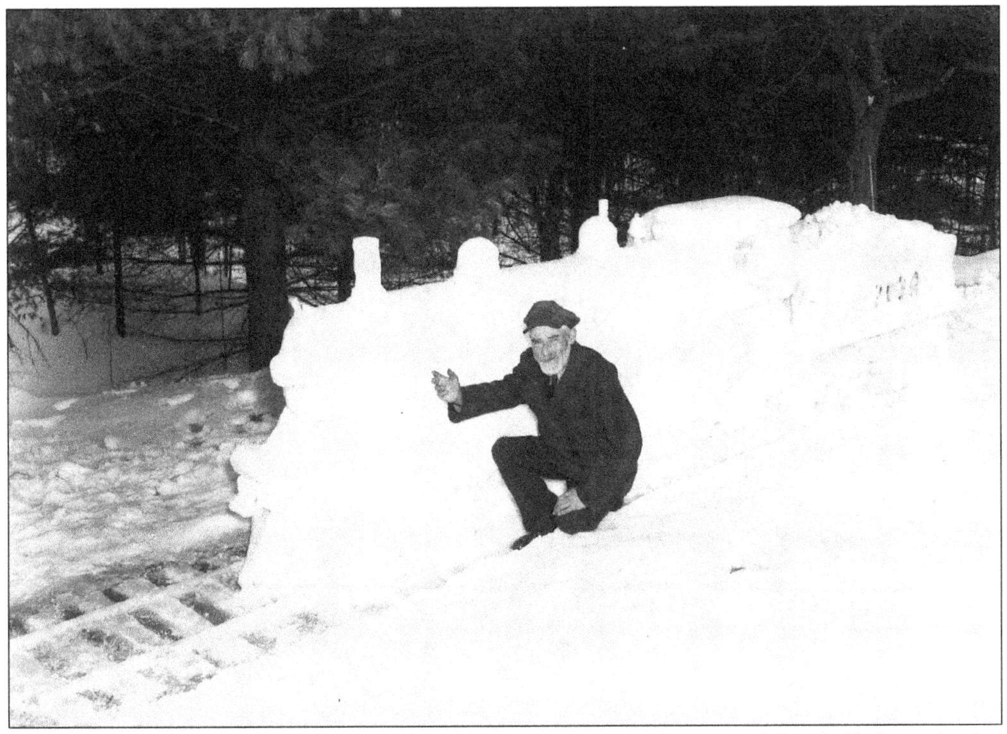

Dean Fifield expressed his artistic talents in a most unusual way in March 1948 with this locomotive snow sculpture.

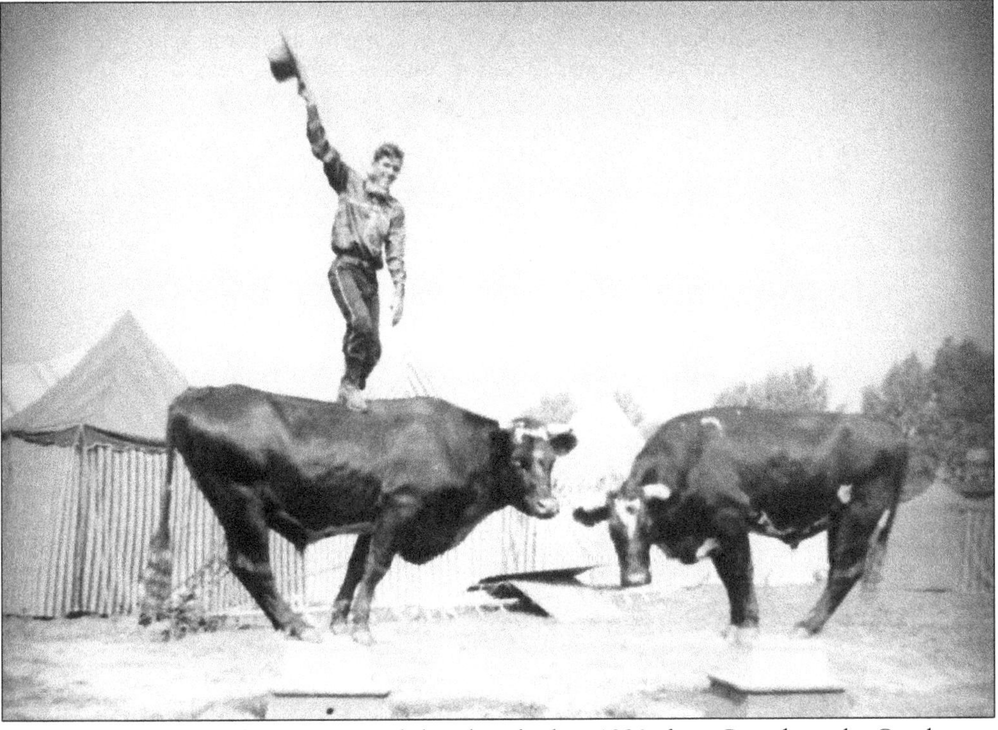

Frank Scruton's trained steers were exhibited in the late 1930s from Canada to the Carolinas.

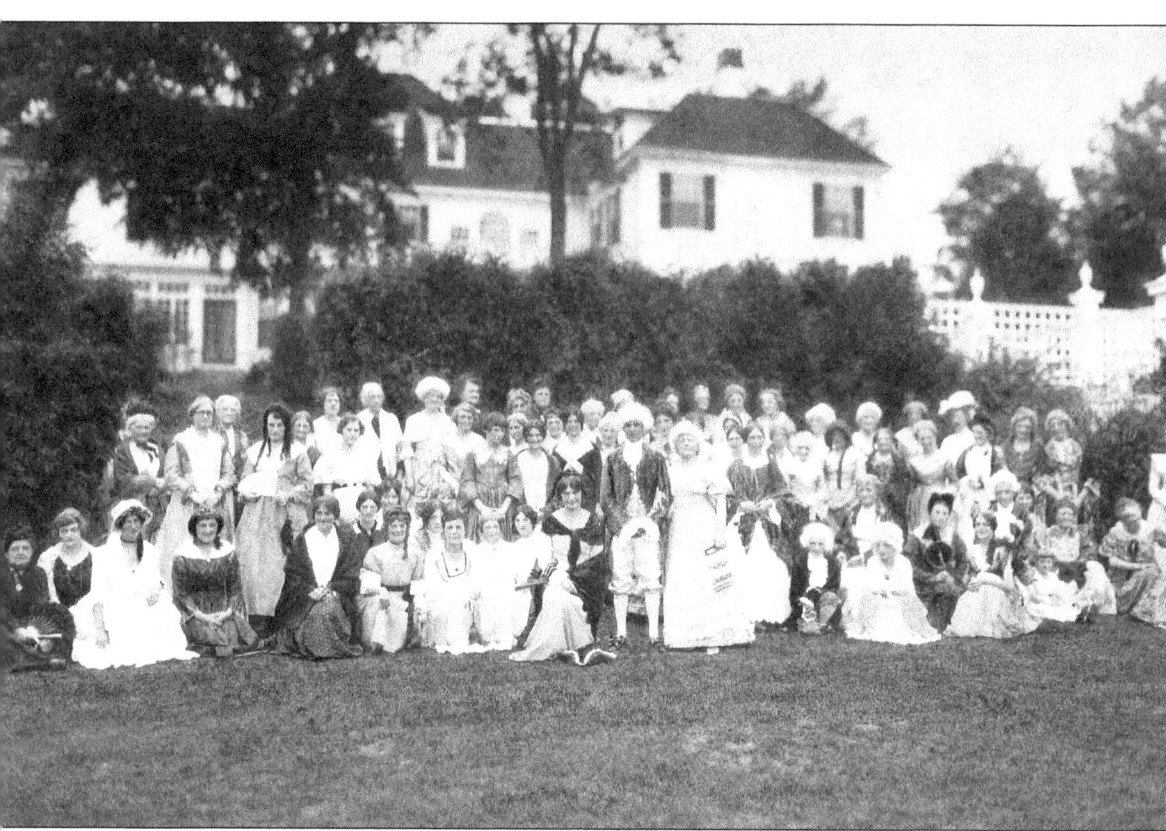

This 1924 "happening" in Farmington was recorded by the famous photographer and author, Wallace Nutting. The young gentleman in knee britches standing next to his mother is James E. Thayer.

www.ingramcontent.com/pod-product-compliance
Lightning Source LLC
LaVergne TN
LVHW081541100826
845153LV00004B/285
* 9 7 8 1 5 3 1 6 6 0 8 1 9 *